TRANSFORMING FOOD SYSTEMS

This book focuses on the contested nature and competing narratives of food system transformations, despite it being widely acknowledged that changes are essential for the safeguarding of human and planetary health and well-being.

The book approaches food system transformation through narratives, or the stories we tell ourselves and others about how things work. Narratives are closely connected with theories of change, although food system actors frequently lack explicit theories of change. Using political economy and systems approaches to analyze food system transformation, the author focuses on how power in food systems manifests, and how this affects whom can obtain healthy and culturally appropriate food on a reliable basis. Among the narratives covered are agroecology, food sovereignty and technological innovation. The book draws on interviews and recorded speeches by a broad range of stakeholders, including international policymakers, philanthropists, academics and researchers, workers in the food and agricultural industries and activists working for NGOs and social movements. In doing so, it presents contrasting narratives and their implicit or explicit theories of change. This approach is vitally important as decisions made by policymakers over the next few years, based on competing narratives, will have a major influence on who will eat what, how food will be produced, and who will have a voice in shaping food systems. The overarching contribution of this book is to point toward the most promising pathways for achieving sustainable food systems and refute pathways that show little hope of achieving a more sustainable future.

This book will be of great interest to students, scholars and policymakers interested in creating a sustainable food system which will ensure a food secure, socially just and environmentally sustainable future.

Molly D. Anderson is William R. Kenan, Jr. Professor of Food Studies at Middlebury College, USA. She is an Honorary Research Fellow in the Centre for Agroecology, Water and Resilience at Coventry University, UK, and a member of International Panel of Experts on Sustainable Food Systems. She is co-editor of *Food Insecurity: A Matter of Justice, Sovereignty and Survival* (Routledge, 2020).

Routledge Studies in Food, Society and the Environment

Evaluating Sustainable Food System Innovations
A Global Toolkit for Cities
Edited by Élodie Valette, Alison Blay-Palmer, Beatrice Intoppa, Amanda Di Battista, Ophélie Roudelle, and Géraldine Chaboud

How to Create a Sustainable Food Industry
A Practical Guide to Perfect Food
Melissa Barrett, Massimo Marino, Francesca Brkic, and Carlo Alberto Pratesi

Food Justice in American Cities
Stories of Health and Resilience
Sabine O'Hara

Sustainable Food Procurement
Legal, Social and Organisational Challenges
Edited by Mark Stein, Maurizio Mariani, Roberto Caranta and Yiannis Polychronakis

American Farming Culture and the History of Technology
Joshua T. Brinkman

Transforming Food Systems
Narratives of Power
Molly D. Anderson

For more information about this series, please visit: www.routledge.com/Routledge-Studies-in-Food-Society-and-the-Environment/book-series/RSFSE

TRANSFORMING FOOD SYSTEMS

Narratives of Power

Molly D. Anderson

LONDON AND NEW YORK

Designed cover image: © martinedoucet / Getty Images

First published 2024
by Routledge
4 Park Square, Milton Park, Abingdon, Oxon OX14 4RN

and by Routledge
605 Third Avenue, New York, NY 10158

Routledge is an imprint of the Taylor & Francis Group, an informa business

British Library Cataloguing-in-Publication Data
A catalogue record for this book is available from the British Library

Library of Congress Cataloging-in-Publication Data
Names: Anderson, Molly D. (Molly DelCarmen), 1955– author.
Title: Transforming food systems : narratives of power /
Molly D. Anderson.
Description: Abingdon, Oxon ; New York, NY : Routledge, 2024. |
Series: Routledge studies in food, society and the environment |
Includes bibliographical references and index.
Identifiers: LCCN 2024006750 | ISBN 9781032196695 (hardback) |
ISBN 9781032196671 (paperback) | ISBN 9781003260264 (ebook)
Subjects: LCSH: Food supply. | Food security. | Nutrition. | Sustainable agriculture. | Agricultural industries.
Classification: LCC HD9000.5 .A5545 2024 | DDC 338.1/9—dc23/
eng/20240403
LC record available at https://lccn.loc.gov/2024006750

ISBN: 978-1-032-19669-5 (hbk)
ISBN: 978-1-032-19667-1 (pbk)
ISBN: 978-1-003-26026-4 (ebk)

DOI: 10.4324/9781003260264

Typeset in Sabon
by codeMantra

CONTENTS

ACKNOWLEDGMENTS

I am grateful to so many people who have helped shape my views on food system transformation over the last few decades—this is a theme with which I've been obsessed for most of my professional life. It's difficult to single out individuals because I am sure to miss some. But I have to thank here the amazing team (panelists and Secretariat) at the International Panel of Experts on Sustainable Food Systems; my collaborators on the International Assessment of Agriculture, Knowledge and Technology for Development; the people who fight passionately for human rights through the Civil Society & Indigenous Peoples Mechanism; the grantees I and staff worked with while at Oxfam America; the wonderful people at the Institute for Agroecology at the University of Vermont who reviewed my draft chapter on grassroots initiatives; Rob Dyball and Barry Newell, who reviewed my chapter on system mapping; and all those students who asked tough questions that made me re-think some glib statement. I also want to thank everyone who agreed to formal interviews: Lauren Baker, Jennifer Clapp, Bruce Ferguson, Melissa Leach, Constanza Monterrubio, Pat Mooney, Helda Morales, Patti Naylor, Raj Patel, Peter Rosset, Ricardo Salvador, Jordan Treakle, Irit Tamir and Martin Wolpold-Bosien. A large number of other people contributed through talks, webinars, conferences and conversations at meals or in hallways. Thanks to Noah Rizika at Middlebury, who breezed through NVivo issues that had me stumped. And thanks to John for his unwavering support, for keeping the home-fires burning (literally) and for feeding me from his garden, and to my children Thea and Peter, who inspire me to keep hoping for a better future.

SECTION 1

The Need for Transformation

1

WHY THIS BOOK?

This book came out of observation over several decades of studying, teaching and listening to others talk about food systems that the need for transformation is widely acknowledged, but the pathway to achieve it is highly contested. Food systems are the biggest transgressor of planetary boundaries and domains where human rights are systematically violated, so one would think that more attention would be focused on how to bring them into alignment with the environmental, social and health goals supported by a large swath of the global population. Yet the connections between food systems and climate change were hardly acknowledged in the Climate Change Summits until COP27 (Weston and Watts 2021), even though the Intergovernmental Panel on Climate Change had reported previously that food systems are responsible for 21–37 percent of greenhouse gas emissions (Mbow et al. 2019). And the United Nations Food System Summit in 2021 to address how food systems could contribute to the Sustainable Development Goals failed to set priorities among the thousands of "solutions" elicited, nor to highlight the pathways promoted by the largest organization of small-scale farmers, La Via Campesina. Transformative solutions are being proposed, but they are ignored or put on the back burner by major international organizations and the meetings they organize.

Why can't we seem to reach agreement on how to transform food systems? Why are well-documented successes of agroecology, food sovereignty and rights-based approaches not trumpeted and emulated across the world? Why are countries regressing on important trends with huge impacts on well-being, such as equality, food security and methane emissions (to which food systems make significant contributions), despite repeated pledges to make progress? These questions have been the subjects of multiple books, papers,

DOI: 10.4324/9781003260264-2

reports and conferences. My hope is that this book will help to consolidate and sort some of this previous work, point toward the most promising pathways for achieving sustainable food systems and refute pathways that show little hope of achieving a more sustainable future.

This book approaches food system transformation through narratives, or the stories we tell ourselves and others about how things work. Narratives are closely connected with theories of change, although food system actors frequently lack explicit theories of change. I use political economy and systems approaches to analyze food system transformation; that is, I am concerned with how power in food systems is manifest and how this affects whom can obtain healthy and culturally appropriate food on a reliable basis. There is enough food produced to nourish everyone (at least for now), but power differentials allow some people to be chronically overfed and keep others chronically food insecure. I argue that narrative conflicts are often at the heart of inability to solve problems and exacerbate the polarization between positions. Of course, failures to find consensus have many other causes beyond not sharing the same stories: real differences of power and opportunity, and unwillingness to share power more equitably, often underpin these conflicts. Yet we can get some insights into directions that have more or less potential for food system transformation by examining their narratives.

I think of power as a dynamic flow through actors and institutions, with reinforcing and balancing loops controlled by feedback, triggers and delays. Trained as a systems ecologist originally, I learned how system diagrams and concept maps could map flows of goods ranging from water to money. Power is also amenable to mapping, to show how it moves through the food system. To learn about how power moves through food systems and how different interests put forth different narratives, I rely on literature reviews, lectures and webinars, attendance at conferences (including the past 13 years of meetings of the Committee on World Food Security or CFS), and interviews with selected people chosen because of their different perspectives on food system transformation, ranging from activists to philanthropists, scholars and farmers. I also participate regularly in meetings of Working Groups of the Civil Society and Indigenous Peoples' Mechanism of the CFS and networks dedicated to food system transformation at the local, state, national and international scales. In each of these spaces, I look for who or what holds power and how it is exercised, with what consequences. I also look for how people talk about transformation. To test my ideas about narratives, I encoded all interviews and a sample of conference presentations, webinars and key texts in the qualitative analytical software program NVivo.

Two clarifications are important in this introductory chapter: what we mean by transformation and what the goal of transformation should be. Do food systems need to transition, or is transformation necessary? These two terms are sometimes used interchangeably, but Patterson et al. (2017, 2) drew on multiple prior authors to define transformation as "fundamental changes in structural, functional, relational, and cognitive aspects of socio-technical-ecological systems that lead to new patterns of interactions and outcomes." Weber et al. (2020, 2) provided a helpful elaboration:

> Transitions are defined as long-term, significant changes of essential social-technical systems. They are often conceptualized from the multi level perspective … and describe change as a process traversing governance levels … Transformations, on the other hand, describe significant changes of essential social-technical systems that disrupt the current state. Transformations to sustainability include substantive change in personal (beliefs, attitudes, values), practical (behaviours, technologies, institutional reform) and political (system-level dynamics and structure) spheres of human interaction with the environment.

Hölscher et al. (2018) claimed that transformation is more commonly applied to refer to large-scale changes in whole societies that involve interacting human and biophysical system components. These may be global, national or local. They pointed out that different research communities have adopted one or the other term.

Food system analysts and activists have been calling for transformation fairly consistently. For example, even the UN Food Systems Summit (one of the fora examined in this book and by no means a radical space) was intended to "transform the way the world produces, consumes and thinks about food" (UN Food Systems Summit 2021). The changes needed are clearly large-scale changes applied over all of society. Béné (2022, 2) wrote specifically about food system transformation:

> We posit that food system transformation is not just about private sector's interest versus public health or environmental considerations; instead it is about the perceptions, believes [sic] and views of individual consumers, institutions, public and private policy-makers, investors, suppliers, interacting all at the same time in a space where structuring factors other than power and dominance are important, including social values, cultural identities or even knowledge and expertise.

In other words, transformation is complex and multi-faceted and involves deep structural and functional changes in many aspects of society. Given the severity and scope of food system impacts, the entrenchment of current political positions, the resilience of practices and policies which are demonstrably harmful and the scale and speed at which change needs to happen in order to avoid catastrophic tipping points in climate change and biodiversity loss, it seems clear that transformation and not transition is the goal.

Many authors agree and press the urgency of this needed transformation. For example, members of the Global Panel on Agriculture and Food Systems for Nutrition wrote in 2016: “Piecemeal action will not do; the trends are so large and interconnected that the entire food system needs overhauling” (Haddad et al. 2016, 31). Some of the same authors followed up with an article in *Nature Food* (Webb et al. 2020) whose title says it all: “The urgency of food system transformation is now irrefutable.” And as the connections between food systems and climate change have become obvious, the call for urgent action to transform agriculture and food systems in response has risen (Campbell et al. 2018). Furthermore, it is the industrialized food system dominating global value chains and production, processing and consumption in most industrialized countries that needs transformation most urgently and most deeply. While countries such as the United States (US) which have supported and facilitated the spread of the industrialized food system globally should take the lead in this transformation, other countries are far ahead of the US in terms of policy and action that will lead to greater sustainability.

What is the goal of “transformation”? While the goal is often stated as greater “sustainability,” this remains a loose concept despite countless attempts to pin it down and general agreement that it has environmental, social and economic dimensions. Some definitions, such as the one developed by the EAT Lancet Commission, focus on health and environmental costs of food production:

> [S]ustainable food production needs to operate within the safe operating space for food systems at all scales on Earth. Therefore, sustainable food production for about 10 billion people should use no additional land, safeguard existing biodiversity, reduce consumptive water use and manage water responsibly, substantially reduce nitrogen and phosphorus pollution, produce zero carbon dioxide emissions, and cause no further increase in methane and nitrous oxide emissions.
>
> *(Willett et al. 2019, 448)*

Other definitions look beyond production to consider the entire food system, yet still with a primary focus on food security and nutrition. Another authoritative source, the High Level Panel of Experts (HLPE) of the Committee on World Food Security, proposed:

> A sustainable food system is a food system that ensures food security and nutrition for all in such a way that the economic, social and environmental bases to generate food security and nutrition of future generations are not compromised.
>
> *(HLPE 2014, 31)*

Building on this definition, the United Nations Food and Agriculture Organization defined a sustainable food system as:

> a food system that delivers food security and nutrition for all in such a way that the economic, social and environmental bases to generate food security and nutrition for future generations are not compromised. This means that:
>
> - It is profitable throughout (economic sustainability);
> - It has broad-based benefits for society (social sustainability); and
> - It has a positive or neutral impact on the natural environment (environmental sustainability).
>
> *(Nguyen 2018, 1)*

Meybeck and Gitz (2017) explored the attempts to define sustainable food systems, moving from a focus on individual diets and nutrition to a global perspective which included environmental, social and economic factors. While the two broad descriptions given above have remained relevant, more recent attention has focused on the potential of specific practices to create sustainable food systems, measuring and monitoring the sustainability of food systems, and exploring policy trade-offs (e.g., Hebinck et al. 2021).

Attempting to find themes and consensus across descriptions of food system sustainability, Eakin et al. (2017, 759) listed their main attributes:

> A sustainable food system achieves and maintains food security under uncertain and dynamic social-ecological conditions, through respecting and supporting the context-specific cultural values and decision processes that give food social meaning, and the integrity of the social-ecological processes necessary for food provisioning today and for future generations.

This definition recognized ecological integrity and the cultural value of food, which provides more nuance to the rather generic FAO definition. The profit-making criterion of FAO's definition of sustainable food systems is perhaps most difficult to handle: who should be profiting, and at whose expense? Is a bit less social or environmental sustainability acceptable, if profits go up as a consequence? I see economic sustainability embedded in and subject to social sustainability, and social sustainability embedded in and subject to environmental sustainability. The latter trumps anything else because it depends on physical properties, planetary boundaries and thresholds or tipping points; social sustainability and economic sustainability are determined by the policies that society sets and how they are enforced. If there is a conflict between environmental or social and economic sustainability, then society's institutions need to be changed to allow people to have healthy food and decent livelihoods that don't degrade the environment or impinge on social sustainability. Allowing environmental degradation so that profits can be enhanced is ultimately self-defeating; profits on a dead planet are worthless.

Although "sustainable" is the most commonly used adjective for socially desirable food systems, I use the term "regenerative" in this book to emphasize that food systems must not only sustain some status quo but also create and restore ecological integrity, social justice, community viability, equity and public health in order to achieve well-being for all. This is congruent with Duncan et al. (2021) in the Routledge Handbook on Sustainable and Regenerative Food Systems, who see regeneration as a "step beyond sustainability" (p. 9) that better reconciles relations between the social and the environmental and focuses less on maintaining systems or simply doing less damage and more on enhancing the ability of living beings to co-evolve in ways that allow for diversity, complexity, and creativity. "We conceptualize regeneration as a holistic approach that moves past neutral environmental impact towards the creation of effects of a mutually supportive symbiosis across the food system" (p. 4).

In Anderson and Rivera-Ferre (2021, 18), my co-author and I suggested that:

> [r]egenerative food systems provide food for human use but also sequester carbon, preserve biodiversity, produce diverse diets to combat malnutrition, and build community well-being by maintaining farming livelihoods and the social reproduction of culture and farming communities, support the dignity and autonomy of the person and allow severing ties of dependence on external inputs and external knowledge.

By endorsing regenerative food systems, I am not voting for regenerative *agriculture*; in fact, I have critiqued the way that term has supplanted agroecology in many contexts (IPES-Food 2023). Although some proponents of regenerative agriculture would agree with the goals that we set forth for regenerative food systems, regenerative agriculture is ill-defined and has been captured by interests that want primarily to avoid reducing fossil fuel use or gain profits from carbon offsets. I use regeneration as a description of the outcomes I hope to see from food system transformation, not as a prescription for specific practices for farmers.

A crucial difference between regenerative and other food systems is the values that underlie them; a regenerative system supports environmental goods including enhancement of biodiversity, sequestration of carbon and clean water. It also supports social goals of justice, equity and human rights, including the right to healthy food. Economic values, which are often considered as the third pillar of sustainability, are not negligible in regenerative food systems—workers should earn enough money to live comfortably and businesses need to stay afloat financially; but they are subsumed under environmental and social goals. The industrialized capitalist food system, which has created so many of the environmental and social problems described in the next chapter, has inflated economic goals at the cost of environmental quality and human health. This is a consequence of capitalism's emphasis on profit and endless growth, even when the natural resources on which the system depends are being degraded.

From the discussion above, we know that food system goals are in dispute, but what about problems associated with them? Chapter 2 of this book asks whether there is really agreement on global food system problems. Chapter 3 introduces the second section by first going deeper into the significance of narratives, their connections with theories of change and how analyzing food systems through these additional lenses helps to discern their strengths and weaknesses. Chapter 4 examines two different narratives of the meaning of food: "food is a commodity," of value primarily for the profits that can be gained by selling or trading it, versus "food is part of a public commons." In the latter view, food has multiple meanings and values: as a way to earn a livelihood, part of culture and religion, an essential contributor to health and nutrition and more. Chapter 5 introduces power analysis to complement analysis of narratives and theories of change. How power is distributed is one of the main distinguishing features between theories of food system transformation, and mapping how power flows can help to show critical differences between theories. Chapters 6 and 7 explore common narratives of food system transformation, based on the different values assigned to food; Chapter 6 focuses on narratives that do not require structural changes to current food systems, and Chapter 7 turns to narratives that do require such a change. These chapters are about *what* causes transformation, but Chapter 8 goes further to ask *who* can cause transformation and who is ultimately responsible. These chapters reinforce the observation by Béné (2022, 1) that:

> …the challenges that such systemic change would induce are not so much about the technological innovations that would be necessary to support the changes, but more about the governance, political-economy constraints and policy trade-offs that are inherent in the system and would need to be addressed.

Chapters 9 and 10 present spaces where food system transformation is the objective, and contested narratives are apparent: Chapter 9 on two international forums, the Committee on World Food Security and its Civil Society and Indigenous Peoples' Mechanism and the Coordination Hub established as a follow-up to the 2021 UN Food Systems Summit. Chapter 10 focuses on grassroots initiatives at the local and sub-national scale. These chapters explore the various competing narratives at play in these spaces and discuss the importance of context to any examination of food system power.

The concluding chapter (Chapter 11) asks whether there is an emerging über-narrative and convergence of opinion on food system transformation and whether that is even a desirable goal.

Through this book, I will analyze my working hypotheses about food system transformation:

1. Transformation toward regeneration will require:
   a. support for entities that already hold regenerative values, such as agroecological farmers, socially responsible businesses and social movements fighting for food sovereignty;
   b. weakening the sources of power upon which extractive food systems draw, such as subsidies for fossil fuels and productivism, and their ability to externalize the costs of workers' well-being and evade environmental regulations and
   c. changing the public narrative so that regeneration becomes normalized and the dangers of the current extractive system are well understood.
2. Assumptions underlying many widely promoted theories of change in food systems are flawed because the likely result is not a regenerative food system with ecological integrity, improved well-being for all and justice; necessary preconditions don't exist; or the logic of how change will happen doesn't hold up to scrutiny.
3. Food systems that engage more actors and especially broad social movements will be more successful in making the transformation.

These hypotheses have come out of nearly three decades of interaction with local, regional, national and international organizations, and actors (including farmers) intent on transforming the food system in their different spheres and through participation in national and international conferences.

I grew up in the American South during a period of civic unrest due to racial discrimination and was part of a family that valued justice and civic engagement to ameliorate oppression. These experiences had a large impact on my values. I have been influenced by seeing deep poverty and how people cope with it or are crushed by it, in the US and other countries. In addition, I lived for more than a decade in a part of the South (the Texas Gulf Coast) that has been badly contaminated by oil refining companies and saw wildlife and human health compromised by pollution of air and water. This helped to drive my love of the natural world, a fierce desire to protect it from further degradation and deep sadness about the prospects for human survival in the face of climate change and pressure from petroleum companies to continue degrading the environment. Like most of my generation in the US, I didn't grow up on a farm but both of my parents did; and I often heard stories about what it was like to live and work on a tobacco farm (Virginia) or an oranges and strawberries farm (Florida). We are lucky to still own a tract of family land in Virginia which I co-manage. I studied systems ecology and natural resources management in graduate school and became interested in interrelationships among components of systems, especially how they are affected by power and knowledge.

I have been fortunate in encountering many wise people who helped to shape my opinions, and being able to work alongside those who are passionate about fighting for human rights and planetary health. People who have other experiences and backgrounds are likely to have other hypotheses, but in this book I will lay out the reasons why these hypotheses seem most plausible to me and the supporting evidence for them from literature and narratives.

References

Anderson, MR and M Rivera-Ferre. 2021. Food system narratives to end hunger: extractive versus regenerative. *Curr Opinion Environ Sustain* 49:18–25.

Béné, C. 2022. Why the Great Food Transformation may not happen – a deep-dive into our food systems' political economy, controversies and politics of evidence. *World Dev* 154:105881.

Campbell, BM, J Hansen, J Rioux, CM Stirling, S Twomlow and E Wollenberg. 2018. Urgent action to combat climate change and its impact (SDG 13): transforming agriculture and food systems. *Curr Opinion Environ Sustain* 34:13–20.

Duncan, J, M Carolan and JSC Wiskerke. 2021. Regenerating food systems: a social-ecological approach. Pp. 1–11 In: J Duncan, M Carolan and JSC Wiskerke (Eds.) *Routledge Handbook of Sustainable and Regenerative Food Systems*. London: Routledge.

Eakin, H, JP Connors, C Wharton, CF Bertmann, A Xiong and J Stoltfus. 2017. Identifying attributes of food system sustainability: emerging themes and consensus. *Agric Hum Values* 34:757–773. https://doi.org/10.1007/s10460-016-9754-8

Haddad, L, C Hawkes, P Webb, S Thomas, J Beddington, J Waage and D Flynn. 2016. A new global research agenda for food. *Nature* 540:30–32. https://doi.org/10.1038/540030a

Hebinck, A, M Zurek, T Achterbosch, B Forkman, A Kuijsten, M Kuiper, B Nørrung, P van 't Veer and A Leip. 2021. A Sustainability Compass for policy navigation to sustainable food systems. *Global Food Security* 29:100546. https://doi.org/10.1016/j.gfs.2021.100546

High-Level Panel of Experts of the Committee on World Food Security (HLPE). 2014. Food Losses and Waste in the Context of Sustainable Food Systems. A Report by the High Level Panel of Experts on Food Security and Nutrition of the Committee on World Food Security. Rome: FAO.

Hölscher, K, JM Wittmayer and D Loorbach. 2018. Transitions versus transformation: what's the difference? *Env Innov and Societal Trans* 27:1–3. https://doi.org/10.1016/j.eist.2017.10.007

International Panel of Experts on Sustainable Food Systems (IPES-Food). 2023. Smoke and Mirrors. Examining competing framings of food system sustainability: agroecology, regenerative agriculture and nature-based solutions. http://www.ipes-food.org/pages/smokeandmirrors

Mbow, C, C Rosenzweig, LG Barioni, TG Benton, M Herrero, M Krishnapillai, E Liwenga, P Pradhan, MG Rivera-Ferre, T Sapkota, FN Tubiello, Y Xu. 2019. Food security. In: PR Shukla, J Skea, E Calvo Buendia, V Masson-Delmotte, H-O Pörtner, DC Roberts, P Zhai, R Slade, S Connors, R van Diemen, M Ferrat, E Haughey, S Luz, S Neogi, M Pathak, J Petzold, J Portugal Pereira, P Vyas, E Huntley, K Kissick, M Belkacemi and J Malley (Eds) *Climate Change and Land: An IPCC Special Report on Climate Change, Desertification, Land Degradation, Sustainable Land Management, Food Security, and Greenhouse Gas Fluxes in Terrestrial Ecosystems*, Chapter 5. Food Security. https://www.ipcc.ch/srccl/chapter/chapter-5/

Meybeck, A and V Gitz. 2017. Sustainable diets within sustainable food systems. *Proc Nutr Soc* 76:1–11. https://doi.org/10.1017/S0029665116000653

Nguyen, H. 2018. Sustainable food systems: concept and framework. https://www.fao.org/3/ca2079en/CA2079EN.pdf

Patterson, J, Schulz K, Vervoort J, Van der Hel S, Sethi M, Barau A. 2017. Exploring the governance and politics of transformations towards sustainability. *Environ Innov Soc Trans* 24:1–16. https://doi.org/10.1016/j.eist.2016.09.001

UN Food Systems Summit. 2021. About the summit. https://www.un.org/en/food-systems-summit/about

Webb, P, TG Benton, J Beddington, D Flynn, NM Kelly and SM Thomas. 2020. The urgency of food system transformation is now irrefutable. *Nature Food* 1:584–585. https://doi.org/10.1038/s43016-020-00161-0

Weber, H, K Poeggel, H Eakin, D Fischer, DJ Lang, H von Wehrden and A Wiek. 2020. What are the ingredients for food systems change towards sustainability? – Insights from the literature. *Environ Res Lett* 15:113001. https://doi.org/10.1088/1748-9326/ab99fd

Weston, P and J Watts. 2021. The cow in the room: why is no one talking about farming at Cop26? *The Guardian*. https://www.theguardian.com/environment/2021/nov/09/the-cow-in-the-room-why-is-no-one-talking-about-farming-at-cop26-aoe

Willett, W, J Rockström, B Loken, M Springmann, T Lang, S Vermeulen, T Garnett, D Tilman, F DeClerck, AWood, M Jonell, M Clark, LJ Gordon, J Fanzo, C Hawkes, R Zurayk, JA Rivera, W De Vries, LM Sibanda, A Afshin, A Chaudhary, M Herrero, R Agustina, F Branca, A Lartey, S Fan, B Crona, E Fox, V Bignet, M Troell, T Lindahl, S Singh, SE Cornell, KS Reddy, S Narain, S Nishtar, CJL Murray. 2019. Food in the anthropocene: the EAT–Lancet Commission on healthy diets from sustainable food systems. *Lancet* 393:447–492. https://doi.org/10.1016/S0140-6736(18)31788-4

2

DO WE REALLY AGREE ON FOOD SYSTEM PROBLEMS AND GOALS?

The unanimous approval of the Sustainable Development Goals (SDGs) in 2015 was a clear indicator of agreement on many of the challenges that humanity faces. Food systems are implicated in almost all of the SDGs as contributors to problems or solutions or both (Olsson 2019). SDG 2, to end hunger, clearly depends on how food systems work; but food systems are also directly connected with SDGs 1 (poverty), 3 (good health and well-being), 5 (gender equality), 6 (clean water and sanitation), 8 (decent work and economic growth), 10 (reduced inequalities), 11 (sustainable cities and communities), 12 (responsible consumption and production), 13 (climate action), 14 (life below water), 15 (life on land) and 16 (peace, justice and strong institutions). In fact, very few spheres of human activity touch the SDGs more powerfully.

The food system framework as an interlinked system of components spanning inputs, food production, processing and packaging, distribution, consumption and waste management (plus the institutions that govern these activities) has become increasingly popular over the past few decades. It is surprising that this concept took so long to catch on, but promoting food systems thinking was a major objective of the 2021 UN Food Systems Summit and remains an objective of the UN One Planet Sustainable Food Systems Program, decades after the concept of a food system was introduced. When the organizers of international programs and summits want to emphasize the utility of the food system concept, we can infer that it is still in dispute. The separation of food-related analyses into different disciplines and departments surely contributed to the failure to understand that food system issues cannot be managed sector by sector or activity by activity (Olsson 2019). Yet similar blinkers prevent many analysts from seeing food systems as intrinsically connected

DOI: 10.4324/9781003260264-3

with other domestic and global systems (health, trade, investment, finance); although food system transformation often depends on the transformation of other systems, be they economic, governance or resource management.

The interlocking and interdependent nature of systems creates tremendous frustration at times for food system activists. For example, the system of governance over immigration blocks labor reforms in many countries, since recent immigrants often work in agricultural production or processing; yet immigration reform depends on which interests control political spaces as well as criminal networks that traffic people and sell drugs and guns across borders. In the US, dairy farms need year-round experienced labor, and US citizens are very seldom willing to do the hard work involved at the pay that farmers can afford. Furthermore, rural areas are losing farmers rapidly through aging, bankruptcy or migration of young people to urban centers. A logical solution would be for the US to open its borders to immigrants willing to work on farms, at least for a period of time, and then grant citizenship. But immigration reform cannot get through the US Congress, and it is often stymied at the state level because it crosses ideological battle-lines influenced by racism and white supremacy, political aspirations of elected officials and resistance from interests that benefit from the status quo.

Despite approval of SDG 2, to end hunger, success in meeting global food needs, which is the core function of food systems, has been stagnant or declining since 2015, with dramatic set-backs during 2019–2020 while a pandemic swept the world and conflicts and climate change impacts escalated (FAO et al. 2023). Growing environmental degradation (e.g., biodiversity loss, soil fertility depletion, greenhouse gas emissions), social issues (e.g., poorly paid labor, dismal working conditions for many in the food system, overwhelming challenges for new farmers and youth) and health issues (e.g., obesity, diet-related diseases) demonstrate that food systems are not functioning well to meet people's needs now and in the future. Increasing concentration of food industries reflects the growing inequality of income within the food system, as well as unequal political power (IPES-Food 2017a). Environmental degradation is perhaps the most indubitable consequence of food systems, closely followed by deterioration of health through the so-called "dietary transition" (Popkin 1999)—unfortunate terminology which makes the slide from healthier traditional diets to processed and ultra-processed foods that dominate the Western diet seem like a natural progression rather than a choice promoted by food industries and allowed by governments that fail to regulate them. In short, food systems which should be nourishing humans, in coexistence with other plants and animals, are killing the planet's capacity to support life and killing people.

Food systems have a more powerful impact on the natural world than any other human activity. For example, agriculture accounts for 70 percent of freshwater extraction worldwide; and agrichemicals, drug residue, organic matter and sediment from farms are major sources of pollution. In the US, agriculture is the main source of pollution in rivers and streams, the second main source in wetlands and the third main source in lakes; and in China, agriculture is responsible for a large share of surface-water pollution and is almost exclusively responsible for groundwater pollution by nitrogen (Mateo-Sagasta et al. 2017). In Europe, 22 percent of surface water bodies and 28 percent of the groundwater area are significantly affected by nutrient and pesticide pollution from agriculture (EEA 2021). Water pollution from agriculture is also severe in developing countries but proportionally less because untreated sewage entering water bodies is common and constitutes a larger percentage.

Agriculture is a major contributor to soil degradation through water and wind erosion after disturbance, which removes the most fertile topsoil and deposits it ultimately in water sources; deforestation to create more cropland or pasture; livestock overgrazing; pollution with agrichemicals; compaction from heavy farm equipment or livestock and salinization from irrigation. According to the most recent estimates, approximately 1/3 of soils globally are already degraded and over 90 percent could become degraded by 2050 (FAO and ITPS 2015; IPBES 2018). Soil erosion from agricultural fields is estimated to be currently 10 to 20 times (with no tillage) to more than 100 times (with conventional tillage) higher than the soil formation rate (IPCC 2019).

Food systems are the main contributor to catastrophic declines in biodiversity (Benton et al. 2021), primarily through deforestation and habitat loss. Planetary studies estimate that the "safe operating space" for humanity has already been exceeded for genetic diversity—with agriculture being the major driver of this transgression (Campbell et al. 2017). Since 1970, the population sizes of mammals, birds, fish, amphibians and reptiles have declined on average 68 percent (Benton et al. 2021). In addition, many domesticated plant and animal species that have historically been food sources have become less widely produced and consumed (FAO 2019). This loss of genetic diversity makes food systems less resilient to threats, such as pests, pathogens and extreme weather due to climate change. Food system contributions to global warming constitute an additional threat to biodiversity, as ecosystems become drier or wetter and species are not able to adapt. But climate chaos caused by greenhouse gas (GHG) emissions has major impacts on human populations as well, leading to mortality from heatwaves, forced migrations and food insecurity.

Deterioration of oceans is also attributable to agricultural activities, with agrichemicals and sediment being carried by almost every waterway. Agriculture, ports and harbors and aquaculture were identified as the major contributors to ocean degradation by the UN Environment Programme (IRP 2021), with impacts on ocean biodiversity the most severe impact. Large "dead zones" caused by eutrophication, which depletes dissolved oxygen in the water and kills marine life, extend from every major river in the world (Altieri and Diaz 2019) and affect all major fisheries. Furthermore, overharvesting of commercial fish species has caused dramatic declines of many species and the collapse of some fisheries. About 90 percent of marine stock is fully exploited or overfished, and fish catches have plateaued or declined since around 1995 (World Bank 2017). Harvesting for meat is the main reason that stocks have declined (Ripple et al. 2019).

Estimates of the amount of greenhouse gases emitted from the food system are still imprecise, not surprisingly given the complexity of making a good estimate. A major shortcoming of all existing estimates to date is that they do not distinguish among types of food systems. However, it seems clear that industrialized food systems reliant on synthetic fertilizers and other agrichemicals emit far more than agroecological systems that eschew such products, given the large contribution to GHG emissions of the production, transport and application of these products. The IPCC estimated in its *Climate Change and Land* report (2019) that agriculture, forestry and other land use accounted for about 13 percent of carbon dioxide (CO_2), 44 percent of methane (CH_4) and 81 percent of nitrous oxide (N_2O) emissions from human activities globally during 2007–2016, which is 23 percent of total net anthropogenic emissions of GHGs. But this is only a portion of emissions from the entire food system. When we include all activities in the food system, the estimate of GHG emissions goes up to 21–37 percent (Crippa et al. 2021). The largest contribution is from agriculture and land use/land-use change activities (71 percent), with the remaining amounts from supply chain activities including retail, transport, consumption, fuel production, waste management, industrial processes and packaging. A full 20 percent of GHG emissions comes just from food miles, mostly from the transport of fertilizer, agricultural machinery and pesticides (Li et al. 2022). Given the magnitude of food system contributions to biodiversity loss and GHG emissions, the lack of attention to food system transformation until quite recently in the meetings of the Convention on Biodiversity and the UN Climate Change Conferences is shocking.

Certainly, the worst problem associated with food systems is that they are failing to nourish everyone on the planet. The most recent report from the UN agencies that deal with food (FAO et al. 2023) estimated that around 735 million people (9.2 percent of the world population) faced chronic undernourishment in 2022, and nearly 30 percent of the world's population experienced moderate or severe food insecurity. Although global hunger levels were relatively unchanged from 2021, 122 million more people went hungry in 2022 than in 2019 before the COVID pandemic. Progress on hunger had already gone into reverse in the five years before the pandemic, with 50 million more undernourished people in 2019 than in 2014. The worst-affected region is Africa, where 64.5 percent of people in rural areas face moderate or severe food security, higher than in urban areas. The increase in cost of living has put the cost of a healthy diet out of reach of nearly half the world population (FAO et al. 2023).

In addition to food insecurity and hunger, obesity and overweight has nearly tripled among children and adults since 1975 (WHO 2021). The health consequences are severe for people who follow a Western or Standard American Diet (aptly called SAD) with high amounts of ultra-processed and processed food, red meat, high-fat dairy products, salt, sugar and fat. Unfortunately, this diet has been exported by food companies eager to expand sales in the Global South and the health and environmental sequelae are apparent in many countries now (Gilmore et al. 2023). Health issues include obesity and a host of diet-related diseases: type 2 diabetes, hypertension, stroke, cancers, dental disease, osteoporosis, cardiovascular diseases and dementia. The latest Global Burden of Disease study found that dietary risks were the third leading cause of death in 2019 for men and the second for women (GBD 2019 Risk Factors Collaborators 2020). In the US, diet-related diseases have been strongly associated with poor health outcomes from COVID-19: people with metabolic disorders such as type 2 diabetes and obesity, heart conditions such as high blood pressure (hypertension) and heart failure were more likely to be hospitalized with COVID-19 (O'Hearn et al. 2021). From a global perspective, the Editorial Board of *Lancet* (2020, 1129) noted early in the pandemic that, "COVID-19 is a syndemic of coronavirus infection combined with an epidemic of non-communicable diseases, both interacting on a social substrate of poverty and inequality."

The health problems associated with diet are only part of the health impacts of the food system. In addition, the ways that food is produced and processed result in poor health (IPES-Food 2017b). For example, anti-microbial resistance has risen due to the practice of feeding livestock antibiotics at sub-therapeutic levels to prevent disease outbreaks in crowded conditions (Manyi-Loh et al. 2018). People living near confined-animal feeding operations suffer from ammonia and particulates in the air, as well as foul smells which can trigger depression (Von Essen and Auvermann 2005). Farmworkers get notoriously poor treatment, sometimes lacking adequate drinking water or decent housing. With climate change, heat is a growing concern for farmworkers; several have died from heatstroke, and safety measures are urgently needed (Kuehn 2021). People working in meat-packing plants have a high incidence of injuries due to unsafe working conditions and unreasonable demands by their supervisors. COVID outbreaks in US meat-packing plants made national news, yet workers were forced by government orders to keep coming into work and lost their jobs if they stayed home because they or family members were sick.

The social problems stemming from food systems are diverse, and highly connected with inequity across and within countries stemming from racism and discrimination against women, marginalized ethnicities, and people with diverse gender identities (Otero et al. 2015). Wealthy white people do not suffer from lack of access to healthy food (although they certainly have diet-related diseases due to poor consumption habits). But poor people throughout the world cannot afford a healthy diet (FAO et al. 2023), and foods with cultural significance are disappearing as diets converge on a limited number of staple crops and products created from them. Traditional crops, often highly nutritious, have been replaced with wheat, corn and rice, which limits availability of Indigenous foods (Mustafa et al. 2019), particularly in urban areas. People around the world are eating more processed and ultra-processed food as supermarkets replace traditional markets (Hawkes 2008).

Particular groups of people are oppressed and marginalized by extractive industrialized food systems. Women are the main food producers in many countries, responsible for both production and reproduction as the main care-givers of children. Despite greater nutritional needs during pregnancy and lactation, they have a higher prevalence of food insecurity and micronutrient deficiencies (FAO et al. 2023). Although they may be the primary food producers, they face unequal access to land and other resources, including agricultural extension, advisory services and financial services such as credit. In many societies, they are unable to own or inherit land. Due to gendered divisions of household labor, women and girls are often responsible for gathering fuel and water—tasks which have become increasingly time-consuming and difficult with climate chaos. Women often have limited opportunities to work outside socially prescribed activities, and they are paid less than men for the same work in almost every country (Kunze 2018; FAO 2023). In addition, women are sexually and physically abused, sometimes with social acquiescence. For example, 25 percent of respondents in the most recent Gender Social Norms Index report said that it is acceptable for a man to beat his wife (UNDP 2023). Transgender and LBGTQIA+ people face even more discrimination and homosexuality is criminalized in 64 countries, with more than half in Africa (BBC 2023). Women were hit harder by COVID than men, losing their jobs more often or being forced to take on new childcare or eldercare responsibilities on top of work (Mooi-Reci and Risman 2021).

Migrant and immigrant workers are another group that is systematically oppressed and marginalized. More than 150 million workers migrate outside their home countries in search of work; they are often exploited by human trafficking and suffer disproportionately from workplace accidents and injuries, low pay, withheld pay and poor mental health (Hargreaves et al. 2019). COVID-19 highlighted the inequitable working conditions of these workers. In many instances, they are employed precariously, and so were ineligible for sick leave, social security or COVID-19 special payments that eased recovery for other workers (Reid et al. 2021). Intersecting with migrant and immigrant workers are people from marginalized ethnicities, who face systematic discrimination in access to food, employment and resources. In the US, enslaved people from Africa and Indigenous people built up enormous wealth for invading settlers from Europe, yet they have been able to retain very little farmland; only 1.4 percent of US farmers are Black now, and Black farmers lost roughly $326 billion worth of acreage during the 20th century due to discrimination by the US Department of Agriculture and inability to inherit land (NASS 2019; Francis et al. 2022).

With the shift to a majority-urban world (as of 2009, according to the Population Division of the Department of Economic and Social Affairs), disconnects between food producers and consumers have widened. This means that people who buy food are usually not aware of how their food is produced nor of hardships that producers face. Especially for youth and beginning farmers, access to good farmland is more and more difficult. Land-grabbing of fertile areas in the Global South to produce food or biofuels for the Global North has been rampant (GRAIN 2016; Yang and He 2021). Similarly, small-scale fishers and pastoralists have lost their traditional territories as they have been sold and privatized. Despite the myth that young people do not want to farm now, many are clamoring for land redistribution so that they can earn a living from land (CSM Youth Working Group 2020). If national policies rewarded farmers for the cost of production (parity), it is likely that many people would start producing food. But in wealthy industrialized countries, only the largest-scale farmers and those who receive generous government subsidies are making a decent living from farming. In 2000, less than half of the 89 percent of US farms where farming is the principal occupation (Whitt et al. 2021) and which sell less than $350,000 had positive farm incomes (USDA 2022). Other food system occupations, such as farmworkers, fish processors, meat packers, cashiers in supermarkets and restaurant workers, offer poverty wages and often dangerous working conditions (Foodprint 2020). In sum, the environmental, health, sociocultural and economic problems in food systems are massive and getting worse.

But which food systems need to change, and which aspects need to change to prevent the devastating damage documented above? Although many people refer to the "global food system," there are many different food systems in the world today that operate in parallel (Anderson 2015). Sometimes foods produced by a farm or caught by a fisherman end up in many different food systems. At one end of the spectrum are subsistence systems, in which producers grow, catch or hunt only for themselves and their households. At the other end of the spectrum are vast global supply lines that bring food across the planet from places where it is relatively cheap to produce to places where it can be sold at high prices. Food, agricultural and agricultural input businesses are rapidly becoming more concentrated and exerting more control over national and international policymakers (IPES-Food 2017a). This means that spaces are shrinking where workers can bargain for better working conditions, and consumers can exercise real choice over food that is available and how it was produced. Industrialized countries are in the grip of the corporate food regime (McMichael 2005), where profit and decision-making are controlled by wealthy corporations.

Although almost all food systems entail some disruption of the natural environment, the industrialized food system is most harmful and also causes the greatest sociocultural damage. While some people refer to industrialized food systems as "conventional," that is a misnomer: this system began to develop in the 1900s and has metastasized to all industrialized countries and many places in the Global South over the last few decades (Wilkinson 2009). The Green Revolution of the 1960s through 1980s (with offshoots such as AGRA, formerly known as the Alliance for a Green Revolution in Africa, still ongoing) invested in crop breeding, hybrid seeds, synthetic fertilizer and pesticides and irrigation in the Philippines, Mexico and South Asia—a massive push to spread industrialized agriculture in the Global South. But the beginnings of this system came much earlier. World War I marked the marriage of military and agricultural technologies: the Haber-Bosch process was discovered shortly before the war broke out and was used to produce explosives as well as fertilizer. The economic mobilization demanded by warfare also created close collaboration between government and private corporations. The US created corporations chartered under state law, such as the Grain Corporation, to manage food commodity markets; and after the war, systems for controlling commodity flows were implemented. Wartime food demands led to more imports and less reliance on local markets. Perhaps one of its biggest impacts was the widespread recognition among policymakers that adequate cheap food is necessary to maintain political and economic stability (Janes et al. 2019). While industrialized agriculture increased production and productivity substantially through synthetic chemical inputs, mechanization and irrigation that replaced human labor and produced cheap (subsidized) food, it did so at the cost of human and environmental health (IAASTD 2009) and massive loss of traditional foodways and the cultural connections based on food.

With projected population growth to 9.7 billion by 2050 and a peak of 10.4 billion by 2080 (UN DESA 2022), many people claim that there is no choice but industrialized agriculture to produce enough food for everyone. Yet the information above shows that industrialized agriculture is rapidly destroying the resource base on which stable food production depends. That is, the industrialized food system is completely unsustainable. The belief that industrialized agriculture can continue to feed large numbers of people ignores the fact that exponential population growth has only been possible due to fossil fuels and the vast increases in production and productivity that their use allowed (Townes 1993). Continuing with current fossil fuel use exacerbates climate chaos, which is already undercutting production, productivity and nutrient content through heat, drought, floods and other extreme weather events (Zhao et al. 2017). Unless substitutes to fossil fuel use to produce, transport, and preserve food can be found quickly (which seems unlikely), a population crash seems to be on the horizon.

Few people argue with the abundant evidence of resource degradation due to agriculture, the growing threat that climate change poses for food systems and the ways that the COVID pandemic exacerbated lack of availability and access to food. Where they run into most disagreement is about whether social inequalities are sufficiently grave that they demand immediate remedies, such as wealthy countries paying poor countries for loss and damages caused by climate chaos. The other major cause of disagreement is regarding the causes of food system problems. At this point, some focus on ways that "development," globalization and capitalism have lifted people out of abject poverty or extended average life-spans and claim that food system problems can be fixed within this modernity paradigm. Indeed, the health of the world's population is steadily improving: global life expectancy at birth increased from 67.2 years in 2000 to 73.5 years in 2019. Healthy life expectancy has increased in 202 of 204 countries and territories. In 21 countries, healthy life expectancy at birth increased by more than 10 years between 1990 and 2019, with gains of up to 19.1 years. The estimated number of deaths in children under 5 years decreased from 9.6 million in 2000 to 5 million in 2019 (*Lancet* 2020). The living standards of millions of people in emerging economies have increased over the last several decades, and most economists see innovation and economic growth as the cause (Broughel and Thierer 2019). The World Bank points to steady declines in extreme poverty (income below $1.90/day) over the past 25 years, until numbers started to increase again in 2020 due to COVID-19. Global poverty resumed its pre-pandemic downward trajectory; yet between 75 million and 95 million additional people could be living in extreme poverty in 2022, compared to pre-COVID-19 projections, because of the lingering effects of the pandemic, the war in Ukraine and rising inflation (World Bank 2022). Of course, country and global averages mask enormous discrepancies across class, race and gender; and inequality within and between countries has risen over the last several decades (Bourguignon 2015)

Others claim that aspects of modernity itself are to blame for failures in the food system: separation of humans from nature and from their local communities, globalization, over-reliance on technology that has unforeseen negative impacts and the exploitation and appropriation associated with capitalism and colonialism (e.g., Rosin et al. 2012; Bradford 2019; Campbell 2020). Many civil society representatives and scholars blame neoliberalism, its rapid rise across industrialized countries since 1980, financialization of agricultural resources and particularly privatization of public goods and deregulation of commodities derivatives (Patel 2012; Russell 2022).

Capital accumulation trumps environmental or social concerns in this system. Harvey (2005, 2) wrote that neoliberalism:

> proposes that human well-being can best be advanced by liberating individual entrepreneurial freedoms and skills within an institutional framework characterized by strong private property rights, free markets and free trade. The role of the state is to create and preserve an institutional framework appropriate to such practices.

That is, the role of the state is limited under neoliberalism to advancing private property rights, free markets and "free trade," even though the state might assume other roles that would enhance regenerative food systems better. Neoliberalism demands the removal of barriers to trade, such as tariffs, regulations, certain standards and laws, and restrictions on capital flows and investment. It also encourages privatization of public services from water to the Internet, an emphasis on individualism rather than the common good and reducing public expenditures for social services such as education and health. Richard Robbins (1999, 100) summarized the main principles behind neoliberalism as follows:

- Sustained economic growth is the way to human progress.
- Free markets without government interference would be the most efficient and socially optimal allocation of resources.
- Economic globalization would be beneficial to everyone.
- Privatization removes inefficiencies of the public sector.
- Governments should mainly function to provide the infrastructure to advance the rule of law with respect to property rights and contracts.

These principles have not been rigorously tested, but there is a plethora of examples of tragic consequences to health, well-being, provision of essential services to the public, environmental quality and national economies when they have been put into practice, such as through "structural adjustments" required for countries to receive loans from the World Bank or the IMF, or through Chile's experiment with neoliberalism under Augusto Pinochet. Wealthy countries play by a different set of rules than poor countries; for example, tariffs were commonly used by the US and other wealthy countries to protect their own fledgling industries; yet the US expects other countries to open up tariffs to allow "free trade." Reijer Hendrikse (2021) has highlighted the alarming rise of "neo-illiberalism," or the symbiosis of neoliberal capitalism and the nationalist far-right. This has allowed wealthy elites to take over liberal-democratic governments and disregard the rule of law, while rolling back protections on independent academia and a free press.

John McMurtry sees capitalism at present having entered a "cancer stage," multiplying out of control and destroying ecological, social and organic life. He described this process as "global ecogenocide" (McMurtry 2013). As part of this uncontrolled growth, food industry in all sectors from seeds and agrichemicals to machinery and retail stores has concentrated power and resists any changes that may impinge on its profits. Christophe Béné (2022) sees this phenomenon as the leading impediment to food system transformation in a positive direction. Others point to challenges to democracy and our collective mental frames (Hassanein 2003; Lappé 2013). These issues feed on and reinforce each other. A common thread in these critiques is that power imbalances between wealthy people and corporations and poor people, often suffering from violation or abuse of human rights, are the fundamental cause of the dismal state of food systems.

The growth of inequality and extractive industry is linked to modernity and the neoliberal path that many industrialized countries have chosen to follow, although there are sharp differences in food systems and access to healthy food between countries that have emphasized greater equality, e.g., socialist countries, and those that have emphasized economic growth at all costs. These disagreements are critical, of course, because they lead to very different ideas for solutions.

But what about agreement on goals, or the characteristics of a *good* food system? The mile-high perspective of the Sustainable Development Goals (SDGs) does not translate to agreement on how food systems must be configured to achieve these goals. Structural transformation of food systems is not part of the SDGs; their objectives are about making changes within existing systems. For example, the targets under SDG 2 (end hunger) are:

1 By 2030, end hunger and ensure access by all people, in particular, the poor and people in vulnerable situations, including infants, to safe, nutritious and sufficient food all year round.
2 By 2030, end all forms of malnutrition, including achieving, by 2025, the internationally agreed targets on stunting and wasting in children under 5 years of age, and address the nutritional needs of adolescent girls, pregnant and lactating women and older persons.
3 By 2030, double the agricultural productivity and incomes of small-scale food producers, in particular women, Indigenous peoples, family farmers, pastoralists and fishers, including through secure and equal access to land, other productive resources and inputs, knowledge, financial services, markets and opportunities for value addition and non-farm employment.
4 By 2030, ensure sustainable food production systems and implement resilient agricultural practices that increase productivity and production, that help maintain ecosystems, that strengthen capacity for adaptation to

climate change, extreme weather, drought, flooding and other disasters and that progressively improve land and soil quality.

5 By 2020, maintain the genetic diversity of seeds, cultivated plants and farmed and domesticated animals and their related wild species, including through soundly managed and diversified seed and plant banks at the national, regional and international levels, and promote access to and fair and equitable sharing of benefits arising from the utilization of genetic resources and associated traditional knowledge, as internationally agreed.

a Increase investment, including through enhanced international cooperation, in rural infrastructure, agricultural research and extension services, technology development and plant and livestock gene banks in order to enhance agricultural productive capacity in developing countries, in particular least developed countries.

b Correct and prevent trade restrictions and distortions in world agricultural markets, including through the parallel elimination of all forms of agricultural export subsidies and all export measures with equivalent effect, in accordance with the mandate of the Doha Development Round.

c Adopt measures to ensure the proper functioning of food commodity markets and their derivatives and facilitate timely access to market information, including on food reserves, in order to help limit extreme food price volatility (UN Department of Economic and Social Affairs, 2022).

These targets are ambitious but say nothing about why they have not been met already, despite years of effort, nor about how failure to meet them violates human rights. Without understanding the barriers, we have little hope of overcoming them. Furthermore, the targets are vague (e.g., what is the "proper functioning of food commodity markets and their derivatives"?) and there are no penalties for countries that do not meet them. We know from the SOFI reports that the world is not on track to end hunger or meet any of these targets, but the SDGs do not specify what must change from the status quo to ensure that they are met.

"Resilience" is an especially problematic goal for food systems, unless the end-goals of resilience are specified carefully. Johns Hopkins University's Center for a Livable Future defined resilient food systems as "able to withstand and recover from disruptions in a way that ensures a sufficient supply of acceptable and accessible food for all" and has created a number of resources about achieving resilience (Center for a Livable Future n.d.). In an era of pandemics, climate change, increasing risks from extreme weather events, sea-level rise and conflict, a sufficient supply of acceptable and accessible food is indeed important. But we need to move beyond this basic criterion to look at how that food is produced and distributed, and who profits from it. COVID-19 demonstrated the fragility of a food system based on national and global supply chains and underpaid, vulnerable labor. The industrialized food system has been hugely resilient, partly through concentration of food industries and their resulting political power, which they use to maintain their dominant position. We need a food system that allows justice and equity to be resilient, which will entail undermining the sources of resilience of existing sources of power.

Many people are content with the FAO definition of sustainable food systems, putting profitability "throughout" as equivalent to economic sustainability. Where I live, farmers will sometimes say, "If it's profitable, it's sustainable!" But profitability depends mostly on policies that affect prices paid for inputs and received for farm products; it has very little to do with long-term social or environmental sustainability. Current actors' constant search for greater profits is precisely what has led to poor public health, poor labor conditions and wages for workers and environmental contamination. By foisting these costs (deemed to be "externalities") onto the public, other countries or future generations, they can realize greater profits. Advocates for degrowth claim that these dismal outcomes can be turned around, however (more about degrowth and what it would mean for the food system in Chapter 4).

The first chapter introduced how regenerative food systems go beyond sustainable food systems. Achieving regenerative food systems requires deep structural transformation of food systems and a reorientation of values so that fairness and contributions to the public good are seen as having more value than profits that accrue to individuals. This implies winners and losers in transformation: losers will be those who profit—often a great deal—from the way that the food system is organized now and its current power relations. Power is concentrated at present in the largest agribusinesses that control food manufacturing, distribution and retailing: they create policies for everything food-system related ranging from whether farmers can save seed to the terms of trade agreements. In essence, they determine who eats what. Distributing power more equitably will lead to enhanced public good by allowing other actors in the food system to have greater autonomy.

Although there is agreement on environmental and to some extent health problems associated with food systems, agreement breaks down when we talk about social inequality and specific goals and even more when we discuss pathways and whether they entail moving away from neoliberal growthism and reining in the current exploitation of resources. The diversity of goals and pathways being proffered toward sustainable (or regenerative) food systems is not surprising. The next chapter explores the significance of narratives in creating and reinforcing different perspectives on problems and solutions.

References

Altieri, AH and RJ Diaz. 2019. Chapter 24- Dead zones: oxygen depletion in coastal ecosystems. Pp. 453–473 In: World Seas: An Environmental Evaluation (2nd ed). *Volume III. Ecological Issues and Environmental Impacts*. https://doi.org/10.1016/B978-0-12-805052-1.00021-8

Anderson, MD. 2015. The role of knowledge in building food security resilience across food system domains. *J Environ Stud Sci* 5:543–559

Béné, C. 2022. Why the great food transformation may not happen – A deep-dive into our food systems' political economy, controversies and politics of evidence. *World Dev* 154:105881. https://doi.org/10.1016/j.worlddev.2022.105881

Benton, TG, C Bieg, H Harwatt, R Pudasaini and L Wellesley. 2021. *Food System Impacts on Biodiversity Loss: Three Levers for Food System Transformation in Support of Nature*. London: Chatham House.

Bourguignon, F. 2015. *The Globalization of Inequality*. T. Scott-Railton (Trans.). Princeton University Press. https://doi.org/10.1515/9781400865659

Bradford, J. 2019. *The Future is Local: Food System Adaptations to the Great Simplification*. Post Carbon Institute. https://www.arc2020.eu/wp-content/uploads/2019/09/Bradford_The-Future-Is-Rural_2019_compressed.pdf

Broughel, J and AD Thierer. 2019. Technological innovation and economic growth: a brief report on the evidence. *Mercatus Research Paper*. https://ssrn.com/abstract=3346495 https://doi.org/10.2139/ssrn.3346495

British Broadcasting Company (BBC). 2023. Homosexuality: the countries where it is illegal to be gay. 31 March 2023. https://www.bbc.com/news/world-43822234

Campbell, BM, DJ Beare, EM Bennett, JM Hall-Spencer, JSI Ingram, F Jaramillo, R Ortiz, N Ramankutty, JA Sayer and D Shindell. 2017. Agriculture production as a major driver of the Earth system exceeding planetary boundaries. *Ecol Society* 22(4):8. https://doi.org/10.5751/ES-09595-220408

Campbell, H. 2020. *Farming Inside Invisible Worlds: Modernist Agriculture and its Consequences*. London: Bloomsbury Publishing.

Center for a Livable Future. N.d. *Food System Resilience*. Johns Hopkins University. https://clf.jhsph.edu/projects/food-system-resilience

Crippa, M, E Solazzo, D Guizzardi, E Monfort-Ferarrio, FN Tubiello and A Leip. 2021. Food systems are responsible for a third of global anthropogenic GHG emissions. *Nature Food* 2:198–209. https://doi.org/10.1038/s43016-021-00225-9

CSM Youth Working Group. 2020. *Youth Demands for a Radical Transformation of Our Food System*. Civil Society and Indigenous Peoples Mechanism, Committee on World Food Security. https://www.csm4cfs.org/csm-youth-policy-declaration-covid-19/

European Environment Agency (EEA). 2021. Drivers of and pressures arising from selected key water management challenges: a European overview. EEA Report Number No 09/2021. https://www.eea.europa.eu/publications/drivers-of-and-pressures-arising

Food and Agriculture Organization (FAO). 2019. The state of the world's biodiversity for food and agriculture. In: J Bélanger and D Pilling (Eds.) *FAO Commission on Genetic Resources for Food and Agriculture Assessments*. Rome. http://www.fao.org/3/CA3129EN/CA3129EN.pdf

Food and Agriculture Organization (FAO). 2023. *The Status of Women in Agrifood Systems*. Rome. https://doi.org/10.4060/cc5343en

FAO, IFAD, UNICEF, WFP and WHO. 2023. *The State of Food Security and Nutrition in the World 2023*. Urbanization, agrifood systems transformation and healthy diets across the rural–urban continuum. Rome: FAO. https://doi.org/10.4060/cc3017en

FAO and ITPS. 2015. Status of the World's Soil Resources (SWSR) – Main Report. Food and Agriculture Organization of the United Nations and Intergovernmental Technical Panel on Soils, Rome, Italy.

Foodprint. 2020. Labor and workers in the food system. https://foodprint.org/issues/labor-workers-in-the-food-system/

Francis, DV, D Hamilton, TW Mitchell, NA Rosenberg and BW Stucki. 2022. Black land loss: 1920–1997. *Amer Econ Assoc Papers and Proceedings* 112:38–42. https://doi.org/10.1257/pandp.20221015

GBD 2019 Risk Factors Collaborators. 2020. Global burden of 87 risk factors in 204 countries and territories, 1990–2019: a systematic analysis for the Global Burden of Disease Study 2019. *The Lancet* 396:1223. https://doi.org/10.1016/S0140-6736(20)30752-2

Gilmore, AB, A Fabbri, F Baum, A Bertscher, K Bondy, H-J Chang, S Demaio, A Erzse, N Freudenberg, S Frield, KJ Hofman, P Johns, SA Karim, J Lacy-Nichols, CM Paes de Carvalho, R Marten, M McKee, M Petticrew, L Robertson, V Tancharoensathien, AM Thow. 2023. Defining and conceptualising the commercial determinants of health. *The Lancet* 401(10383):1194–1213. https://doi.org/10.1016/S0140-6736(23)00013-2

GRAIN. 2016. The global farmland grab in 2016: how big, how bad? https://grain.org/article/entries/5492-the-global-farmland-grab-in-2016-how-big-how-bad

Hargreaves, S, K Rustage, LB Nellums, A McAlpine, N Pocock, D Devakumar, RW Aldridge, I Abubakar, KL Kristensen, JW Himmels, JS Friedland and Cathy Zimmerman. 2019. Occupational health outcomes among international migrant workers: a systematic review and meta-analysis. *Lancet Glob Health* 7:e872. https://doi.org/10.1016/S2214-109X(19)30204-9

Harvey, D. 2005. *A Brief History of Neoliberalism*. Oxford: Oxford University Press.

Hassanein, N. 2003. Practicing food democracy: a pragmatic politics of transformation. *J Rur Stud* 19:77–86. https://doi.org/10.1016/S0743-0167(02)00041-4

Hawkes, C. 2008. Dietary implications of supermarket development: a global perspective. *Dev Pol Rev* 26(6):657–692. https://doi.org/10.1111/j.1467-7679.2008.00428.x

Hendrikse, R. 2021. The rise of neo-illiberalism. *Krisis* 1:65–93. https://doi.org/10.21827/krisis.40.2.37158

Intergovernmental Science-Policy Platform on Biodiversity and Ecosystems Services (IPBES). 2018. The IPBES assessment report on land degradation and restoration. In: L Montanarella, R Scholes and A Brainich (Eds.) *Secretariat of the Intergovernmental Science-Policy Platform on Biodiversity and Ecosystem Services*. Bonn, Germany. https://doi.org/10.5281/zenodo.3237392

International Assessment of Agricultural Knowledge, Science & Technology (IAASTD). 2009. Agriculture at a Crossroad: Global Report. https://wedocs.unep.org/20.500.11822/8590

International Panel of Experts on Sustainable Food Systems (IPES-Food). 2017a. Too big to feed: exploring the impacts of mega-mergers, consolidation and concentration of power in the agri-food sector. https://ipes-food.org/_img/upload/files/Concentration_FullReport.pdf

International Panel of Experts on Sustainable Food Systems (IPES-Food). 2017b. Unravelling the food–health nexus: addressing practices, political economy, and power relations to build healthier food systems. https://ipes-food.org/_img/upload/files/HEALTH_FULLREPORT(1).PDF

International Resource Panel (IRP). 2021. Governing coastal resources: implications for a sustainable blue economy. S Fletcher, Y Lu, P Alvarez, C McOwen, Y Baninla, AM Fet, G He, C Hellevik, H Klimmek, J Martin, R Mendoza Alfaro, G Philis, N Rabalais, U Rodriguez Estrada, J Wastell, S Winton, JA Yuan. Report of the International Resource Panel. United Nations Environment Programme. Nairobi, Kenya.

Intergovernmental Panel on Climate Change (IPCC). 2019. Summary for policymakers. In: PR Shukla, J Skea, E Calvo Buendia, V Masson-Delmotte, H-O Pörtner, DC Roberts, P Zhai, R Slade, S Connors, R van Diemen, M Ferrat, E Haughey, S Luz, S Neogi, M Pathak, J Petzold, J Portugal Pereira, P Vyas, E Huntley, K Kissick, M Belkacemi and J Malley (Eds.) *Climate Change and Land: An IPCC Special Report on Climate Change, Desertification, Land Degradation, Sustainable Land Management, Food Security, and Greenhouse Gas Fluxes in Terrestrial Ecosystems.* https://www.ipcc.ch/site/assets/uploads/sites/4/2020/02/SPM_Updated-Jan20.pdf

Janes, L, A Merleaux, HZ Veit, A Weinreg and S Yamshita. 2019. World War I and the origins of the modern food system. *Glob Food Hist* 5(3):224–238. https://doi.org/10.1080/20549547.2019.1666647

Kuehn, BM. 2021. Why farmworkers need more than new laws for protection from heat-related illness. *JAMA* 326(12):1135–1137. https://doi.org/ 10.1001/jama.2021.15454

Kunze, A. 2018. The gender wage gap in developed countries. Pp. 369–394 In: SL Averett, LM Argy and SD Hoffman (Eds.) *The Oxford Handbook of Women and The Economy*. Oxford: Oxford University Press.

Lancet. 2020. Global health: time for radical change? *The Lancet* 396(10258):1129. https://doi.org/10.1016/S0140-6736(20)32131-0

Lappé, FM. 2013. *Ecomind: Changing the Way We Think, to Create the World We Want*. New York: Bold Type Books.

Li, M, N Jia, M Lenzen, A Malik, L Weil, J Yutong and D Raubenheimer. 2022. Global food-miles account for nearly 20% of total food-systems emissions. *Nature Food* 3:445–453. https://doi.org/10.1038/s43016-022-00531-w

Manyi-Loh, C., S Mamphweli, E Meyer and A Okoh. 2018. Antibiotic use in agriculture and its consequential resistance in environmental sources: potential public health implications. *Molecules* 23(4): 795

Mateo-Sagasta, J, SM Zadeh and H Turral. 2017. *Water Pollution from Agriculture: A Global Review*. UN Food & Agriculture Organization and International Water Management Institute. https://www.fao.org/3/i7754e/i7754e.pdf

McMichael, P. 2005. Global development and the corporate food regime. Pp. 265–299 In: FH Buttel and P McMichael (Eds.) *New Directions in the Sociology of Global Development* (*Research in Rural Sociology and Development, Vol. 11*). Bingley: Emerald Group Publishing Limited. https://doi.org/10.1016/S1057-1922(05)11010-5

McMurtry, J. 2013. *The Cancer Stage of Capitalism: From Crisis to Cure*. 2nd edition. London: Pluto Press.

Mooi-Reci, I and BJ Risman. 2021. The gendered impacts of COVID-19: lessons and reflections. *Gender Soc* 35(2):161–167. https://doi.org/10.1177/08912432211001305

Mustafa, MA, S Mayes and F Massawe. 2019. Crop diversification through a wider use of underutilised crops: A strategy to ensure food and nutrition security in the face of climate change. Pp. 125–149 In: A Sarkar, SR Sensarma and GW vanLoon. (Eds.) *Sustainable Solutions for Food Security. Combating Climate Change by Adaptation*. Cham: Springer. https://doi.org/10.1007/978-3-319-77878-5

National Agricultural Statistics Service (NASS) 2019. Black producers – 2017 census. https://www.nass.usda.gov/Publications/Highlights/2019/2017Census_Black_Producers.pdf

O'Hearn, M, J Liu, F Cudhea, R Micha and D Mozaffarian. 2021. Coronavirus disease 2019 hospitalizations attributable to cardiometabolic conditions in the United States: a comparative risk analysis. *J Am Heart Assoc* 10(5):e019259. https://doi.org/10.1161/JAHA.120.019259

Olsson, EGA. 2019. The transformative potential of the food system concept. Pp. 199–216 In: EGA Olsson and P Gooch (Eds.) *Natural Resource Conflicts and Sustainable Development*. London: Routledge.

Otero, G, G Pechlaner, G Liberman and E Gürcan. 2015. The neoliberal diet and inequality in the United States. *Soc Sci Medicine* 142:47–55.

Patel, R. 2012. *Stuffed and Starved: The Hidden Battle for the World Food System*. Brooklyn, NY: Melville House.

Popkin, BM. 1999. Urbanization, lifestyle changes and the nutrition transition. *World Dev* 27(11):1905–1916. https://doi.org/10.1016/S0305-750X(99)00094-7

Reid, A, E Ronda-Perez and MB Schenker. 2021. Migrant workers, essential work, and COVID-19. *Amer J Indust Med* 64(2):73–77. https://doi.org/10.1002/ajim.23209

Ripple, WJ, C Wolf, TM Newsome, MG Betts, G. Ceballos, F. Courchamp, MW Haywards, B van Valkenburgh, AD Wallach and B Worm. 2019. Are we eating the world's megafauna to extinction? *Conserv Lett* 12:e12627. https://doi.org/10.1111/conl.12627

Robbins, R. 1999. *Global Problems and the Culture of Capitalism*. Boston: Allyn and Bacon.

Rosin, C, P Stock and H Campbell. 2012. *Food Systems Failure: The Global Food Crisis and the Future of Agriculture*. London and New York: Earthscan.

Russell, R. 2022. *Price Wars: How the Commodities Markets Made Our Chaotic World*. New York: Doubleday.

Townes, HL. 1993. The hydrocarbon era, world population growth and oil use--a continuing geological challenge: Presidential Address. *Amer Assoc Petrol Geol Bull* 77(5):723–730.

UN Department of Economic and Social Affairs (UNDESA). 2022. World Population Prospects 2022: Summary of Results. https://www.un.org/development/desa/pd/sites/www.un.org.development.desa.pd/files/wpp2022_key_messages.pdf

UN Development Programme (UNDP). 2023. A decade of stagnation: new UNDP data shows gender biases remain entrenched. https://www.undp.org/press-releases/decade-stagnation-new-undp-data-shows-gender-biases-remain-entrenched

US Department of Agriculture (USDA), Economic Research Service. 2022. *Farm Household Well-being: Farm Household Income Estimates,* December 1, 2022. https://www.ers.usda.gov/topics/farm-economy/farm-household-well-being/farm-household-income-estimates/

Von Essen, SG and BW Auvermann. 2005. Health effects from breathing air near CAFOs for feeder cattle or hogs. *J Agromedicine* 10(4):55–64. https://doi.org/10.1300/J096v10n04_08

Whitt, C., JE Todd and A. Keller. 2021. *America's Diverse Family Farms*. 2021 Edition. Economic Research Service Economic Information Bulletin Number 231. USDA.

Wilkinson, J. 2009. The globalization of agribusiness and developing world food systems. *Monthly Review* 61(4). https://monthlyreview.org/2009/09/01/globalization-of-agribusiness-and-developing-world-food-systems/

World Bank. 2017. Life below water. SDG 14 Atlas Data Topics. https://datatopics.worldbank.org/sdgatlas/archive/2017/SDG-14-life-below-water.html

World Bank. 2022. Overview. https://www.worldbank.org/en/topic/poverty/overview

World Health Organization (WHO). 2021. Obesity and overweight. https://www.who.int/news-room/fact-sheets/detail/obesity-and-overweight

Yang, B and J He. 2021. Global land grabbing: a critical review of case studies across the world. *Land* 10:324. https://doi.org/10.3390/land10030324

Zhao, C, B Liu, S Piao, Z Wang, DB Lobell, Y Huang, M Huang, Y Yao, S Bassu, P Ciais, J-L Durand, J Elliott, F Ewert, IA Janssens, T Li, E Lin, Q Liu, P Martre, C Müller, S Peng, J Peñuelas, AC Ruane, D Wallach, T Wang, D Wu, Z Liu, Y Zhu, Z Shu and S Asseng. 2017. Temperature increase reduces global yields of major crops in four independent estimates. *Proc Nat Acad Sci* 114 (35):9326–9331. https://doi.org/10.1073/pnas.1701762114

SECTION 2

Competing Food System Narratives

3

SIGNIFICANCE OF NARRATIVES AND THEIR CONNECTIONS WITH THEORIES OF CHANGE

Narratives give structure and meaning to people's lives. We search for intelligible patterns to make sense of our perceptions and experiences because without them, we would be overwhelmed with perception.

> [W]e pick out bits of the stream of experience and give them boundaries and significance by labeling them. Like all talk and all action, narrative is socially and epistemologically constructive: through telling, we make ourselves and our experiential worlds.
>
> *(Johnstone 2015, 644–645)*

Narratives allow us to sort perceptions into repeating patterns and ignore extraneous details, once we have fit perceptions into a familiar form. We swim through a sea of narratives, and they shape our perceptions of food and food systems. In trying to disentangle narratives from frames, two concepts that are often conflated, Aukes et al. (2020, 2) define the narrative as:

> a course of action with a beginning, a middle (often a complication) and an end (often a resolution) used by humans to make sense of experiences. Narratives include a chronicle, a sequence of events, as well as the interpretation of these events' meaning.

Frames are more general and perhaps more important for what they *do* than for what they *are*. "Framing" can be defined as "select[ing] some aspects of a perceived reality and mak[ing] them more salient in a communicating text, in such a way as to promote a particular problem definition, causal interpretation, moral evaluation, and/or treatment recommendation for the item

DOI: 10.4324/9781003260264-5

described" (Entman 1993, 52). As an example, the 2022 invasion of Ukraine by Russia led to national food shortages, particularly in Africa and the Middle East, and raised fears of global food shortages. In this case, the common framing was the risks of food insecurity caused by this conflict while neglecting many other conflicts, the impacts of climate change around the world that have led to regional food insecurity and structural problems in the global food system that were never addressed adequately after the two previous food crises which occurred since 2007.

Narratives can be true or false, but false narratives can be quite compelling if they are promoted by charismatic figures or serve powerful interests. A common narrative about food system transformation in the US and the EU has been productivist, with the claim that producing more wheat and corn will alleviate food insecurity around the world and that restrictions on planting imposed by conservation programs should be lifted to allow maximum production. This is a false narrative, since (1) greater availability of wheat and corn will not lead automatically to greater access by people who lack food; (2) conservation programs are part of a suite of measures that will help to protect current and future food security and (3) most US corn becomes animal feed or ethanol or feedstock for industry, not human food. Going back to the Russian invasion of Ukraine, great hopes were placed on the Black Sea Grain Initiative, a UN-brokered deal to allow ships to get Ukrainian wheat past the Russian blockade. The US Agency for International Development claimed that the deal "helps people in need across the globe by delivering desperately needed grains to lower income countries and bringing down food prices" (USAID 2022). Similarly, the European Commission celebrated the initiative as "a critical step forward in efforts to overcome the global food insecurity caused by Russia's aggression against Ukraine" (European Commission 2022). Yet analysis by the Oakland Institute of where the grain was actually sold showed that only three percent went to low-income countries and two percent went to the World Food Program for food aid. Forty-four percent and thirty-six percent went to upper-income and upper-middle income countries, respectively. The grain exporters were large agribusinesses and oligarchs associated with European and North American financial interests, and grain sales seem to have been driven by the need to service their debts (Mousseau 2023). So despite the lofty rhetoric about helping people in desperate need, the motivation for this deal was financial dealings.

How stories are framed is quite significant, because it directs our attention to what we can safely ignore. In this book, I am especially concerned with narratives because they steer the public and policymakers toward certain transformational possibilities by constricting or enlarging imagination. Paul Levy (2013, 250) notes,

> How we experience life is determined by the meaning we place on it, how we view it, the metaphors we use to contextualize it, and the story we tell

> ourselves about it. When we "tell our stories" about ourselves, both to ourselves and others, it is important to differentiate: there's a way of telling our story that solidifies and reinforces the spell we are under, and conversely, there's a way of telling our story that liberates us from our spell.

That is, our narratives can keep reinforcing false perceptions of why things happen as they do, so that we fail to see other possibilities; or they can point to new ways of doing things. Without that imaginary, perceiving new realities and realizing new systems is very difficult. Paul Stock (2021) argued that utopian thinking is important to imagine and begin to realize better alternative futures. Utopian thinking can combine critique, experimentation and new processes for moving toward a care-centered agriculture—part of regeneration—and away from one focused just on production.

A popular (but fanciful) story is that when European ships first appeared off the coast of Caribbean islands, Australia, and South America, the Indigenous inhabitants either literally could not see them or believed that they were giant birds because they had no frame of reference for large sailing ships. The "myth of the invisible ships" seems to have originated with Sir Joseph Banks, botanist on Captain James Cook's 1770 voyage, who commented that Indigenous people paid no attention to the 106-foot long *Endeavour* as it passed near the Australian cost. This was the observation that took hold, even though in the same journal, Banks recorded several encounters with Indigenous people who very obviously perceived them and their boat (Banks 2005). Although we cannot know at all what Indigenous people in the 1770s perceived, we can know more about how people in the US react to news of rapid climate change. Such news is often met with denial or it quickly fades into the backdrop of media noise, despite the fact that climate change is having calamitous impacts on society. Perhaps we have trouble seeing a future in which the technologies responsible for greenhouse gas emissions have been eliminated, or reckoning with the awareness that missed policy opportunities over the last several decades have consigned our children to a largely uninhabitable planet. Seeing those alternative futures and working toward them with all of our might is vital, even though the chance to avoid awful consequences of climate change is no longer here.

These three examples (the Black Sea Grain initiative, the myth of the invisible ships and ignoring factual data about climate change) illustrate an important point: narratives serve and uphold certain perspectives, values and interests. The notion that wheat freed by the UN-brokered Black Sea Grain Initiative flowed directly into the mouths of hungry people in Ethiopia, Afghanistan, Somalia and Yemen assuaged concerns that the UN was not being sufficiently pro-active and bolstered the view that Russian aggression was causing a tremendous increase in hunger. The myth of the invisible ships may have endured because many people wanted to believe that Indigenous people were simple and innocent, unable to even see what is right in front of them.

This can serve to exculpate those who have lied to and cheated Indigenous people since their first encounters with Europeans. Ignoring climate change exonerates inaction, strong anti-science biases and the belief that people in some regions will be protected from its impacts. Until recently, the worst impacts of climate change were restricted to certain regions and time-periods and thus could be dismissed with anecdotal observations that droughts and floods have always occurred. The myth that some people will be immune to climate change's devastation is dissipating rapidly, as droughts, floods and heatwaves are affecting all regions of the world.

Powerful narratives drive support for particular beliefs about food and approaches to food system transformation. One of the strongest has been the Green Revolution narrative, which claims in brief that "improved" seeds, synthetic fertilizers, pesticides and irrigation which were made available from the 1940s to 1970 in India, Mexico and the Philippines were responsible for preventing the deaths of millions of people and similar technologies could have equally beneficial effects in Africa. Pingali (2012, 12302) wrote,

> The developing world witnessed an extraordinary period of food crop productivity growth over the past 50 y, despite increasing land scarcity and rising land values. Although populations had more than doubled, the production of cereal crops tripled during this period, with only a 30 percent increase in land area cultivated. Dire predictions of a Malthusian famine were belied, and much of the developing world was able to overcome its chronic food deficits.

Numerous authors (including Pingali, in the above-cited paper) have punched holes in the narrative of the resounding success of the Green Revolution. Benefits went largely to wealthier farmers; inequity increased in rural areas; malnutrition (especially of micronutrients) persisted; and the use of fertilizer, pesticides and ostensibly high-yielding varieties of crops led to dependence on seed and agrochemical manufacturers, higher debt and suicide rates among farmers, loss of biodiversity and Indigenous crops and environmental degradation (Paddock 1970; Pimentel and Pimentel 1990; Shiva 2016; Kumar et al. 2017; Raeboline et al. 2019). Yet the Green Revolution narrative lives on in the AGRA program in Africa, supported by the Bill & Melinda Gates Foundation and the Rockefeller Foundation, and in other development initiatives (Patel 2013). Its proponents believe that they can prevent problems this time around, and the benefits will far outweigh the risks. However, proponents are often people from the Global North and the corporations that will profit from increased sales of agrochemicals. There is active resistance to AGRA in African countries (Akanshumbusha 2021; Belay 2021) and in the US; and recent analyses of its impacts have demonstrated that the AGRA emperor has no clothes: the projected increases in productivity and declines in poverty have failed to materialize despite millions of dollars invested (Mkindi et al. 2020; Wise 2020).

Cabral et al. (2022) and Cabral and Sumberg (2022) introduced the concept of "epic narratives," in which an individual assumes (or is given) a heroic persona facing extraordinary challenges, overcoming them through persistence and resolving to found a new approach to solving a problem. Examples include Norman Borlaug with the Green Revolution, Masanobu Fukuoka with natural farming and Alan Savory with Holistic Resource Management. Epic elements associated with founders include an awakening to a crisis, a quest for meaning, a solution guided by higher principles and efforts to apply the solution widely. The focus on key individuals is similar to the hero-as-protagonist in multiple story lines (Brooks 2004), and the epic narrative follows some of the most pervasive story lines, such as the quest. But an epic narrative is more than a story line: it has the power to capture imagination and inspire others to follow the example or recommendations of the founder. This is both its strength and its danger.

Narratives are associated not only with deep stories, those which people have told each other since the beginnings of civilization, but also with theories of change. Theories of change became popular first in evaluation literature, examining impacts of development interventions; but have since been applied more broadly. A theory of change differs from a narrative in that it is explicitly designed to explain *why* certain interventions will lead to certain outcomes. Narratives have a plot, even if somewhat incoherent; but their purpose is to impose a pattern on experience and not to explain why that pattern results in certain outcomes.

Stein and Valters (2012, 5) define a theory of change as "a way to describe the set of assumptions that explain both the mini-steps that lead to a long-term goal and the connections between these activities and the outcomes of an intervention or program." They have consistent elements: a desired outcome (sometimes called impact) and often intermediate outcomes, pre-conditions for achieving that outcome, an intervention of some kind, and assumptions that must be met for the desired outcome to happen. Ultimately, the theory of change describes how we get from the current state to the desired state.

Making the theory of change explicit allows an examination of the intermediate steps between the current and desired state and the reasonableness of pre-conditions and assumptions; but most of the literature on food systems transformation lacks an explicit theory of change, based instead on taken-for-granted conventional wisdom (Gready 2013). In contrast to food system transformation, international development and social change literature (particularly dealing with evaluation of impact) has an abundance of theories of change, many rooted in sociological, political science, communications and social psychology literature (Stachowiak 2013). Applications to food system transformation are largely lacking, with a few exceptions: one is the theory of change developed by CGIAR and used to structure the 5th Global Science Conference on Climate-Smart Agriculture (Campbell et al. 2018; Dinesh et al. 2021). This theory emphasizes digitalization, public-private partnerships and "innovative finance" as key factors in success without much analysis of who wins and who loses from these strategies. In addition, TEEBAgriFood authors articulated a range of theories of change (May et al. 2018). They looked at policy changes to reduce external costs or give incentives for positive behavior, a requirement for financial institutions to meet sustainability criteria, pressure from large buyers for sustainability guarantees, consumers' willingness to pay for sustainability and NGOs or the media publicizing unsustainable or sustainable business practices. They examined the impacts of coalitions among civil society actors, progressive business organizations, consumers, taxpayers and labor advocates as well as international agreements such as the SDGs. Although these studies included theories of change, their underlying assumptions were not pulled out and examined for plausibility.

Even though many food system transformation narratives are missing a theory of change, a plethora of ideas, theories or sets of recommendations has been proposed. Some scholars have analyzed the differences and intersections of narratives dealing with specific food system concepts and practices relevant to transformation, such as sustainability versus food security (El Bilali et al. 2019), food security versus food sovereignty (Carney 2012; Elkharouf and Pritchard 2019; Weiler et al. 2015), regenerative versus extractive approaches (Anderson and Rivera Ferre 2021) and agroecology versus climate-smart agriculture and nature-based solutions (Hrabanski and Le Coq 2022). These studies usually rely on textual analysis and interviews to show the origin of various narratives, key discrepancies, and consequences of each narrative. In the following chapters, we will examine common narratives of food system transformation by identifying their accompanying theories of change and assumptions. But first, we will turn to contrasting narratives of the meaning and importance of food itself, which underlie those stories of transformation.

References

Akanshumbusha, J. 2021. Faith leaders call on the Gates Foundation to drop AGRA. *The Cooperator*. https://thecooperator.news/faith-leaders-call-on-the-gates-foundation-to-drop-agra/

Anderson, M and MG Rivera Ferre. 2021. Food system narratives to end hunger: extractive versus regenerative. *Curr Opin Env Sustain* 49:18–25. https://doi.org/10.1016/j.cosust.2020.12.002

Aukes, EJ, LE Bontje and JH Slinger. 2020. Narrative and frame analysis: disentangling and refining two close relatives by means of a large infrastructural technology case. *Forum Qualitative Sozialforschung* 21(2):Article 28.

Banks, J. 2005. The endeavour journal of Sir Joseph Banks, Journal from 25 August 1768–12 July 1771. *Project Gutenberg Australia Booker*. https://gutenberg.net.au/ebooks05/0501141h.html#apr1770

Belay, M. 2021. Africa is not a monoculture, we reject the plan to make it one. *Al Jazeera*. https://www.aljazeera.com/opinions/2021/9/22/africa-is-not-a-monoculture-we-reject-the-plan-to-make-it-one.

Brooks, C. 2004. *The Seven Basic Plots: Why We Tell Stories*. London & New York: Continuum.

Cabral, L and J Sumberg. 2022. The use of epic narratives in promoting 'natural agriculture'. *Outlook on Agriculture* 51(1):129–113. https://doi.org/10.1177/00307270221077708

Cabral, L, P Pandey and X Xu. 2022. Epic narratives of the Green Revolution in Brazil, India and China. *Agric Human Values* 39:249–267. https://doi.org/10.1007/s10460-021-10241-x

Campbell, BM, J Hansen, J Rioux, CM Stirling, S Twomlow and E Wollenberg. 2018. Urgent action to combat climate change and its impact (SDG 13): transforming agriculture and food systems. *Curr Opin Environ Sustain* 34:13–20. https://doi.org/10.1016/j.cosust.2018.06.005

Carney, M. 2012. "Food security" and "food sovereignty": what frameworks are best suited for social equity in food systems? *Agric, Food Syst Comm Dev* 2(2):1–88. https://doi.org/10.5304/jafscd.2012.022.004

Dinesh, D, DLT Hegger, L Klerkx, J Vervoort, BM Campbell and PPJ Driessen. 2021. Enacting theories of change for food systems transformation under climate change. *Glob Food Sec* 31:100583. https://doi.org/10.1016/j.gfs.2021.100583

El Bilali, H, C Callenius, C Strassner and L Probst. 2019. Food and nutrition security and sustainability transitions in food systems. *Food Energy Sec* 8:e00154. https://doi.org/10.1002/fes3.154

Elkharouf, O and B Pritchard. 2019. How do grassroot NGOs in rural Myanmar express their visions for the food system? Food security and food sovereignty as entangled narratives within NGO struggles and strategies. *Asia Pac Viewpoint* 60(3):402–415. https://doi.org/10.1111/apv.12246

Entman, RM. 1993. Framing: towards clarification of a fractured paradigm. *J Communication* 43(4):51–58.

European Commission. 2022. Russia/Ukraine: statement by High Representative Josep Borrell on the agreement on export of grains. European Union External Action https://www.eeas.europa.eu/eeas/russiaukraine-statement-high-representative-josep-borrell-agreement-export-grains_en

Gready, P. 2013. Organisational theories of change in an era of organizational cosmopolitanism: lessons from ActionAid's human rights-based approach. *Third World Quart* 34 (8):1339–1360. https://doi.org/10.1080/01436597.2013.831535

Hrabanski, M and JF Le Coq. 2022. Climatisation of agricultural issues in the international agenda through three competing epistemic communities: climate-smart agriculture, agroecology, and nature-based solutions. *Env Sci Policy* 127 (2022):311–320. https://doi.org/10.1016/j.envsci.2021.10.022

Johnstone, B. 2015. Discourse analysis and narrative. Pp. 635–649 In: D Schiffrin, D Tannen and HE Hamilton (Eds.) *The Handbook of Discourse Analysis*. 2nd ed. Hoboken, NJ: Wiley Blackwell.

Kumar, P, T Lorek, TC Olsson, N Sackley, S Schmalzer and G Soto Laveaga. 2017. Roundtable: new narratives of the Green Revolution. *Agric Hist* 91(3):397–422. https://doi.org/10.3098/ah.2017.091.3.397

Levy, P. 2013. *Dispelling Wetiko: Breaking the Curse of Evil*. Berkeley, CA: North Atlantic Books.

May, P, G Platais, M Di Gregorio, J Gowdy, LFG Pinto, Y Laurans, COFO Cervone, A Rankovic and M Santamaria. 2018. The TEEBAgriFood theory of change: from information to action. Pp. 333–375 In: S O'Neill (Ed.), A Mueller (Project Manager). *TEEB for Agriculture & Food: Scientific and Economic Foundations*. Geneva: UN Environment.

Mkindi, AR, A Maina, J Urhahn, J Koch, L Basserman, M Goïta, M Knetani, R Herre, S Tanzmann, TA Wise, M Gordon and R Gilbert. 2020. False Promises: The Alliance for a Green Revolution in Africa (AGRA). Rosa-Luxemburg-Stiftung, Biba, Bread for the World, FIAN Germany, Forum on Environment and Development, INKOTA-netzwerk, IRPAD, PELUM Zambia, Tabio, and TOAM. https://www.rosalux.de/en/publication/id/42635

Mousseau, F. 2023. *The Black Sea Grain Initiative: when the United Nations brokers profits for corporations, bankers, and oligarchs*. Oakland Institute. https://www.oaklandinstitute.org/blog/black-sea-grain-united-nations-profits-corporations-bankers

Paddock, WC. 1970. How green is the Green Revolution? *BioScience* 20(16):897–902. https://doi.org/10.2307/1295581

Patel, R. 2013. The long Green Revolution. *J Peasant Stud* 40(1):1–63. https://doi.org/10.1080/03066150.2012.719224

Pimentel, D and M Pimentel. 1990. Adverse environmental consequences of the Green Revolution. *Pop Dev Review* 16(Supplement: Resources, Environment, and Population: Present Knowledge, Future Options):329–332. https://doi.org/10.2307/2808081

Pingali, PL. 2012. Green Revolution: impacts, limits, and the path ahead. *Proc Nat Acad Sci* 109(31): 12302–12308.

Raeboline, A, LE Nelson, K Ravichandran and U Antony. 2019. The impact of the Green Revolution on indigenous crops of India. *J Ethnic Foods* 6:8. https://doi.org/10.1186/s42779-019-0011-9

Shiva, V. 2016. *The Violence of the Green Revolution: Third World Agriculture, Ecology, and Politics*. Lexington: University Press of Kentucky.

Stachowiak, S. 2013. Pathways for Change: 10 Theories to Inform Advocacy and Policy Change Efforts. Center for Evaluation Innovation. https://www.syrialearning.org/system/files/content/resource/files/main/2013-10-ors-10-theories-to-inform-advocacy-and-policy-change-efforts.pdf

Stein, D and C Valters. 2012. Understanding theory of change in international development. JSRP Paper 1, The Justice and Security Research Programme and The Asia Foundation, London School of Economics.

Stock, P. 2021. Food utopias, (mature) care, and hope. *Int J Soc Agric Food* 27(2):89–107. https://doi.org/10.48416/ijsaf.v27i2.92

US Agency for International Development (USAID). 2022. The Black Sea Grain Initiative. https://www.usaid.gov/sites/default/files/2022-12/Black_Sea_Grain_Initiative_Fact_Sheet_November_2022.pdf

Weiler, AM, C Hergesheimer, B Brisbois, H Wittman, A Yassi and JM. Spiegel. 2015. Food sovereignty, food security and health equity. *Health Policy Plan* 30(8):1078–1092.

Wise, TA. 2020. *Failing Africa's Farmers: An Impact Assessment of the Alliance for a Green Revolution in Africa*. Working Paper No. 20–01. Medford, OR: Global Development and Environment Institute, Tufts University.

4

THE VALUE OF FOOD

Commodity or Commons

We could direct food system transformation more effectively if we understood why food systems have changed in the past. Graeber and Wengrow's (2021) account of the rise of agriculture and how societies have shifted their means of subsistence from agriculture to hunting and gathering, sometimes on a regular seasonal basis, disrupts the theory of a steady progression from "primitive" hunting and gathering to agriculture. Reading Graeber and Wengrow also calls into question the linear narrative of "traditional" agriculture being superseded by "mixed" and then "modern" food systems (e.g., HLPE 2017). That linear narrative echoes the notion of progress driven by science and technology, instead of recognizing the many different food systems that co-exist today with different strengths and vulnerabilities (Anderson 2015). In the ideal, people have a choice of food system in which they participate, depending on which embodies their own values best. But the assumption that societies should or must progress toward "modern" food systems does not leave that choice open. And different actors benefit and bear the costs, depending on the choice of food system.

At the macro-scale, food systems have been determined by geopolitical forces, environmental factors, resource availability, government policies and colonialism. Food regime theory as developed by Harriet Friedmann and Philip McMichael (Friedmann 1987; Friedmann and McMichael 1989) explains how food systems change as a function of geopolitics and the rise and fall of different imperial powers. Although theories of why and when agriculture arose and food regime theory are quite useful as *post facto* analyses, they do not help us to direct food system change since the forces leading to food regime change are at such a grand scale that they are not amenable to

DOI: 10.4324/9781003260264-6

nudging or intervention. However, the "development project" over the past century does afford opportunities to test theories of change.

The development project has consisted of deliberate attempts to change food systems in order to bring "backward" farmers and countries into the globalized food system. Over the past century, wealthy countries that have colonized and impoverished countries in Africa, Asia and Latin America (and often continue to do so) have embarked on the development project, usually to promote their own self-interests but ostensibly to help countries that have failed to industrialize. Development projects afford laboratories to test different theories because they take place on a smaller scale (national or regional) and over a shorter timespan (until the money runs out). Unfortunately, development projects have proceeded more on the basis of assumptions than as deliberate tests of how food system transformation can best proceed. The proponents of the Green Revolution, initiated in Latin America, Southeast Asia and India in the 1960s and bankrolled by the Rockefeller and Ford Foundations, assumed that increasing productivity was the best way to prevent food insecurity. They also assumed that countries where food insecurity was high would be especially vulnerable to take-over by communism, so the US could position itself and its socioeconomic system of capitalism as bringers of technology providing abundant food, thereby forestalling the encroachment of communism in countries where the Green Revolution was implemented. Early well-documented refutation of these assumptions was developed by Amartya Sen (1981) in Poverty and Famines; and subsequent research revealed that Green Revolution technologies by-passed poor farmers who suffered most from food insecurity (Pingali 2012).

Accurately discerning trends, causal factors and consequences of different interventions in the food system is vitally important, especially given the increasing challenges of nourishing a population of perhaps ten billion people on a degraded planet undergoing rapid climate change. Narratives embed different perspectives about which causal factors and which kinds of interventions are most significant. Chapters 6 and 7 will describe different narratives of *what* drives food system transformation, and Chapter 8 describes *who* must be involved. But these different narratives can be collapsed into "meta-narratives" that rest on different meanings that people assign to food and different purposes that they believe food systems should serve.

According to Sheila Jasanoff (2002, 256),

> For much of the twentieth century, a single grand narrative has underwritten most of the ambitious, planned interventions undertaken by rich, technologically advanced nations to improve the condition of poorer societies, in short, to promote *development*. This is the story of progress, driven largely by advances in science and technology. As time's arrow points

> inexorably forward, so too, it was unproblematically assumed, do scientific discovery and its technological spinoffs, bringing only the possibility of gain and betterment.

This "grand narrative" of linear progress driven by technology and innovation lives on in the world of food systems, expressed by entities such as the World Economic Forum (WEF) in its vision of "transformative technologies" including digitalization, drones, robots, precision agriculture, nanotechnology, the Internet of things and use of Big Data (WEF 2018). It is also alive in some philanthropic organizations, such as the Bill and Melinda Gates Foundation and its work to "modernize" African agriculture. And it is supported by the United Nations in initiatives such as the UN Food Systems Summit of 2021, which was organized after a Memorandum of Understanding between the WEF and the Deputy Secretary-General of the United Nations.

Food Values and Meta-Narratives

The choice of how food systems should change depends considerably on how people value food and the meanings they ascribe to it. In Chapter 1, I proposed that regenerative food systems are the desirable outcome of transformation, going beyond "sustainable" to restore degraded resources and create thriving communities. In this chapter, I propose that two meta-narratives of the value of food compete for attention today within and between governments, intergovernmental organizations, policymakers, civil society organizations and actors who participate directly in food system activities. The first meta-narrative portrays food as a commodity, valued largely for its monetary exchange value and potential for realizing profits. The second meta-narrative portrays food as holding multiple values: a necessity for subsistence, a human right, a cultural mainstay, a means of expression, a renewable resource and a part of enacting religious rituals and building community. This meta-narrative can be described as "food in the commons," where food security is understood to be a public good.

> Commons are a system of decision-making, collective ownership and value-based purposes that challenge the for-profit ethos of the market and the state's pretense to a monopoly on the definition of the common good and to acting 'parens patriae' in the name of the whole polity. Commons are not about maximizing individual utilities, selfish individualism or legitimizing the use of force but rather collective decisions, institutions, property and shared goals to maximize everybody's wellbeing.
>
> *(Vivero-Pol et al. 2019, 8)*

There are other possible choices for meta-narratives, such as industrialized food or productivism for the "food as commodity" narrative and food sovereignty or agroecology for the "food in the commons" meta-narrative. My choice is influenced by wanting to emphasize how power is held and how it circulates in each meta-narrative. In the meta-narrative of "food as commodity," power is held primarily by businesses that control food distribution, access, trade and technology. In "food in the commons," power is distributed among those who participate in the commons as food producers, buyers, and eaters but also as analysts and policymakers. Other important dimensions of difference are sources of knowledge, who is involved in decision-making, how much agency food producers and small businesses have and who benefits from the system. That is, the actors who have a voice in each meta-narrative are not just incidental, but key to differentiating them. Each meta-narrative has its own logic, assumptions and rules of operation, described in more detail below.

Meta-narratives are bound by the values and assumptions of those who espouse them: whether people are committed to maintaining the status quo of food systems or envision better alternatives that will or may result in better outcomes than the current systems. The meta-narrative of food as commodity is promoted by people and organizations with a financial stake in current food system operations, such as agribusiness and the WEF, and thus somewhat suspect. On the one hand, they have a strong interest in accurately assessing risks and appealing to end-users; but on the other hand, they have an incentive to keep in place ways of doing business from which they are profiting, even if these cause damage to the public good. We know from many sources that "business as usual" in food systems is not an option, if we sincerely hope for a just and sustainable world. Many business leaders today consider that they are being "innovative" and going far beyond "business as usual." But often the innovations consist of doubling down on technological fixes and promises of future technological breakthroughs. Many of the technologies in WEF's vision of the future are in nascent form and not widely accessible to the farmers and fishers who are among the most food-insecure and impoverished people in the world. This seems to be a risky extension of "business as usual," compared with implementing social innovations and new forms of production and consumption. For example, agroecology helps poor farmers because it reduces use of external inputs, in addition to encouraging diversification which provides nutritious diets and protection from risks of crop failure. Territorial markets that serve local or regional areas instead of forcing peasant farmers to compete on a global scale, or worker-owned food cooperatives that share profits and decision-making among workers, already exist and have documented advantages to improve livelihoods and access to healthy food.

The Food as Commodity Meta-Narrative

To be exchangeable in global markets, food stuffs are standardized and quality-controlled to ensure their uniformity and safety for consumers who can afford to be discriminating. Food production, as well as distribution and sales, is privatized. Knowledge needed for food production also is increasingly privatized (Maskus and Reichman 2004; Anderson 2019) and knowledge of food reserves, distributional channels and profits accrued at each stage of food systems is often proprietary. In this system, food goes to people who can pay for it and healthy, sustainably produced food is only for those able to pay a premium or grow it themselves. Profits of farming or fishing go to whomever owns the means of production (i.e., land, machinery, water, fishing fleets, etc.) and controls access to them. Commodity traders send vast quantities of standardized grains around the world, seeking the biggest differential between cost of production and sale price but also betting on present and future scarcity or perceived scarcity. Commodification allows for futures markets and speculation on sale prices as well as spot markets, which can create huge disruptions and volatility in food prices and markets (Russell 2022); and commodity traders fight hard against regulations that would limit increased production or speculation.

The standardization of food as commodity creates tremendous waste, in addition to narrowing the choices available to the public. For example, at a Costa Rican farm I watched workers tossing at least six bananas out of ten onto a giant waste pile because they were not the "right" shape and size to be exported to European markets. McDonald's has tried to make uniformity a virtue, by promising customers that they will get exactly the same experience from a Big Mac whether they buy it in Singapore or St. Louis. Commodification is part of industrialization, or the application of "rational," efficient, mechanized and transferable methods of growing, packing and distributing food. Deborah Fitzgerald comprehensively explained the rise of industrialism in the US Great Plains starting in the 1920s, resulting in vast wheat fields that were the envy of Soviet agricultural experts, in Every Farm a Factory: The Industrial Ideal in American Agriculture (2003). The commodification of food and the policies that support it create hunger, debt and scarcity because everyone must eat, whether they have money or not. Yet food is produced for and distributed to those who can afford it, not for everyone. In addition, this system creates incentives for overproduction, waste and cutting corners on environmental and labor regulations to increase profits.

Capitalists are the primary people who benefit from food-as-just-a-commodity, although often the system is justified as one that can provide low-cost food to everyone. In fact, low cost to consumers often depends on underpaying producers, cutting corners or externalizing environmental and social harms onto people who are marginalized and politically powerless, or future generations. In industrialized capitalist societies, low costs of food are subsidized by the government in many ways, including direct payments to commodity producers; low-cost access to resources such as water, roads and energy; and publicly funded research and development that benefit large-scale industrial producers (Stone 2022). In the US, subsidies also include federal food assistance to workers who are paid at rates below a living wage. These benefits do not extend to the undocumented workers who dominate field-work and meatpacking and do not cover the cost of a healthy diet. That is, workers create the food system's wealth but do not share it. Capitalists are under pressure to exploit labor (including that of the family unit) to maximize profits. Marketing is often non-transparent, with no way to know how much each buyer is adding to costs before selling the product to another user: the food-as-commodity perspective involves extracting as much as possible at each stage for private gain.

The perception of food as a commodity is intrinsically linked with racialized capitalism, patriarchy and colonialism. Capitalism depends on the expansion of imperial power over the lives and property of others via processes such as accumulation by dispossession (Harvey 2003). Commodification is part of a shift to market economies where basic human needs are met through impersonal markets rather than within the household or community (Magdoff 2012). In capitalism, commodities are exchanged for profit rather than for their use-value. The lifestyles of wealthy people are propped up by taking food, land, water and other resources from less powerful people, often those of another race or country. The first wave of colonialism in the 1500s and 1600s has been replicated in more recent land-grabs, water-grabs and other instances of neocolonialism which allow scarcity and food insecurity to persist in the midst of abundant supplies of food. Neocolonialism promulgates the racialization and feminization of poverty unless the racialized "other" becomes an agent of imperialism and oppresses other racialized subjects, as has happened in corrupt governments of many countries. The same dynamic is in effect in the US food industry, where Mexican labor contractors oppress Mexican farmworkers and where the few women who rise to the top of food industries do so by acquiescing to the existing power dynamics within the corporation. By creating scarcity through dispossession, capitalism demands competition to survive. Commodification extends throughout society, as Raj Patel and Jason Moore described in A History of the World in Seven Cheap Things (2018), showing how the commodification and "cheapening" of everything from food to care and labor has underwritten "progress."

Despite its shortcomings of not being able to nourish people, the view of food as a commodity is still dominant, at least in the Minority World, with the assumption that markets will regulate food supply and price. State intervention is only supposed to be necessary in capitalist economies under conditions of market failure; but in fact, states intervene regularly through policies and programs that affect food supply and price, both for their own citizens and for people outside their boundaries. Although the weaponization of food is prohibited by international humanitarian law, conflicts routinely result in destruction of farmland (e.g., by placing landmines), interrupted markets and disrupted trade flows. So engaging in warfare in itself is an intervention that affects food supplies and prices. Imperialist policies have often led to starvation, especially when combined with drought or other natural disasters. Mike Davis showed in Late Victorian Holocausts (2002) how droughts in India, Northern China and Northeastern Brazil led to massive famines, when crop failure was exacerbated by destructive policies enacted by ruling elites. Millions of peasants died so that capitalist modernization could proceed.

Allowing one's own people to starve, or undermining the ability to produce food, is quite dangerous for a state and threatens the social contract between state and citizens. In the worst case, higher food prices or decreased ability to produce food will lead to the overthrow of the government, as happened in Haiti and many other countries during the 2007–2008 food price crisis (Jarocz 2009). The assumption that markets are sufficient to regulate food prices adequately was severely tested by the spread of COVID-19, then again by the Russian invasion of Ukraine in 2021. In both cases, market-based "solutions" alone were insufficient to allay growing food insecurity until they were augmented with public policies and government aid to people who were suffering, with positive results in countries wealthy enough to pay for vaccines and food and income supplementation for their citizens.

The Food in the Commons Meta-Narrative

Although food and resources have been largely commodified, food in the commons persists in many traditional societies, in the unwritten rules of hospitality to guests and newcomers, in religious customs, and within households. Countless other examples of commoning exist today, as ways to organize social life and allocate goods (Bollier and Helfrich 2012). David Bollier has been one of the strongest advocates for commons thinking in the US; he and his colleague Silke Helfrich have both advanced scholarship and publicized commoning as a viable alternative to neoliberalism. José-Luis Vivero Pol has been the most outspoken scholar working on food in the commons, recently co-editing the Routledge Handbook of Food as a Commons (2019).

According to a "food in the commons" view, everyone deserves food even if they lack income to pay for it; and the resources needed to produce food may also be managed as commons. This does not mean unregulated access to land, water, seeds, etc., but that people who use and depend on these goods for survival develop their own system of governance to make sure that no one takes advantage of the public interest. Similarly, food in the commons does not imply collective farms under state control but a voluntary collective of people producing and distributing food for livelihoods and care of each other. While surplus not required by the community may be sold or exchanged, this is at use-value rather than to obtain profits. Elinor Ostrom, in her pioneering work on commons, identified principles of commons management that seem to apply in all cases, including clearly defined boundaries, participatory decision-making, graduated sanctions for those who abuse the commons, and easily accessible mechanisms of conflict resolution (Ostrom 2009). For food to be in the commons, participants must actively engage in "commoning" or protecting the boundaries from encroachment by other food economies. Therefore, they must understand the vulnerability of their alternative food system to take-over by food-as-commodity actors.

The call for food to be in the commons, or at least to be treated differently than other commodities, has emerged with increasing frequency from sources including the 2015 *Laudato Si* of Pope Francis, Bill Clinton, activists and academics, and the Group of Chief Scientific Advisors to the European Commission (Rosset 2006; Vivero Pol 2017; Vivero Pol et al. 2019; European Commission et al. 2020; Jackson et al. 2021). The call comes from moral grounds (i.e., a basic necessity for existence should not be withheld because of loss of profits or inability to pay), the recognition that food systems prioritizing profits are failing to nourish people adequately, and growing awareness of the destruction of nature and communities that accompanies the food as commodity perspective with its mandate to exploit.

The value of food in the commons is supported by scientific evidence as well: the 2019 report by the High Level Panel of Experts of the Committee on World Food Security analyzed the contributions of agroecology and related food systems to food security and nutrition. This report contrasted the systems related to agroecology (organic agriculture, agroforestry, permaculture, food sovereignty) with a set of approaches related to sustainable intensification (climate-smart agriculture, nutrition-sensitive agriculture and sustainable food value chains) and concluded that the agroecological systems are superior overall in terms of resource efficiency, resilience and social equity/responsibility. While agroecology does not map directly onto the commons, it shares many features including a focus on the whole system, attention to integration of practices and principles, regenerative production practices, co-generation of knowledge, democratic governance by resource users and an emphasis on equity (HLPE 2019). Food production in agroecology is for food security and producers' livelihoods, not primarily for profit. Food sovereignty, in particular, draws on principles of commoning by restoring control over food systems to food producers and their communities. In contrast, the practices lumped with sustainable intensification are consistent with commodification, not requiring any change in how food is valued.

Knowledge in the commons system is shared and co-generated. In addition, diverse sources of knowledge are usually respected, with the recognition that Western intellectual traditions are one among many ways of knowing. This means that Indigenous and traditional knowledge is upheld and the holders of that knowledge are compensated for their contributions to shared management of commons. This happens more frequently in the commons because of the explicit aim to include all "users" of the commons in decision-making, leading to a built-in respect for diversity of perspectives.

The concepts of "care" and "reciprocity" are central to commons and key to its transformative power. "Care then can serve as an umbrella for various liberatory and emergent examples, including the categories of equity, justice, sovereignty, flourishing, and community" (Stock 2021, 94). Commoners care for people who are marginalized as well as those who need food and try to overcome impediments to agency and political participation. Coming from a position of recognizing the damage that racialized capitalism causes, Monica White advanced the Collective Agency and Community Resilience framework, which provides a telos of care that is "working toward and practicing freedom—freedom to participate in the political process, to engage in an economic model that [is] cooperative and fair, and to exchange ideas with others who [share] their goals" (White 2018, 5). Commoning allows people to actively care for their community and environment by working collectively to formulate their protocols for self-governance and governance of their landscapes.

Beginning with food production and the inputs that it requires, commoning prohibits the exploitation of any resource for private gain at the cost of the collective. Seeds, water, land, knowledge and other inputs are shared by the community (Pettanati et al. 2019). Depending on how the commons is set up, labor, food produced and profits may be shared as well. A commoner may have a private enterprise, but the critical point is that exploitation of collectively owned goods is never permitted and each participant's rights are respected. Commoning involves giving back due compensation, whether this means using regenerative practices that protect ecosystem health or providing fair wages to workers and fair prices to end-consumers. This is the significance of reciprocity for the commons. Commoning is a fight against enclosure and expropriation and also a counter-hegemonic fight against both the power of government and the power of the market.

> From the very moment that we accept that the community has an instituting power to create a commons (resource, property regime, governing institution and purpose), we accept that the community is bestowed with legal and political powers to regulate the resources important to it, making commoning transformational and counter-hegemonic, since the state aims to retain those instituting powers to issue policies and enact laws and the market aims to retain its supremacy to allocate and govern scarce resources.
>
> *(Vivero-Pol et al. 2019, 9)*

The commodification of what has previously been in the commons, i.e., its reduction to market value, is necessary for capitalism. Thus, food systems in the commons are alternatives to capitalist food systems, although a food commons may be embedded in a capitalist society. John McMurtry pointed to the commons as a "social immune system" constructed of social life organizations and universal goods necessary for humanity that can resist the cancer of capitalism (McMurtry 2013). Nick Rose (2021) picked up this idea by referring to systemic crises of capitalism, with the most recent in the 1970s creating conditions for the emergence of neoliberalism, which ushered in the cancer stage of capitalism. He wrote (954):

> Capitalism is once more in profound, systemic crisis. The political far right is, once more, in the ascendancy. The drums of war are being beaten ... At the same time, the yearning for profound change in the direction of greater equality and ecological integrity is both powerful and substantial... Hence the significance, relevance and importance of proposals for transformative change in both food systems governance and in the social relations that underpin the food system.

Food in the commons is closely aligned with the degrowth movement and its aspirations. Degrowth is an auspicious alternative to the extractive economy, based on the recognition that people can enjoy comfortable and satisfying lives without the massive flows of material and energy that characterize modern industrialized societies. Furthermore, by reducing these flows to what is actually useful and enhancing of well-being, we can achieve greater equality within and between countries. Gerber (2020) began his article about intersections of degrowth and critical agrarian studies by clarifying common misperceptions of degrowth. First, degrowth is not about just reversing GDP growth rates but about organizing appropriation, extraction, production, distribution, consumption and waste differently. Second, it does not impose austerity but rather evaluates carefully which economic activities serve the common good and which should be eliminated. Third, it does not resist technology; and fourth, it does not only apply at the local scale. Fifth, it is fundamentally post-capitalist. All of these claims apply to food in the commons as well.

Degrowth proponents point to the destruction of nature that "growthism" has caused particularly in the Global South. By assuming that economic growth is essential to avoid recessions and focusing on increasing it at all costs, policymakers have created a monster that consumes more and more of the earth's productivity. Indigenous peoples have several names for this monster including Geewakwa, Wetiko or Wendigo. He is described as a cannibalistic spirit that feeds on greed, excess and unchecked consumption. He infects humankind with an illness that leads to a suicidal path of endless consumption in which people eventually dance themselves to death (Mitchell 2018). He is an apt personification of growthism. Since Minority World peoples have already exhausted most of the resources in lands they have settled, they turn to Majority World countries for the materials they need to keep growing: fossil fuels, minerals, land, etc. The claim that "advanced" industrialized societies have decoupled economic growth from increased material consumption is false (Hickel and Kallis 2020) and seems unlikely to be possible. The consumption has simply been displaced onto poor countries unable to resist businesses that want to mine their resources. Degrowth fights neocolonialism and can redress some of the lasting harms of colonialism (Hickel 2021).

The ways that societies feed themselves are targets for degrowth, since so much of nature is absorbed into food production and degraded in the process. Degrowth advocates point to many alternatives that can radically decrease the use of materials, land and water yet nourish societies (Fitzpatrick et al. 2022). Agroecology is a prominent example among production systems; and its coupling with food sovereignty leads to alternative production, distribution, business and consumption patterns (e.g., community-supported agriculture, food cooperatives that invest in their communities, production on land reclaimed from imperialist thefts, decreased food waste, consumption of more local and seasonal foods) that build social capital, health and local power. Food sovereignty advocates fight at many levels for "degrowing" food systems, by forcing land redistribution to peasants and away from wealthy landowners in the case of the Movimento dos Trabalhadores Rurais Sem Terra (Landless Workers' Movement) in Brazil to rebuilding public stock and food reserves at the community level to unrelenting advocacy for the UN Declaration on the Rights of Peasants and Other People Working in Rural Areas at the international level. People from social movements that promote food sovereignty, notably La Via Campesina, are resisting displacement and the destruction of their livelihoods by extractive agriculture (Plank 2022).

Commoning and degrowth both draw on a fundamentally different view of human relationships with nature, in which humans learn to take only what is essential for survival and to respect planetary boundaries and the rights of other beings, rather than exploiting nature for profit. This mindset is a huge leap away from the dominant Western view of human exceptionalism; but it may be necessary to allow human survival on the planet, given that our quality of life depends on protecting biodiversity, ecological integrity and non-renewable resources that future generations will need to live (Kemp et al. 2022). Commoning is a utopian vision but also a very pragmatic alternative that exists in many societies today, from the Mondeggi Bene Comune in Italy to agrarian commons in the US. Stock (2021, 96) argued for the importance of a utopian imagination in words that connect immediately with narratives:

> Utopias offer us powerful stories that help us read our own world for difference. Rather than just looking at the stories that we can critique as bad and unhelpful for enacting social change, a utopian imagination helps us to look for the small and the experimental as potential change agents in our world.

These small and experimental projects may be the seeds of survival for a world that has commodified the most important elements of life.

We need to ground an analysis of the potential of food system projects and policies to foster regeneration not only in decommodification, but also in degrowth, equity and ecological integrity, all within the framework of human rights (Figure 4.1). Degrowth is necessary to stop environmental degradation and exploitation. Equity is necessary to maintain a focus on marginalized people and just transitions that promote well-being instead of perpetuating neoliberalism's tendency to enrich the already wealthy. Ecological integrity is necessary to allow for environmental restoration. And human rights are necessary to ensure healthy food for all, decent working conditions and attention to women and other groups that have not benefited from the current food systems. Growing movements to support degrowth, equity and ecological integrity support regeneration of food systems, and advocates for regeneration need to lend their voices to these movements to build greater political power.

In Section 3, "Narratives of Transformation: What and Who Will Drive Change?", we will examine specific notions of food system transformation and their supporters. I use the term "notions" here rather than theories, since

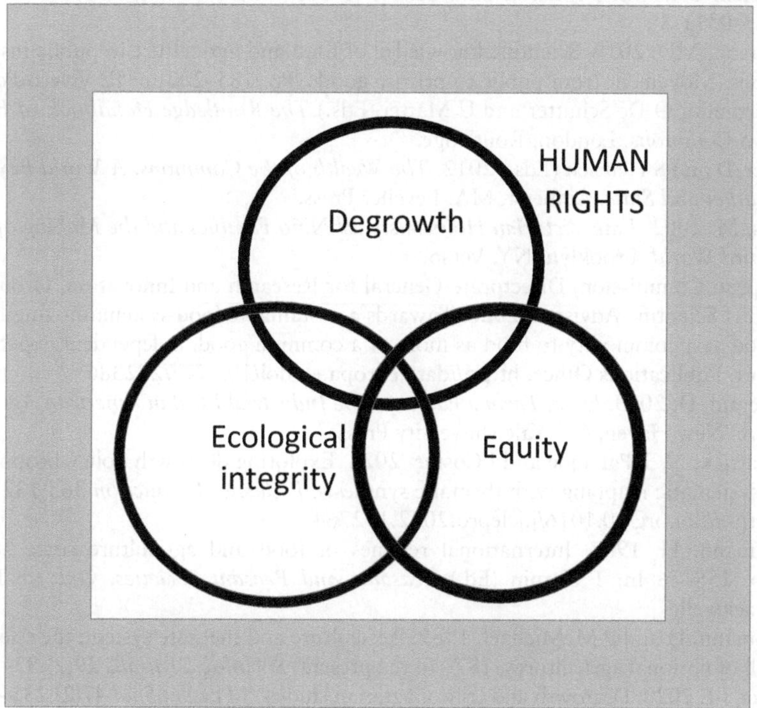

FIGURE 4.1 Movements interlinked with regenerative food systems.

a theory of change is not always well articulated. The "food as commodity" meta-narrative expands to numerous market-based approaches to food system transformation, such as "voting with your fork," use of technological innovation, data intensification and private labels created by multistakeholder initiatives. These approaches are promoted by businesses, governments, intergovernmental organizations, scholars and policymakers. The "food as commons" meta-narrative is upheld by social movements fighting for agroecology and food sovereignty, by many human rights advocates, by efforts to promote democratization of the food system and by efforts to include smallholders and marginalized people in food system governance. They are supported by numerous scholars and people working within civil society. Food-as-commons narratives tend to see cultural change as being more important than technological innovation, although people who are commoning do not reject technology. They are paying attention to who benefits from the technology under different circumstances and who owns it, however, not seeing it as unqualified progress.

References

Anderson, MD. 2015. The role of knowledge in building resilience across food system domains. *J Environ Stud Sci* 5:543–559. https://doi.org/10.1007/s13412-015-0311-3

Anderson, MD. 2019. Scientific knowledge of food and agriculture in public institutions. Movement from public to private goods. Pp. 185–202 In: JL Vivero-Pol, T Ferrando, O De Schutter and U Mattei (Eds.) *The Routledge Handbook of Food as a Commons*. London: Routledge.

Bollier, D and S Helfrich (Eds.) 2012. *The Wealth of the Commons: A World Beyond Market and State*. Amherst, MA: Leveller Press.

Davis, M. 2002. *Late Victorian Holocausts. El Niño Famines and the Making of the Third World*. Brooklyn, NY: Verso.

European Commission, Directorate-General for Research and Innovation, Group of Chief Scientific Advisors. 2020. Towards a sustainable food system: moving from food as a commodity to food as more of a common good: independent expert report. Publications Office. https://data.europa.eu/doi/10.2777/282386

Fitzgerald, D. 2003. *Every Farm a Factory: The Industrial Ideal in American Agriculture*. New Haven, CT: Yale University Press.

Fitzpatrick, N, T Parrique and I Cosme. 2022. Exploring degrowth policy proposals: a systematic mapping with thematic synthesis. *J Cleaner Production* 365:132764. https://doi.org/10.1016/j.jclepro.2022.132764

Friedmann, H. 1987. International regimes of food and agriculture since 1870. Pp. 258–76 In: T Shanin (Ed.) *Peasants and Peasant Societies*. Oxford: Basil Blackwell.

Friedmann, H and P McMichael. 1989. Agriculture and the state system: the rise and fall of national agricultures, 1870 to the present. *Sociologia Ruralis* 29(2):93–117.

Gerber, J-F. 2020. Degrowth and critical agrarian studies. *J Peasant Stud* 47(2):235–264. https://doi.org/10.1080/03066150.2019.1695601

Graeber, D and D Wengrow. 2021. *The Dawn of Everything: A New History of Humanity*. London: Penguin Books.
Harvey, D. 2003. *The New Imperialism*. Oxon: Oxford University Press.
Hickel, J. 2021. The anti-colonial politics of degrowth. *Polit Geog* 88:102404. https://doi.org/10.1016/j.polgeo.2021.102404
Hickel, J and G Kallis. 2020. Is green growth possible? *New Polit Econ* 25(4):469–486. https://doi.org/10.1080/13563467.2019.1598964
High Level Panel of Experts (HLPE). 2017. Nutrition and Food Systems. Report #12, Committee on World Food Security. https://knowledge4policy.ec.europa.eu/sites/default/files/a-i7846e.pdf
High Level Panel of Experts (HLPE). 2019. Agroecological and Other Innovative Approaches for Sustainable Agriculture and Food Systems that Enhance Food Security and Nutrition. Report #14, Committee on World Food Security. https://www.fao.org/3/ca5602en/ca5602en.pdf
Jackson, P, MG Rivera Ferre, J Candel, A Davies, C Derani, H de Vries, V Dragoviç-Uzela, AH Hoel, L Holm, E Mathijs, P Morone, M Penker, R S'piewak, K Termeer and J Thøgersen. 2021 Food as a commodity, human right or common good. *Nature Food* 2:132–134. https://doi.org/10.1038/s43016-021-00245-5
Jarocz, L. 2009. Energy, climate change, meat, and markets: mapping the coordinates of the current world food crisis. *Geog Compass* 3(6):2065–2083. https://doi.org/10.1111/j.1749-8198.2009.00282.x
Jasanoff, S. 2002. New modernities: reimagining science, technology and development. *Environ Values* 11:253–276.
Kemp, L, C Xu, J Depledge and TM Lenten. 2022. Climate endgame: exploring catastrophic climate change scenarios. *Proc Nat Acad Sci* 119(34):e2108146119. https://doi.org/10.1073/pnas.2108146119
Magdoff, F. 2012. Food as a commodity. *Monthly Review* 63(8). https://monthlyreview.org/2012/01/01/food-as-a-commodity/
Maskus, KR and JH Reichman. 2004. The globalization of private knowledge good and the privatization of global public goods. *J Int Econ Law* 7(2):279–320. https://doi.org/10.1093/jiel/7.2.279
McMurtry, J. 2013. *The Cancer Stage of Capitalism: From Crisis to Cure*. 2nd edition. London: Pluto Press.
Mitchell, S. 2018. *Sacred Instructions: Indigenous Wisdom for Living Spirit-based Change*. Berkeley, CA: North Atlantic Books.
Ostrom, E. 2009. *Governing the Commons: The Evolution of Institutions for Collective Action*. Cambridge: Cambridge University Press.
Patel, R and JW Moore. 2018. *A History of the World in Seven Cheap Things A Guide to Capitalism, Nature, and the Future of the Planet*. Davis: University of California Press.
Pettanati, G, A Toldo and T Ferrando. 2019. The food system as a commons. Pp. 42–56 In: JL Vivero-Pol, T Ferrando, O DeSchutter and U Mattei. *Routledge Handbook of Food as a Commons*. Oxon and New York: Routledge.
Pingali, PL. 2012. Green Revolution: impacts, limits, and the path ahead. *Proc Nat Acad Sci* 109(31):12302–12308. https://doi.org/10.1073/pnas.0912953109
Plank, C. 2022. An overview of strategies for social-ecological transformation in the field of food. Pp. 200–218 In: N Barlow, L Regen, N Cadiou, E Chertkovskaya, M Hollweg, C Plank, M Schulken and V Wold (Eds.) *Degrowth and Strategy: How to Bring about Social-Ecological Transformation*. London: Mayfly Books.

Rose, N. 2021. From the cancer stage of capitalism to the political principle of the common: the social immune response of "food as commons". *Int J Health Policy Manag* 10(1):946–956.

Rosset, PM. 2006. *Food is Different: Why We Must Get the WTO Out of Agriculture*. London: Zed Books.

Russell, R. 2022. *Price Wars: How the Commodities Markets Made Our Chaotic World*. New York: Doubleday.

Sen, A. 1981. *Poverty and Famines. An Essay on Entitlement and Deprivation*. Oxford: Oxford University Press.

Stock, P. 2021. Food utopias, (mature) care, and hope. *Int J Soc Agric & Food* 27(2):89–107. https://doi.org/10.48416/ijsaf.v27i2.92

Stone, GD. 2022. *The Agricultural Dilemma. How Not to Feed the World. London: Routledge*.

Vivero-Pol, JL. 2017. Food as commons or commodity? Exploring the links between normative valuations and agency in food transition. *Sustainability* 9:442. https://doi.org/10.3390/su9030442

Vivero-Pol, JL, T Ferrando, O De Schutter and U Mattei. 2019. The food commons are coming... Pp. 1–21 In: JL Vivero-Pol, T Ferrando, O De Schutter and U Mattei (Eds.) *The Routledge Handbook of Food as a Commons*. London & New York: Routledge.

White, MM. 2018. *Freedom Farmers: Agricultural Resistance and the Black Freedom Movement*. Chapel Hill: University oof North Carolina Press.

World Economic Forum (WEF). 2018. Innovation with a purpose: The role of technology innovation in accelerating food systems transformation. https://www3.weforum.org/docs/WEF_Innovation_with_a_Purpose_VF-reduced.pdf

5

MAPPING POWER FLOWS IN FOOD SYSTEMS

Changing power dynamics is crucial to allow regenerative food systems to become more prevalent than extractive food systems. How power flows and where power is concentrated in the food system have tremendous impacts on food security, environmental quality, public health, wages and other attributes. Transforming the food system in the direction of regeneration entails transforming flows of power from the agribusiness corporations that now dominate markets and governance to a more democratic system in which all people affected by food system policies share power and have agency to achieve their human rights and in which people who care about ecological integrity and non-human species have the agency to protect these. At the deepest level, power dynamics determine whether people starve or obtain sufficient quantities of healthy food in political systems where food security is a public good and a right, embedded in common access and ensured by the government.

Many authors point to power asymmetries between the private sector (particularly transnational corporations) and people, as citizens or members of civil society, as a fundamental cause of environmental and social problems in food systems (e.g., Fuchs 2007; De Schutter 2017; Rossi et al. 2019; Swinburn 2019; Clapp and Purugganan 2020). Swinburn (2019, 4) explains:

> Since food systems have been principally designed to feed those who can pay, they are heavily oriented towards economic outcomes—profits for people and companies within the food system and economic growth, exports and productivity for the countries. However, this prosperity has been unevenly distributed and there is now a considerable concentration of global market power held by a handful of large transnational corporations.

DOI: 10.4324/9781003260264-7

> Small and medium enterprises, smaller landowners, and family food businesses are being squeezed by the increasingly globalized food systems that work to the advantage of the oligopolies.

Concentration of market power is problematic for a number of reasons: concentrated firms have the power to shape markets and set prices, require that certain technologies and safety standards be used by producers, control availability and access to seeds and breeds, set workers' wages and working conditions and increase the availability of processed or ultraprocessed foods more than fresh foods. Furthermore, they have privatized several public functions including food procurement by public agencies, agricultural research and extension, school meals and data on land records. These activities further reinforce their power and leave producers, consumers and competing businesses with limited choices (Guttal 2021). Neoliberalism, through its push to deregulate economies around the world, forces open national markets to trade and capital and reduces governments' reach via austerity or privatization, thus enabling and exacerbating the global power of corporations (Harvey 2005).

Power in its most fundamental form is the ability to accomplish goals. Walls et al. (2021, 810), in describing the impacts of power dynamics on malnutrition, describe power as:

> what allows or prevents … actors from realizing their interests, why and how systems including food systems tend to favor particular groups over others over time; why resources accrue to some and not others; who gets to set social norms and beliefs and how this affects individuals or groups; and how people may struggle against and resist this.

They noted (p. 812):

> Power dynamics (and imbalances) within global and national food systems have led to many ineffective and incoherent policy decisions, decisions which have failed to address malnourishment, leaving many people under-served, under-voiced, and unable to hold the powerful to account.

In analyzing power, scholars have distinguished instrumentalist, structuralist and discursive forms (Levy and Egan 1998; Fuchs 2007; Clapp and Fuchs 2009). The definition from Walls et al. refers to instrumentalist power, or the ability to carry out one's own will. Corporations have leveraged their economic power into political power, muscling into governance spaces to create policies in their favor (IPES-Food 2023). They have undermined political commitment to act for the public good through lobbying and public relations activities, such as fighting against taxes on sugary beverages (Swinburn

2019). Structuralists emphasize the material structures and institutional processes that pre-determine actors' ability to exercise power. In food systems, the growth of corporations through mergers and acquisitions means that they are often larger in economic importance than national budgets. Their ability to provide jobs, investments and tax revenues gives them considerable bargaining power with governments, relative to small and medium-sized companies (Baker et al. 2021). Discursive perspectives emphasize the importance of ideas, frames, norms, discourses and beliefs. Agrichemical corporations have pushed a productivist narrative of "feeding the world" through continued use of their products, based on the (flawed) FAO estimate that global agricultural production would need to grow by 50–60 percent by 2050 (De Schutter 2017). This narrative serves the extractive industrialized food system.

Avelino and Rotmans (2009) and Avelino and Wittmayer (2016) further identified innovative, constitutive and transformative power in the context of sustainability transitions. Innovative power refers to the capacity of actors to create or discover new resources; constitutive power is the capacity to establish, enforce or reproduce existing structures and institutions that affect how people distribute resources (similar to structural power). Transformative power is the capacity to transform how resources are distributed by developing new institutions, structures or rules. Innovative power in food systems could include using solar energy to power tractors; constitutive power would be exemplified by a merger of two large seed companies; and transformative power might be the creation of a community-supported agriculture operation or a food cooperative in places where these don't exist.

Frameworks of power in the literature focus on social interactions or how people relate to each other individually or in groups. Another crucial form of power in food systems may be how people relate to the environment. Food systems are social-ecological systems with their own dynamics that affect human survival. By expanding human activities well beyond planetary boundaries, humans are reducing the planet's capacity to continue producing food. We see this vividly with climate change's impacts on sea-level rise in low-lying countries and the increasing frequency and severity of heat waves, droughts and floods. Some might argue that human impacts on the environment are part of structural power, in setting the context for other forms of power. But an argument could be made that domination of nature by violating Daly's three operational principles for sustainable development is qualitatively different because it can trump or negate other forms of power. Daly's principles are (1) exploit renewable resources no faster than they can be regenerated; (2) emit wastes no faster than they can be assimilated and (3) deplete non-renewable resources no faster than renewable substitutes can be developed to replace them (Daly 1990). Extractive activities—mining, overgrazing, soil depletion, water contamination and overuse—foreclose the opportunity for others to exercise any kind of power, thus shrinking the domain in which food system power functions. We will come back later to the extractive mindset as something that must be transformed to enable regenerative food systems.

Food system actors use power "to," power "with," power "over" and power "within" (VeneKlasen and Miller 2008) to achieve their purposes. They also use different levels of power: visible, invisible and hidden (Gaventa 2006). People and institutions may exert their power openly (visible power), behind closed doors or in privileged spaces such as global food and nutrition fora or trade negotiations (hidden power). Invisible power is the ability to shape agendas and narratives, such that certain political decisions are perceived to be legitimate; this is a form of discursive power.

Power is not static. It is constantly moving between actors and institutions as a consequence of dominance and resistance. Michel Foucault (1980, 93, 98) expressed a similar idea:

> Power must be analyzed as something which circulates, or rather as something which only functions in the form of a chain. It is never localized here or there, never in anybody's hands, never appropriated as a commodity or a piece of wealth. Power is employed and exercised through a net-like organization... [I]ndividuals are the vehicles of power, not its points of application.

Food system power can serve the purposes of actors who are implementing regenerative or extractive systems. It might consist of monetary flows, such as bribes offered to politicians to support a particular policy, or financial incentives provided to producers to use rotational grazing. It might consist of information, technology or access to resources. It might consist of regulations that inhibit or permit certain actions, social pressures to act or direct violent pressure to act (or not act). It may also consist of opportunities to participate in decision-making or to choose public officials.

Valeria Sodano and Maria Teresa Gorgitano (2022) distinguished four fields where power conflicts can occur: economic; formal institutions (governments, NGOs, international bodies); informal institutions (civil society) and science and technology. Food systems conflicts occur in each arena. The same authors described the following sources of power: economic; institutional; informative/knowledge (human capital, expertise and information) and socio-cultural (cultural attitudes to cooperation, civil mobilization and social capital). I would add socio-cultural attitudes to gender, race, sexual orientation, disability and other factors, in addition to poverty (an economic source), that are used to marginalize some people or exclude them from opportunities. These attitudes are weapons used by wealthy and privileged people to marginalize others. Poor and marginalized people, especially those living in rural areas, are of particular concern in food systems transformation, since they have the highest degree of food insecurity and lack of access to land and other resources (FAO et al. 2023). They also have the least agency to maneuver in the food system to increase their access to healthy food and resources to obtain it. Opening up opportunities for marginalized people does not exclude relatively wealthy and powerful people, but the opposite is seldom true.

In the neoliberal food system, corporations and wealthy people use power to exclude people from goods and services. Businesses, government officials and mainstream media, through a narrative promoted by business, often place responsibility on the individual to acquire goods and services and attribute their lack to deficiencies at the individual level rather than recognizing and dealing with systemic problems. Food insecurity is largely due to lack of money by large groups of people (for example, the 2023 SOFI report claimed that 3.1 billion people in the world cannot afford a healthy diet; FAO et al. 2023) and lack of access to resources needed for food production. These gaps persist because of deliberate impoverishment and exclusion of some people from the commons. Power is used in the food system not only to starve people but to silence them. As Arundhati Roy said, "there is no such thing as the 'voiceless'; there are only the deliberately silenced, or the preferably unheard" (Roy 2006, 330).

Tools of systems analysis can help to reveal power dynamics, show the impacts of different power flows on transformation and help us to see which actions are critical for transformation. Systems analysis sets boundaries around a system of interest (in this case, a food system) and examines the dynamics of components inside that boundary. Most people in the US, even those who advocate for local food systems and purchase most of their food from producers nearby, are part of a global food system in which products such as coffee, tea, spices, fish and cheese from across the world reach US retailers' shelves and US households. Sometimes products are imported to the US because they cannot be produced here, but not always: I can buy apples from New Zealand in New England, even though we produce abundant quantities of apples and their quality is maintained through the year with controlled atmospheric storage. Usually trade flows are driven by relative costs of production in different regions, which are affected by climate, insect and disease pressure, economies of scale, cost of labor and more. Even though we cannot easily draw a boundary on the US food system, I will focus on its dynamics and potential for transformation to a regenerative system. However, such transformation will entail changing trade rules and practices because of the intrinsic interconnections in the global food system.

Systems analysis developed from fields as diverse as electrical engineering, computer science and military strategy. Its applications to food systems have been relatively recent, but food production was one of the components of the hugely influential 1972 Limits to Growth study which modeled interactions between resource consumption and earth's limits. My view of systems analysis was shaped by one of this study's authors, Donella Meadows. She explained her approach elegantly in Thinking in Systems: A Primer (2008). While she had a deep interest in food systems, her approach to systems analysis has wide applications beyond food systems. In particular, her ideas about the kinds of interventions that have the most leverage to change systems have been picked up by many disciplines.

Some common terms in system models are stocks and flows: a stock is a supply of a good or service that can increase or decrease, such as land in farming, the strength of social movements, or the amount of social capital in a community. A flow is an action which leads to the increase or decrease of a stock, such as providing funds to increase the number of farmers or generating distrust which erodes social capital. Delays and rates affect flows and may be extremely important to food system actors. An example of a common delay in agriculture is farmers' need to invest up-front in seeds and other inputs for a season's crop, although they don't receive payment until the crop is sold. Rates are factors that influence the strength of a flow, possibly cutting it off completely. A crop sold at a price below operating costs may trigger bankruptcy, unless the farmer receives crop insurance or has buffer funds set aside to cover bad harvests. The farmer's inability to pay debts because her crop cannot augment her assets sufficiently will cut off the flow of future lending from a bank, a critical input.

Symbols used in stock and flow diagrams include the following:

□ = Stock, accumulation
⟹ = Flow
–X⟹ = Rate of flow
⟶ = Information or influence link
☁ = Unspecified source or sink

The simplest tools for systems analysis are conceptual diagrams that show linkages between different parts of the system and feedbacks that encourage stocks to keep growing or remain stable. Feedback loops occur when changes in a stock affect flows in and out of that stock. A simple example is interest on a bank account, in which wealth is added to the stock (the bank account) with each calculation of interest depending on how much is in the account. Another example is population growth, in which the birth of kittens results in increasing numbers of cats very quickly. These are both reinforcing loops (R) and the stocks of money in the bank or cats in the barn increase exponentially unless another type of feedback intervenes to stabilize growth and balance the reinforcing loop. Balancing loops (B) are created when there is a gap between reality (e.g., exploding numbers of cats) and a desired objective (e.g., just enough cats to catch mice). Examples of balancing loops would be

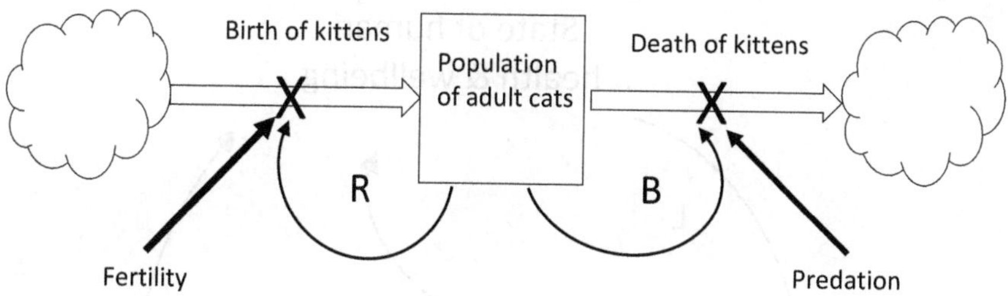

FIGURE 5.1 Example of reinforcing and balancing loops.

regular withdrawals from the bank or fox predation on some of the kittens when numbers are large (Figure 5.1).

System diagrams show the stocks and flows in a system conceptually or quantitatively. Primary stocks and flows must be identified as the first step in a quantitative model. Polly Ericksen (2008) developed an early conceptual diagram of the main activities within a food system (stocks of food at different stages) relevant to food security under global environmental change. Other authors depict these activities as a "value chain" since one link leads to the next. Conceptual diagrams can either show stocks and flows, as affected by rates and influence links, or just influences; the latter is called a causal link diagram. Causal link diagrams are useful when flows might go both ways (i.e., the direction of flow is difficult to determine) or in very complex systems where the number of influences are large. Examples of sophisticated causal loop diagrams are the US food system maps produced by Gregory Keoleian and Martin Heller at the University of Michigan (Heller and Keoleian 2001) showing how much US grain is produced, fed to livestock, exported and consumed domestically in different ways. They assigned quantitative estimates to each stock, but this is still a causal loop diagram and not a dynamic model. To use system diagrams to predict future scenarios, modelers must assign values to stocks, determine rates and identify delays. When this is done, static conceptual models can dynamically predict what will happen if various stocks and flows are changed. The Limits to Growth team designed the World3 model to make its predictions, which have proven to be remarkably accurate (Heinberg 2022). Similarly, the scientists working on the Intergovernmental Panel on Climate Change use very complex models to predict different scenarios of increasing greenhouse gases.

Rob Dyball and Barry Newell (2023) augmented Meadows's ideas about system dynamics in important ways. They added the cultural narrative (which they called cultural paradigms) into social-ecological systems and asserted that the key components of any system are the paradigms, the "state of institutions," the state of human health and well-being and the state of the

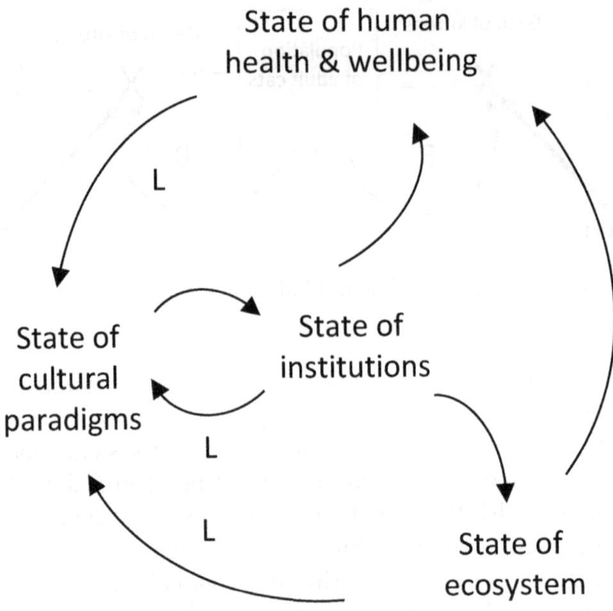

FIGURE 5.2 Cultural adaptation feedback template (from Dyball and Newell 2023, used by permission of authors).

ecosystem. The "state of institutions" includes shared goals, decision rules and action policies based on the cultural paradigms. Their "cultural adaptation template" which shows how these components influence each other is (Figure 5.2).

Three of the influences feeding back into the paradigm in this diagram are learning loops, marked with "L," which allow society to adapt its dominant paradigm as it recognizes that the state of the ecosystem, the state of human health and well-being, or the state of institutions is suffering negative impacts. These learning loops are how human societies adapt to changing conditions: first, the cultural paradigm changes in response to feedback. As the cultural paradigm changes, it modifies social institutions such as political and economic arrangements, resulting in changes to the impacts on the state of human health and the environment. Unfortunately, each of these learning loops is blocked in a neoliberal capitalist political system so that the cultural narrative remains static even while tremendous harm is being done to human health and the environment. This is precisely what we see in the food system. Its most powerful actors are intent on perpetuating their grasp on power, which requires blocking feedback needed to change the cultural narrative.

The food system is full of reinforcing loops. Lock-ins occur in any system when reinforcing loops are not balanced sufficiently. IPES-Food (2016) identified eight lock-ins that keep the extractive industrialized food system in place, including the concentration of power by food industries. In this lock-in, large corporations seek mergers and acquisitions to increase their wealth, as well as selling their products or services. They also use a number of tactics to block learning loops by influencing legislators, public opinion and the dominant cultural narrative itself. Rapid concentration in every food system activity from processing through retailing over the last few decades has become a reinforcing loop. Several potential balancing loops might be implemented, but they have either not happened or have been too weak to combat the growth of corporate power and its resistance to being reined in.

In Figure 5.3, corporations gain power (financial and political assets) by mergers and acquisitions, as well as by re-investing profits back into the company and with subsidies. They gain products from deliveries and lose them through sales, taxes and depreciation of their inventory. Mergers and acquisitions are enabled by lenient enforcement of anti-trust law, and sales are strengthened by advertisement. Although sales deplete the inventory of the company, they generate profits (i.e., income minus costs). Companies have many ways to invest their profits. They might distribute more value to producers; but they are far more likely to invest in enhancing their political power. They can do this by donating to political campaigns, lobbying for policies to their benefit or influencing the cultural narrative by purchasing

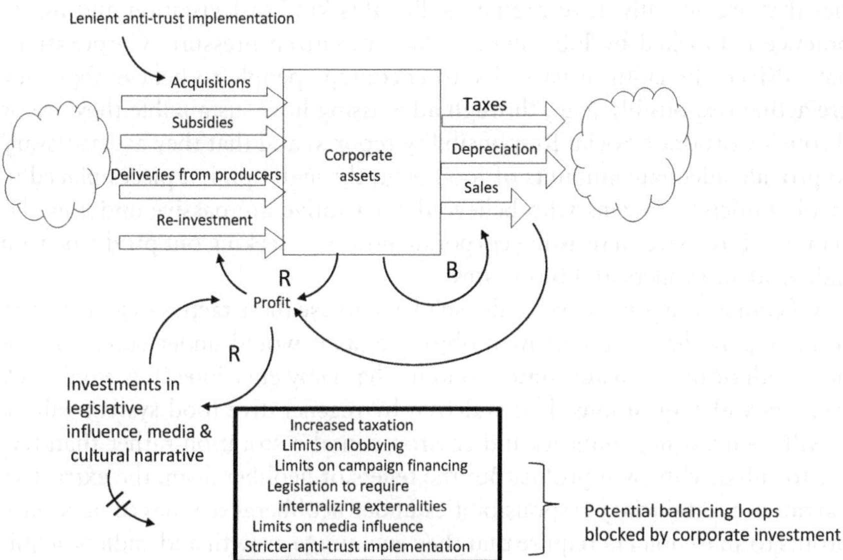

FIGURE 5.3 Reinforcing and (potential) balancing loops on corporate power.

media space and advertising. All of these tactics increase the company's power; sharing profits more equitably would obviously diminish its power. Although not shown on this diagram, corporations are further supported by banks and investors, which increase their profits through commodity speculation and investment in projects with quick returns rather than long-term regeneration.

The block of text at the bottom of Figure 5.3 is opportunities that legislators could seize to limit corporate influence (this is not an exhaustive list). They include enforcement of anti-trust policy to restrict the further consolidation of corporations and increased taxation so that corporations are paying into the public coffers to support programs in the public interest. These steps to limit the profits of concentrating agribusiness would be fair compensation for the "pass" that corporation board members receive of not being held personally liable for abuses for which the corporation is responsible. Legislators might also limit the many ways that corporations are influencing their actions, such as by lobbying and extracting tit-for-tat promises with campaign donations, and influencing customers through advertising. In particular, advertising aimed at children is an egregious practice which is outlawed in the EU but not in the US. Finally, legislators could impose "circular economy" policies on corporations so that they were forced to internalize damage to the environment or society, thus diminishing profits. Beyond public policy, journals and media outlets could tighten up on conflict-of-interest policies so that corporations would not be able to plant "independent" stories that are actually advertisements. But this kind of legislation and media practice is blocked by lobbying and lack of citizen pressure. Corporations have driven the cultural narrative to encourage people to believe that they are acting responsibly (e.g., through advertising how sustainable they are or through Corporate Social Responsibility reports) and that they are necessary to provide adequate amounts of food (e.g., through opinion pieces placed in media outlets). Citizens who believe this narrative are passive and complacent, not interested in resisting corporate power or seeking out products from independent farmers and businesses.

Of course, the private sector doesn't have to use these tactics to gain power. If a company has a zero-growth objective (as it would under conditions of degrowth or in the steady-state economy that Daly envisioned), it won't seek mergers and acquisitions. If it is driven by regenerative food system values, it will re-invest in producers and environmental restoration rather than trying to enhance its own profits. But the tenets of neoliberalism, the extractive narrative and fiduciary responsibilities under neoliberal regimes to maximize profits to shareholders require that they encourage growth and endless acquisition of profits rather than restoration or regeneration. And policymakers face considerable pressure to be "business-friendly," even when this results in deterioration of ecological integrity and social harms.

The most important stocks and flows in food systems for determining whether the system is dominated by extractive or regenerative practices are the relative power wielded by the following actors and the actions that they take:

Policymakers (local to national) → Creating and implementing policy.
Civil society (social movements and NGOs) → Advocating and helping to build public awareness of the dynamics in the food system. For my purposes, I consider civil society that advocates for and builds awareness of regenerative food systems; but in reality, civil society may serve many purposes.
Citizens → Purchasing food, electing policymakers and advocating for specific policies.
Media (newspapers, television, trade magazines, social media, etc.) → Informing the public about positive and negative aspects of different food systems.
Donors (individuals, philanthropic organizations, government programs that give grants) → Providing private and public funding.
Producers (farmers, fishers, ranchers, hunters, foragers) → Producing food.
Food businesses (packers, processors, distributors, wholesalers & retailers) → Moving food from producers to eaters and advocating for a favorable cultural narrative.

Each of these actors is influenced by a number of factors; how they respond to those influences determines whether the food system is regenerative or extractive. A food system is never entirely regenerative or extractive, of course. Although I've been referring to it in those terms, the important thing is which narrative is dominant and whether the system is tipping toward one or the other narrative. This raises another issue for system dynamics: how stocks toggle back and forth from dominance by one narrative to another. For example, the more producers who use regenerative practices, the fewer who use extractive practices. The more regenerative businesses, the fewer operate in an extractive mode. The more policymakers who are dedicated to the public interest and the common good, the fewer who are padding their own retirement accounts and satisfying donors who contributed big campaign donations. We can think of toggles as rates; they serve the same purpose in the system of speeding up or slowing down certain power flows from one actor to another. The question for policymakers and everyone advocating for regenerative food systems is what drives those rates.

With one final causal link diagram, we're ready to move into specific narratives of transformation (or in systems language, drivers of rates). Figure 5.4 pulls together the major stocks listed above to show how flows of power between them influence the food system, building on Dyball and Newell's

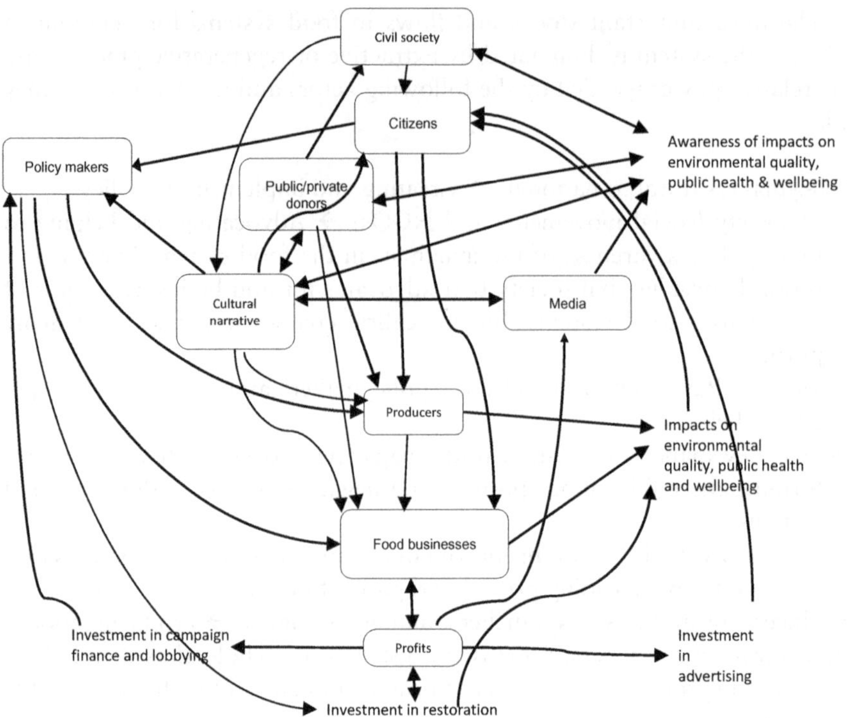

FIGURE 5.4 Patterns and potentials in the food system.

cultural adaptation template (Figure 5.2) and the diagram of corporate influence (Figure 5.3). In Figure 5.4, I separated actors who are combined into "state of the community" in Dyball and Newell's schema into the legislative engine of policy-makers, the economic engine of producers and food businesses, and the political engine of citizens and civil society. And I divided the "state of the cultural paradigm" into the cultural narrative and media. I made these changes to show that different information flows affect each of these actors or stocks.

The dominant cultural narrative sits near the middle of this system, affecting many of the actors' willingness and ability to support regenerative or extractive practices. The cultural narrative is unusual in the number of other actors and stocks that it affects (producers and food businesses, citizens, donors, policymakers, media, awareness of impacts from the food system); but it is directly affected, in turn, by fewer influences: donors; media; civil society; and awareness of impacts on environmental quality, public health and well-being. Those impacts are one of the "learning loops" that the food system has neglected; they may be overlooked or drowned by other power flows. Several influences can go both ways: for example, civil society may advocate for a regenerative narrative, but if other pressures are pushing for extraction, civil society's influence may be too weak to flip the narrative. Civil society can dramatically increase awareness of food system impacts on the environment and society, and awareness of these impacts can strengthen civil society by encouraging more participation. Donors may want to support a regenerative narrative; but if the feedback concerning awareness of impacts of the food system on social and environmental factors is weak and boards, advisors or fund managers are influenced by pro-extractive forces, they may support extractive projects and practices instead.

A cultural narrative supporting regeneration leads to (a) the expectation that policymakers will act in the public interest by supporting ecological integrity, public health and well-being. It also (b) strengthens independent media (i.e., not tied to a pre-determined agenda written by the private sector); (c) strengthens citizen engagement directly by normalizing active democratic participation and indirectly through encouraging civil society; (d) strengthens civil society because engaged citizens want to improve their food system; (e) increases awareness of impacts of the food system; (f) influences public and private donors to support regenerative food systems; and (g) strengthens producers and businesses using regenerative practices because citizens expect pro-social behavior from both actors and avoid producers and businesses that are not regenerative. Producers (farmers, foodworkers, fishers, ranchers, pastoralists) can exert power to favor regeneration by using agroecological practices and by preferentially selling to businesses that use regenerative practices (e.g., fair compensation for workers and products, genuine environmental stewardship) rather than trying to cut corners to accumulate greater profits for other kinds of investment.

In Figure 5.4 (as in Figure 5.3), food businesses can invest their profits back into the business, into advertising which will affect sales, into campaign finance and lobbying to affect whether policy-makers support extractive or regenerative practices and policies and into media which, in turn, affects the cultural narrative. But they might also invest profits into environmental or social restoration (e.g., land back to Indigenous people, building local food system infrastructure, providing resources to build soil health), which would affect their impacts on environmental quality, public health and well-being. Investing in restoration would not be acceptable to shareholders under capitalism, however, unless it also increased profits. Citizens affect power in the food system by (a) electing politicians, (b) purchasing from producers or food businesses and (c) responding to civil society's messages about impacts of the food system and alternatives. In a food system that is in transformation to being regenerative, citizens will elect pro-social legislators and preferentially purchase from regenerative producers and businesses.

Policymakers who understand the imperative of regeneration are essential in the food system because of what they encourage and what they prohibit:

they support producers and businesses that use regenerative practices through incentives, loans and grants. They prohibit harmful practices including farming that degrades the environment and health (such as confined animal feeding operations and wetland draining), labor abuses and unfair taxation. And they do not allow industry to grow in power by concentration or to leverage its market power into political power by lobbying and campaign contributions. Policymakers may invest in restoration as well as producers and food businesses, but they will be responsive to industry investment in campaign finances and lobbying in addition to direct influence from citizens who elect them. If industry investment is large, they will favor policies and practices that increase the power of food businesses and the largest producers on whom food businesses rely for products.

Policymakers direct the power flows of the food system so that they include or exclude people from the commons by creating, maintaining or disabling exclusionary legal structures such as private property, patents, intellectual property rights and Investor State Dispute Resolution mechanisms (which allow corporations to sue a government if its policies diminish expected profits). They can enact policies and programs that deliberately impoverish people (e.g., failing to tie minimum wages to increases in the cost of living, failing to stimulate the creation of jobs with decent working conditions and pay) or spread wealth (e.g., fair tax policies, closing down tax havens). Many policymakers, such as ones dealing with trade rules and property rights, are not elected directly but appointed by elected officials, which highlights the responsibility to ensure that elected officials are competent to uphold the public interest.

There are several reinforcing feedback loops in this system to note. First, investment in campaign finance and lobbying increases food businesses' power. Similarly, business profits that are invested in media affect the cultural narrative to strengthen food businesses' power. We see both of these trends in effect in the US now: politicians are routinely bought off with corporate donations and "dark money," and the most popular media are controlled by arch-conservative business interests such as the Koch brothers and the Murdoch family. Bought media weakens the cultural narrative in support of regeneration, which weakens policy-makers' ability to pass legislation to support environmental and labor regulation, which reinforces the power of the largest food businesses.

Advertisements and industry propaganda circulated through media result in citizens buying from businesses that are not regenerative; having little awareness of food system impacts and alternatives and accepting the narrative that food industries are necessary and sustainable, even when they are not. The money going to regenerative businesses in the US is much less now than what is spent at extractive retailers such as Walmart or other large grocery chains. For example, Walmart is the largest food retailer in the US and accounts for 45 percent of food purchases; grocery stores combined make up 91.1 percent of food sales (Kolmar 2023). Walmart is an extractive retailer that does not provide living wages to its employees and extracts wealth from communities by supplanting smaller stores that have a multiplier effect by which money spent at smaller local stores stays in the community and re-circulates. Walmart is one of the largest employers of recipients of federal food assistance in the US (Rosenberg 2020). Given food industry efforts to influence public opinion, civil society and donors have great difficulty affecting the dominant narrative and subsequently advocating for regenerative policies. Relatively few US producers and businesses are truly regenerative, they control a small market share of food, and most citizens are disengaged from food systems issues and unaware of their full impacts. Because of the lack of sufficient policy support, producers and food businesses usually cannot operate in a regenerative way even if they want to do so because they would be out-competed by peers that are cutting corners on safe, humane labor standards and environmental regulations to make higher profits.

On the other hand, we also see increasing citizen interest in the food system and increasing awareness of how business practices affect public health, environmental quality including climate change, and well-being. Independent investigative journalism is steadily uncovering stories of corporate and governmental malfeasance; and at least in the US, it can be accessed fairly easily by curious citizens. Some citizens seek out and buy from regenerative producers and businesses that protect the environment, pay workers fairly, and produce healthy foods. The more citizens that become engaged in their food system, the closer the cultural narrative comes to toggling toward regeneration. Citizens' purchases affect the environment, public health and well-being; these in turn affect the cultural narrative, which gives important feedback to citizens about what kinds of purchases to make (unless they are overwhelmed by advertising and private sector media messaging).

Figure 5.4 would be drawn in different ways by different people, but there might be agreement on the major stocks that are important to regeneration and on Figure 5.3, how investment by agribusiness and the largest food businesses can subvert regeneration. I will use system diagrams of a few transformation narratives in subsequent chapters, such as "vote with your fork," to show that market-based "solutions" that employ the "food is just a commodity" value narrative involve a small subset of the entire food system and do not affect the cultural narrative directly, while transformation narratives that employ the "food as commons" value narrative involve most of the system because they change the cultural narrative. This ties back to my hypothesis that involving more food system actors and sharing power increases the likelihood that a transformation narrative will be successful in moving toward regeneration because different actors reinforce and balance each other. Other authors have noted that activism and advocacy needs to focus on multiple forms and spaces of power, and at different scales, to be effective (Gaventa 2021). Meadows (2008) claimed that changing the goals and mindset from which a system arises are the most powerful levers to change a system. Narratives are an expression of that mindset, and the next three chapters explore some of the common ones in circulation.

References

Avelino, F and J Rotmans. 2009. Power in transition: an interdisciplinary framework to study power in relation to structural change. *Eur J Soc Theory* 12(3):543–569. https://doi.org/10.1177/1368431009349830

Avelino, F and JM Wittmayer. 2016. Shifting power relations in sustainability transitions: a multi-actor perspective. *J Environ Pol Plann* 18(5):628–649.

Baker, P, J Lacy-Nichols, O Williams and R Labonté. 2021. The political economy of healthy and sustainable food systems: an introduction to a special issue. *Int J Health Policy Manag* 10(12):734–744. https://doi.org/10.34172/ijhpm.2021.156

Clapp, J and DA Fuchs. 2009. *Corporate Power in Global Agrifood Governance.* Cambridge, MA: MIT Press.

Clapp, J and J Purugganan. 2020. Contextualizing corporate control in the agrifood and extractive sectors *Globalizations* 17(7):1265–1275. https://doi.org/10.1080/14747731.2020.1783814

Daly, H. 1990. Commentary: toward some operational principles of sustainable development. *Ecol Econ* 2:1–6.

De Schutter, O. 2017. The political economy of food systems reform. *Eur Rev Agric Econ* 44(4):705–731. https://doi.org/10.1093/erae/jbx009

Dyball, R and B Newell. 2023. *Understanding Human Ecology. A Systems Approach to Sustainability*, 2nd Edition. London: Routledge.

Ericksen, PJ. 2008. Conceptualizing food systems for global environmental change research. *Global Env Change* 18(1):234–245.https://doi.org/10.1016/j.gloenvcha.2007.09.002

FAO, IFAD, UNICEF, WFP and WHO. 2023. *The State of Food Security and Nutrition in the World 2023*. Urbanization, agrifood systems transformation and healthy diets across the rural–urban continuum. Rome: FAO. https://doi.org/10.4060/cc3017en

Foucault, M. 1980. *Power/Knowledge: Selected Interviews and Other Writings.1972–1977*. C Gordin (Ed.). New York: Pantheon.

Fuchs, D. 2007. *Business Power in Global Governance*. Boulder: Lynne Rienner.

Gaventa, J. 2006. Finding the spaces for change: a power analysis. *IDS Bull* 37(6):23–33. https://doi.org/10.1111/j.1759-5436.2006.tb00320.x

Gaventa, J. 2021. Linking the prepositions: using power analysis to inform strategies for social action. *J Pol Power* 14(1):109–130. https://doi.org/10.1080/2158379X.2021.1878409

Guttal, S. 2021. Re-imagining the UN Committee on World Food Security. *Development* 64:227–235.

Harvey, D. 2005. *A Brief History of Neoliberalism*. Oxford, UK: Oxford University Press.

Heller, MC and GA Keoleian. 2001. *CSS Factsheets, U.S. Food System*. Ann Arbor: University of Michigan, 1–2.

Heinberg, R. 2022. The Limits to Growth at 50: from scenarios to unfolding reality. *Resilience.org*. https://www.resilience.org/stories/2022-02-24/the-limits-to-growth-at-50-from-scenarios-to-unfolding-reality/

IPES-Food. 2016. From Uniformity to Diversity. A Paradigm Shift from Industrial Agriculture to Diversified Agroecological Systems. https://ipes-food.org/_img/upload/files/UniformityToDiversity_FULL.pdf

IPES-Food. 2023. Who's Tipping the Scales? http://www.ipes-food.org/pages/tippingthescales

Kolmar, C. 2023. 25 Appetizing U.S. food retail industry statistics [2023]: facts about the stores where we shop. Zippia. https://www.zippia.com/advice/us-food-retail-industry-statistics/

Levy, D and D Egan. 1998. Capital contests: national and transnational channels of corporate influence on the climate change negotiations. *Politics and Society* 26(3):337–361.

Meadows, DH. 2008. *Thinking in Systems: A Primer*. White River Junction, VT: Chelsea Green Publishing.

Meadows, DH, DL Meadows, J Randers and WW Behrens III. 1972. *The Limits to Growth. A Report for the Club of Rome's Project on the Predicament of Mankind*. New York: Universe Books.

Rosenberg, E. 2020. Walmart and McDonald's have the most workers on food stamps and Medicaid, new study shows. *The Washington Post*. https://www.washingtonpost.com/business/2020/11/18/food-stamps-medicaid-mcdonalds-walmart-bernie-sanders/

Rossi, A, S Bui and T Marsden. 2019. Redefining power relations in agrifood systems. *J Rural Stud* 68:147–158. https://doi.org/10.1016/j.jrurstud.2019.01.002

Roy, A. 2006. *Ordinary Person's Guide to Empire*. Gargaon: Penguin Books India.

Sodano, V and MT Gorgitano. 2022. Framing political issues in food system transformative changes. *Soc Sci* 11:459. https://doi.org/10.3390/socsci11100459

Swinburn, B. 2019. Power dynamics in 21st-century food systems. *Nutrients* 11:2544. https://doi.org/10.3390/nu11102544

VeneKlasen, L and V Miller 2008. *A New Weave of Power, People and Politics*. Boston, MA: Just Associates.

Walls, H, N Nisbett, A Laar, S Drimie, S Zaidi, J Harris. 2021. Addressing malnutrition: the importance of political economy analysis of power. *Int J Health Policy Manag* 10(12):809–816. https://doi.org/10.34172/ijhpm.2020.250

SECTION 3

Narratives of Transformation

What and Who Will Drive Change?

6

WHAT DRIVES FOOD SYSTEM TRANSFORMATION TOWARD REGENERATION? NARRATIVES THAT DO NOT REQUIRE STRUCTURAL TRANSFORMATION

The questions of what drives food system transformation in the direction of greater regeneration and justice, and how such a transformation might happen, have preoccupied scholars and activists for decades. The literature on sociotechnical and sustainability transitions is well-developed, but its applications to food systems are just beginning. Equally important to the *what* and *how* questions is *who* can drive food system transformation in the direction of regeneration, which has received less attention except from civil society. This chapter introduces narratives of what drives food system transformation toward regeneration and how it will happen, focusing on narratives that do not require structural transformation. Since I think that deep structural changes in power dynamics are necessary to create regenerative food systems, I see the narratives in this chapter mainly as window-dressing or green-washing; but they need to be considered because they are promoted widely.

The next chapter turns to narratives that do require structural transformation to create regenerative food systems, and Chapter 8 addresses who is responsible for and capable of transformation. However, the what and the who are often intermeshed. For example, what value do good policies have if policymakers cannot or do not push them through the legislative process to create programs or other tangible results, and people on the ground cannot or do not put them into practice?

For each narrative described in this chapter, I focus on the underlying (often implicit) theory of change and its assumptions, then cite available evidence that this theory of change works or does not work as anticipated. We can analyze assumptions for their congruence with current realities and

DOI: 10.4324/9781003260264-9

trends to discern which assumptions are backed with solid evidence and most likely given what we know.

The most frequently cited theory of sociotechnical transformation is the multi-level transitions pathway or multi-level perspective (MLP; Rip and Kemp 1998; Geels 2002; Geels and Schot 2007), which is relevant to several ideas described below. In this theory, sociotechnical transitions occur as outcomes of the alignment of developments at three expanding levels: niche-innovations, sociotechnical regimes and the sociotechnical landscape. Niches are the micro-level where innovations emerge, supported by networks of actors. These niche innovations build momentum and are able to break through the customary thought processes, regulations and other stabilizing institutions of the regime (a community of interacting actors), if changes in the landscape level (exogenous variables that are not influenced directly by actors in the regime or niche) create windows of opportunity. In some ways, the MLP is a generic refinement of Joseph Schumpeter's theory of creative destruction, which posits that capitalism is always in a dynamic flux with new products, new methods of production or transportation, new markets and new forms of industrial organization that capitalist enterprise creates. These new products and processes replace the products and processes that are now deemed obsolete (Schumpeter 1942). Why and how certain niches "succeed" is a vital field of investigation.

The MLP elicited criticisms and further elaborations as soon as it appeared in literature. Frank Geels and Johan Schot, early advocates of this approach, as well as other authors, have responded to many of the criticisms, such as the lack of agency, the emphasis on technological niches, a bias toward bottom-up change models and neglect of power dynamics (Geels and Schot 2007; Geels 2011, 2019). The MLP is in widespread use. Hamid El Bilali (2019) reviewed its applications in food systems at the time and assigned agroecology, organic agriculture, permaculture, urban agriculture, conservation agriculture, integrated farming, care farming and alternative food networks to the niche category, with potential to alter the regime of intensive industrial, "conventional" agriculture. He called for more attention to understanding interactions between levels and recognition of the complexity and diversity of pathways to transformation.

The *Beacons of Hope* project (Biovision and GAFF 2019) and Olivier De Schutter and Tom Dedeurwaerdere (2022) used the MLP especially well to develop hypotheses of why certain types of food system innovations scale up from niches to regime-changers, although many others have applied it in specific case studies. The *Beacons of Hope* project covered 21 initiatives from around the world. Its authors developed a framework of successful initiatives that grow in consistent stages, from promoting agroecology to improve health and livelihoods, through confronting existing policies that need to be changed, through establishing legitimacy for the project, to anchoring the project so that it can be sustainable. Each of these steps has clear strategies that were used in multiple initiatives.

De Schutter and Dedeurwaerdere pointed out that regime change is difficult because its components have co-evolved, it is path-dependent because of facilitating infrastructure, and incumbents have disproportionate weight. They posited four scenarios under which niches can scale up to change the regime: (1) collapse and reconstruction (echoing resilience theory [Cumming and Peterson 2017]), (2) sociodiversity in which multiple social innovations reconfigure social norms, (3) co-optation by actors in the mainstream regime and (4) subversion in which niche actors deliberately seek to transform the regime's end goals. They argued that regime change is only possible if all of the actors share an understanding of sustainability challenges and economic democracy ensures that a different kind of economic system is given form.

Sustainable Intensification

> Doubling food production in developing countries by 2050 might seem impossible, but we have the technologies to achieve it. From simple farming techniques like microdosing, to GPS and mobile technology, applying new innovations and methods at the small scale can have a significant impact on food production in developing nations. By focusing on 'Sustainable Intensification', we can ensure that the progress we make will feed the world in many generations' time, not just today.
>
> *(Conway 2017, n.p.)*

Implicit Theory of Change

- If more food is made available by increasing production and productivity, more people will be fed.

Implicit Assumptions

- The reason many people are not getting enough to eat is lack of food availability.
- Demands on food production will increase because of population growth, rising incomes and increasing demand for meat.
- The primary task of food system transformation is to increase production and productivity of food crops and animals.
- It is possible to increase production and productivity without causing environmental damage.

Sustainable intensification (SI) was introduced originally by Jules Pretty (1997), who emphasized that policies should create enabling conditions for locally generated and adapted technologies that allow them to cut their use of external inputs. However, it has become a "green" variant of productivism, the idea that food producers and businesses must boost production and productivity by all means possible to meet the needs of a growing population.

Exactly how much global food demand will rise is subject to debate but very important to the argument for intensification. The most cited figure for increases in global food demand, originating from a 2009 FAO briefing paper (FAO 2009a), states that world food production needs to increase by 70 percent from 2005 to 2007 levels to feed the world population in 2050. This number was reduced to 60 percent in a revision of the original study, but it continues to be used by companies and scientific papers. In another widely cited paper, David Tilman et al. (2011) gave a much higher estimated increase in global food demand of 100–110 percent between 2005 and 2050. Michiel van Dijk et al. (2021) conducted a meta-analysis and concluded that solid estimates range from a 35 to 56 percent increase between 2010 and 2050, depending on the method used to estimate. But others point to reducing the one-third of food that is wasted from production through consumption stages, shifting land from livestock production to growing crops for people, dietary changes to plant-based diets and introducing algae-based food products, insects or foods created from other media as ways that the amount of resources available for growing food for people can be effectively increased without increasing production or converting more non-agricultural land.

Although food availability is indeed limiting food security in some places, financial and physical access to food is much more important: wealthy people don't starve. Susan George argued in 1976 that hunger was the result of human policies, not absolute limits on food: wealthy elites control the food supply, poor farmers do not have a voice in determining trade rules and foreign agribusinesses replace local farmers growing food with cash crops. Amartya Sen (1980) demonstrated that bundles of entitlements (to land, money and other resources) are the key to food security, not the amount of food that is produced. While it is possible to point to lower numbers of food-insecure people in some areas that correspond with investment in increasing food production and productivity, the global prevalence of hunger has risen since 2015. That is, focusing on food availability and the means to increase it has not been sufficient to ensure food security.

"Sustainable" in the context of SI means minimizing environmental harm; SI advocates seldom mention social aspects of sustainability such as equity or gender justice. The Global Panel on Agriculture and Nutrition (GLOPAN 2020, 15) defined SI as:

> A process or system where agricultural yields are increased without adverse environmental impact and without the conversion of additional non-agricultural land. The concept does not articulate or privilege any

> particular vision or method of agricultural production. Rather, it emphasizes ends rather than means, and does not pre-determine technologies, species mix or particular design components.

GLOPAN (2020, 16) went on to state that the goals of SI are "improving efficiency, substituting more environmentally beneficial practices for environmentally harmful ones, and redesigning production systems" and that "novel technologies—including improved agronomy, digital innovations, and new breeding methods—have an important role to play in fostering sustainable productivity growth, diversity, and resilience in agricultural production systems." The World Economic Forum (2023, 14), in comparing transitions to more sustainable food systems in countries where smallholder farms (<2 ha) are dominant, claimed that "food systems transformation is first and foremost … economic … and it must start with the sustainable intensification of agriculture, done in a way that minimizes land-use change and environmental degradation." Although this sounds fine in theory, it results in opportunity costs as policies emphasize research, development and implementation of practices that increase productivity rather than social justice or access. And the uncritical acceptance of a broad array of technologies ignores important questions of who has access to them and who owns and profits from them. The answers to these questions can determine whether the technologies are in fact "sustainable" or not in social, economic, cultural and environmental dimensions.

SI goes hand-in-glove with the idea that technological innovation will drive greater sustainability (see below). As mentioned in Chapter 4, the High Level Panel of Experts of the Committee on World Food Security's report on *Agroecological and other innovations for sustainable agriculture and food systems that enhance food security and nutrition* (HLPE, 2019) grouped climate-smart agriculture, nutrition-sensitive agriculture and sustainable food value chains with SI, contrasting them with agroecology and related approaches such as agroforestry, organic agriculture and food sovereignty. In their report, SI had the fewest documented benefits, in terms of resource efficiency, resilience, social equity and responsibility. The authors claimed that, in practice, SI advocates "privilege technological and productivity-oriented innovations in order to improve resource efficiency while reducing the negative environmental and health impacts of current food systems" (p. 61).

Rachel Bezner Kerr, who has studied farming systems in Malawi for several years, wrote that sustainable intensification there is part of a colonial "plantation mentality" (2023, 1):

> A kind of plantation imaginary circulates among foreign donors, government representatives, and scientists, which contrasts modern industrial monocrops grown by entrepreneurial business-oriented farmers with

> illiterate, difficult, intransigent, tribal, small-scale African farmers, ignorant in the face of evidence of the benefits of modern technological farming. Modernization theory abounds in this narrative, which conjures up the savvy entrepreneurial farmers who deploy genetically modified seeds, pesticides, and fertilizer, and sell their crops at a profit—with the help of scientists and companies. As the story goes, Africa was "left out" of the Green Revolution, but their time has arrived, with the Africa Green Revolution.

She contrasted SI with agroecology, which uses ecological and social principles to produce food in ways that sustain nature and people's well-being. "While plantation logic reinforces persistent patterns of delegitimizing Black agrarian knowledges and practices, agroecological plots provide hopeful alternatives, but face fierce opposition, dangers of cooptation and limited support" (2023, 1).

SI is interpreted in many ways and often used to support "land-sparing" arguments (the idea that land must be protected and "set aside" from any human use to meet biodiversity targets). The encroachment of cropping and grazing on forest, in addition to deforestation and road-building by the timber industry, are among the biggest contributors to the spread of diseases from wildlife to humans, and have been implicated in several recent zoonoses as well as COVID-19 (Plowright et al. 2021). Replacing forest with monocultures is undoubtedly bad for biodiversity, but mosaics of small diverse cultivated plots can enhance biodiversity (Wanger et al. 2020).

Since SI does not prescribe production systems but rather the end result of using resources and inputs more efficiently, it was quickly taken up by a number of governments and organizations that favor flexibility and endorsed in numerous high-level reports (Bernard and Lux 2017). For example, it was Strategic Objective A of FAO's Strategic Framework 2010–2019 (FAO 2009b) and is still recommended in the context of aquaculture in the current FAO Strategic Framework 2022–2031 (FAO 2021). It is a weak approach to transformation, however, because it leaves out so many crucial aspects of sustainability and justice including access to seeds and land for small-holders, equity for women, and compensation for the theft of land and biological resources. It can easily become business as usual, if proponents argue that the use of technologies such as synthetic pesticides and fertilizers are necessary to increase production without expanding into additional land. However, with heat, floods and drought due to climate chaos reducing crop productivity and nutritional content, and growing awareness of the need to maintain reservoirs of biodiversity for human as well as ecosystem health, it is likely that SI will continue to be a dominant narrative.

Technological Innovation

> Technological change is perhaps the deepest driver of global change. We need the new technologies to confront the crises of climate change, hunger, education, and health.
>
> *(Sachs 2023, n.p.)*

Implicit Theory of Change

- If farmers adopt prescribed technological innovations, their productivity and production will increase with few deleterious side-effects.

Implicit Assumptions

- Technological innovations are beneficial and the main reason that modern production methods have higher productivity and yields.
- Technological innovations are adopted and welcomed by producers and businesses.
- Benefits of technological innovation are widely available and trickle down to others.

Some people foresee the end-point of technological innovation as a dystopian world of "farming without farmers," whether farmers are no longer needed because they can be replaced with robots and their products replaced with precision-fermented yeast and other foodstuffs manufactured by corporations or because their practices produce too many greenhouse gases. Concerns about the loss of biodiversity and climate change lead to arguments that the world needs far fewer farmers, especially livestock farmers (e.g., Monbiot 2022); but others hold a vision in which society is radically decentralized and far <u>more</u> farmers using agroecological practices that conserve the natural environment are needed to nourish local food systems (e.g., Donahue et al. 2014; Bradford 2019; Smaje 2023). These two narratives are in sharp contrast: technological innovation might serve both, but it would be essential for the first vision.

Technological innovation is the bedrock of many transformation narratives—referring either to innovations that have already been developed (such as genetic engineering of crops and livestock) or to the promise of new and widely available technological innovations (e.g., feedstuffs for cattle that will reduce methane production, robotic weeding systems). Technological innovations are often beneficial; for example, few would argue that digging sticks are better than metal shovels or that solar cookstoves aren't better than open cooking fires that release particulates leading to respiratory problems for many Majority-World women. But in every case, it is important to ask who is benefiting from the technology, who is paying the costs, and what those costs are. This step is often missing. Early adopters usually reap the most benefits from technological innovation and it can easily widen the gap in income between early adopters and others. Adoption is a multi-step process: producers and businesses need to have the wherewithal to make changes and invest in whatever infrastructure is required by the technological innovation. Wealthier producers and businesses usually get more from technological innovation because they can afford to make this investment and they are less risk-averse.

In addition to the question of who has access to innovations, there are big issues related to who develops, owns and profits from them. Some people argue that farmers are the biggest innovators; they can be very adaptable when circumstances require it—retrofitting tools and equipment, repurposing supplies, and trying different ways to handle production problems ranging from insect pests to floods. Domestication of plants and animals was one of the biggest food innovations, and farmers were responsible for all of this. They seldom get credit for their innovations, however; the system of Intellectual Property Rights can be used to rob farmers of innovations that they started (as has happened in cases of bio-piracy), or to privatize profits from innovations that began with public funding (as happened with COVID vaccines).

States promote and reward technological innovation, but innovators are not usually rewarded for sharing their discoveries or research materials. Patents and Intellectual Property Rights law explicitly prohibit sharing, but in the process increase the market dominance of industries that can afford to invest in research and development, discourage competition and lock in current technology. The glorification of technological innovation shifts attention away from behavioral changes and social innovations, which may be far more significant in terms of movement toward regenerative food systems (De Schutter and Dedeurwaerdere 2022). The adulation of technological innovation has been advanced through public-private partnerships, including partnerships between public media and the agrifood industry. An example is *Follow the Food*, a series of videos produced by the British Broadcasting Company in partnership with the agricultural chemical and seed giant Corteva (Carlile 2023). Technological innovations such as the use of drones to plant cover crops and sophisticated greenhouses are presented glowingly in the videos as the future of food systems, with no space given to alternatives or criticism.

Innovation has taken on a value of its own:

> [L]eading economic thinkers have even begun to frame it in terms of the "innovation imperative", elevating the fetish for novelty and technological "progress" into an existential ultimatum familiar in developmental discourse: modernize or disappear.
>
> *(Anderson and Maughan 2021, 3)*

Technological innovations may not result in anticipated sustainability improvements because of rebound effects (Zink and Geyer 2017). With increasing efficiency or availability of products because of innovation, people may simply consume more, leading to increased material throughput and scarcity (the Jevons Paradox). The goal of technological innovation should be to decrease overall resource extraction and throughput, as well as increasing efficiency of resource use. Advocates for "green growth" believe that economic growth can happen in conjunction with increases in sustainability. But degrowth proponents have shown conclusively that increased resource consumption accompanies economic growth (Hickel and Kallis 2020).

In response to the question of whether technological innovation can drive transformation toward regenerative food systems, the answer is maybe but probably not. In some circumstances, such as poor farmers' use of cellphones to track crop prices or monitor weather, it is relatively accessible and can help livelihoods of small-scale producers. But technological innovations are seldom designed with the poorest people who are least served by current food systems in mind. This question has assumed increased importance over the last decade with a clamor of voices calling for digitalization and increased use of data in farming, such as the so-called 4th Industrial Revolution. Proponents claim that this will be "revolutionary," but social scientists are far more skeptical and note that digitalization is being driven by large private sector companies (e.g., Birner et al. 2021; Duncan et al. 2021; Rose et al. 2023). One of the most astute social scientists studying patterns of agricultural development, Philip McMichael, observed that "the emergent digital frontier continues capital's re-valuation of its landed relations across food regime space-time: from confiscation (via colonization) through conversion (through agro-technologies), to cyberization (via digitalization)" (McMichael 2023, 744).

"Revolutionary" technology has elicited regular protests, from the British Luddites who smashed powered weaving looms in the early 1800s because they would put people out of work to farmhacks who circumvent exclusionary licenses on who can fix tractors to citizens who are concerned about loss of privacy with social media platforms and other manifestations of "surveillance capitalism" (Zuboff 2019; Stone 2022). Although concerns are often ridiculed as evidence that a person is simply not willing to keep up with the times and accept "progress," they come down to questions of what kind of future we want, who will be better off and who will be worse off. At present, technological innovation is clearly serving the interests of the most powerful people and companies in the world. However, there is no objective reason that technological innovation, in the form of appropriate technology, might not serve small-scale agroecological farmers and marginalized people. Many of the tasks of food production and processing are time-consuming and arduous. Appropriate technology, such as hand pumps for wells or cultivators and planters designed for small-scale farms, could make the lives of small-scale farmers easier. Equipment for small acreages often is not available, however. For example, an innovative rice farmer living near me in Vermont had to ship a rice-planter from Japan because the only planters available in the US were designed for large-scale farms. Ideally, end-users are involved in designing and evaluating the technology for it to be appropriate; and the goals of regeneration demand that fossil fuel dependence and environmental degradation be minimized if not entirely eliminated, technology be free or low-cost, the choice of whether to adopt the technology be decided democratically and people be able to maintain the technology that they acquire. Technology without agency creates dependence, but appropriate technology could be liberating.

Scientific Knowledge

> We focus on the key role of science and research, as they are essential for innovations that accelerate the transformation to healthier, more sustainable, equitable, and resilient food systems. The problems of food systems are to a significant extent due to long delays between scientific warnings and policy responses, innovation-stifling regulatory regimes, low levels of science investments, and a lack of effective communication by science communities themselves.
>
> *(von Braun et al. 2021, 4)*

Implicit Theory of Change

- Using methodologies refined in universities of the industrialized Minority World to conduct scientific studies is the best way to analyze food system transformation alternatives and find solutions to global problems.

Implicit Assumptions

- "Science" is a unified approach to knowledge which can uncover truth.
- Knowledge relevant to food system transformation is divided logically into "disciplines," and disciplines have a hierarchy with the value of natural science and economics above other social sciences.
- Scientific research in the Minority World (Global North) has relevance in the Majority World as well.
- People who criticize evidence produced by scientific knowledge are ignorant or misguided (or both).
- People who are trained as scientists are qualified to speak authoritatively about issues outside the disciplines in which they were trained.

Scientific knowledge about the detrimental effects of current dominant agricultural and food-system practices is important to help guide food system policy and monitor the impacts of interventions. But "evidence-based" policy is a code phrase for policy with Western scientific underpinnings, and the demand for it is sometimes used as a cudgel to bully international negotiators. For example, the 2023 US demands that Mexico allow imports of genetically engineered corn that will end up in tortillas, and lift its prohibition on glyphosate, are supposedly driven by a lack of scientific evidence for associated damages. However, Mexico provided ample scientific evidence of the harms due to glyphosate and genetically engineered corn, and it is allowed to use the precautionary principle to avoid likely harm, according to the US-Mexico-Canada free trade agreement (Wise 2023a). This dispute over "science" is clearly politically motivated: the US grows excessive amounts of corn, farmers overwhelmingly use corn seed that is genetically engineered so that the plant can tolerate glyphosate, and the US wants to export more to satisfy farmers and increase its balance of trade.

Scientists, scientific associations and intergovernmental agencies look to science for answers to some of the biggest sustainability challenges; and indeed scientific knowledge has led to innumerable advances in well-being, ranging from modern medicine to the basic science behind innovative technologies. Scientists are vociferous about needing more funding; and research focused on challenges such as global warming can be very costly. Scientists sometimes scoff at growing approval of the value of other forms of knowledge, such as Indigenous and traditional; but Western science cannot solve all of our problems. This was part of the reason that many scholars and people within civil society were concerned about the narrow expertise of the scientific advisory group of the UN Food Systems Summit of 2021 (described further in Chapter 9). Scientific knowledge is sometimes overrated, but it can be the best way to solve disputes about various food system practices. For example, the questions of whether grass-fed cattle or confined cattle emit more greenhouse gases, or whether intensive rotational grazing sequesters more carbon and promotes more biodiversity than re-wilding pasture are best answered with careful scientific studies. Anecdotal evidence is not strong enough to justify government funding to promote specific practices, although sometimes personal experience is contrary to the results of randomized controlled trials, the gold standard for scientific evaluations of interventions. Scientific studies do not always take into account all of the factors that can make an intervention work or not, such as local environmental context, farmers' experience and their ability to adapt their practices.

Numerous scholars have critiqued the view that science is a source of objective truth. Science is socially and institutionally embedded, such that the questions asked, methods used and interpretations of results depend on who is doing the work, where, and for what purposes. The knowledge produced by scientists is always socially constructed and viewed through subjective lenses, despite attempts to erase the role of the individual and subjective. Lorrae van Kerkhoff and Louis Lebel wrote (2006, 12):

> Technical-rational ways of approaching policy, management, and development—including particularly the natural sciences and economics—have long been a subject of criticism for concentrating power in those who can lay claim to scientific knowledge and its interpretation and implementation in practice.

Thus, science reflects existing inequalities and cultural biases. The results of scientific studies may be used selectively, distorted or misreported if they do not fit with some actors' agendas. Their results must be disseminated to receptive audiences, whether this is to the public through independent trustworthy media or to scientific communities through journals that have strict standards regarding conflicts of interest. One of the ways that food and agricultural industries try to promote their interests is by funding studies to test their products and exercising veto power over results that do not verify that their products are effective. Agribusiness has also been guilty of deliberately discrediting scientists and their findings, such as the notorious defamation of Tyrone Hayes when he discovered that the pesticide atrazine was an endocrine system disruptor (Rohr 2021). Agribusiness may attempt to suppress scientific results that are inconvenient, such as the relationship between neonicotinoids and deaths of beneficial insects and birds. The tobacco industry developed a repertoire of ways to falsify science or delay policy action; these tactics have been adopted by food industries as well (Hamerschlag et al. 2015; UCS 2018).

Despite its value to reveal new knowledge and solve various disputes, scientific knowledge alone is never sufficient to promote action. Behavioral shifts require a suite of incentives beyond simply knowing what we should do. We have no need to look farther than climate change to recognize that people have a remarkable ability to ignore inconvenient facts, which fossil fuel companies have exploited to their benefit.

Scientific knowledge in conjunction with Indigenous and traditional knowledge can be tremendously valuable in food systems transformation. Scientists can test ideas that come from food producers and other knowledge holders to find out how well they work under different circumstances, and sometimes hypothesize why they work such that results can be applied in other domains. For example, Indigenous and traditional societies often rely on native plants as medicine without being aware of the specific compounds that have medicinal properties. Scientists have extracted quinine from the bark of the cinchona tree of South America, where it had been used to treat fever and malaria for centuries (Achan et al. 2011) and formulated antimalarial drugs from it. Unfortunately, the use of traditional and Indigenous knowledge has seldom been compensated fairly; two international conventions, the Convention on Biological Diversity and the International Treaty on Plant Genetic Resources of the Food and Agriculture Organization, are intended to combat biopiracy. Yet it has been so prevalent that many Indigenous and traditional communities are wary of any kind of collaboration with scientists. Successful collaboration requires humility on the part of scientists and transparency about motives and results, mutual respect, sharing any profits or other gains from the partnership, willingness to trust on the part of Indigenous and traditional partners and willingness from all partners to invest the substantial amounts of time needed to build that trust.

Scientific knowledge about the environmental, social, economic and health impacts of extractive food systems and comparisons with regenerative systems is extremely important to build up the evidence base for regenerative systems, especially given the esteem that scientific studies garner. Unfortunately, far less money has been invested in regenerative than in extractive food system research and development. Several studies have examined the proportion of research funding that has gone to organic agriculture and found very low levels compared with non-organic agriculture. In Germany (with high organic acreage and sales) only two percent of the agricultural research funds were dedicated to organic, and the global average for organic research funding was only 0.04 percent in previous decades (Rahmann et al. 2017). In the US, the Organic Farming and Research Foundation found that only 0.1 percent of the total agricultural research budget of US$24 billion was dedicated to organic agriculture (Lipson 1997) despite earmarked funding for organic research.

If we look for agroecological or even "sustainable agriculture" research, we find a similarly low proportion of federal funding: only 0.6–1.5 percent of the 2014 federal research, education and extension budget was applicable (DeLonge et al. 2016). Because of this skew in the topics that institutions fund and scientists tackle, science has supported large-scale farms and imperial domination far more than small-scale farms and the public interest (Ghosh 2022). Yet small-scale farms are more productive and biodiverse than large-scale farms, and more impoverished (Ricciardi et al. 2021). Civil society resistance to public research funding priorities, such as mechanized lettuce-pickers and tomato-pickers that put farmworkers out of jobs, were prevalent in the 1970s and 1980s (Buttel 2005), but has changed in the decades since to calls primarily to increase public research funds as private research has become more dominant. Groups including the National Campaign for Sustainable Agriculture in the US have steadily campaigned for more public research money; this should be spent on the public interest.

Just as with technological innovation, whom will be served by scientific research and whom will be harmed are essential questions to answer before embarking on the research.

Multistakeholder Initiatives

> [T]he future of global governance will not be based on worldwide unity or top-down control, but rather on connectivity across distinct domains, communities, and spheres of influence. To be people-centred, it also must be radically and systematically inclusive, offering meaningful opportunities for participation in global decision-making by all States, civil society, private sector actors, local and regional governments, and other groups that have been traditionally excluded from global governance
>
> *(UN High Level Advisory Board (HLAB) 2023, 13)*

Implicit Theory of Change

- Food systems can be transformed if all actors who are involved cooperate as partners in broad inclusive initiatives where they can discuss and implement potential solutions to problems, with each partner providing its unique resources and knowledge.

Implicit Assumptions

- People and organizations that hold very different levels and kinds of power in the food system can establish meaningful partnerships of value to all.
- Benefits of these partnerships will be shared by all participants.

Multistakeholder initiatives (MSIs) are defined as a practice of governance that brings multiple "stakeholders" including corporations, corporate platforms and business associations, donors, academics and civil society actors together to participate in dialog, decision-making and implementation of responses to jointly perceived problems (Chandrasekaran et al. 2021). They are sometimes called coalitions of the willing and able, a phrase first used by the World Economic Forum. MSIs have come under increasing criticism by civil society, especially since the UN Food Systems Summit demonstrated what happens when they have power. The UN Secretary-General prepared *Our Common Agenda* (UN 2021), a strategy proposal, followed up by recommendations from an appointed High Level Advisory Board, to move the entire UN system to multistakeholderism and away from multilateralism. The latter is the current operating principle of UN agencies, in which member states make decisions on a one-country/one-vote basis, albeit often with heavy lobbying or influence by corporations.

The problems with MSIs have been spelled out clearly in reports from civil society organizations (e.g., Chandrasekaran et al. 2021; Food Systems 4 People 2023), many of which oppose MSIs vehemently. In addition, scholars and the High Level Panel of Experts have explained their limitations and deficiencies, when it comes to democratic participation and governance (McKeon 2017; Gleckman 2018; HLPE 2018; MSI Integrity 2020).

> MSIs are not effective tools for holding corporations accountable for abuses, protecting rights holders against human rights violations, or providing survivors and victims with access to remedy. While MSIs can be important and necessary venues for learning, dialogue, and trust-building between corporations and other stakeholders—which can sometimes lead to positive rights outcomes—they should not be relied upon for the protection of human rights. They are simply not fit for this purpose.
>
> *(MSI Integrity 2020, 4)*

While inclusive participation in governance is a game-changer in the search for regeneration, MSIs are not the way to achieve this. "Inclusion" should focus on the people who have not benefited from food systems and have been left out of governance forums, not those who are already at the table and eating their fill. Yet industry and some NGOs favor MSIs and they provide a veneer of legitimacy to policies and actions that benefit industry. Membership is usually open and there are no restrictions on participation due to financial conflicts of interest. Corporate actors hold the most power in MSIs because they bring financial assets to implementation of decisions, they can always afford to pay participants (unlike civil society) and they can remain engaged until the outcomes meet their needs. Human rights play a negligible role in MSI deliberations. The processes of discussion and negotiation in MSIs are tilted in favor of the largest and wealthiest participants; meetings may occur at times and places that are hard for civil society representatives to join and lack translation into multiple languages beyond English. Outcomes of MSI tend to be watered down so that they do not disrupt the status quo, and accountability to people who are affected by decisions is weak or missing (IPES-Food 2023). MSIs blur the distinction between the public interest and corporate profit and take power away from governments that bear the duty of accountability for respecting, protecting and fulfilling their peoples' human rights.

MSIs often decide to create private standards to change production and business practices and to raise the bar for business-to-business transactions. More recent criticism of MSIs and their movement into international food system governance is in line with evaluations of earlier MSIs in the food system realm, such as the Roundtable on Sustainable Palm Oil (Ruysschaert and Salles 2014) and Field to Market, the Stewardship Index for Specialty Crops and the National Sustainable Agricultural Standard Initiative (Konefal et al. 2019). These were deemed to be weak mechanisms for encouraging or enforcing more sustainable practices. This has been demonstrated with food and beverage companies that continued to promote junk food to children despite pledges to desist and breast-milk substitute manufacturers that continued to market substitutes to mothers despite international codes of conduct created through MSIs prohibiting this.

We will return to MSIs in Chapter 9, where we discuss the UN Food Systems Summit and its aftermath (creation of a "Coordination Hub," coalitions, national pathways and Summit+2), to examine what they have and have not accomplished to address global food systems challenges. MSIs are of particular concern at present because the UN Secretary-General seems intent on converting the entire United Nations governance structure to MSIs. As MSI Integrity noted, MSIs do have value in facilitating learning from shared information or experimentation, although even there the assumption that information will be shared equitably may not be fulfilled. The problem at present is that they are infiltrating governance spaces that are far beyond their capacity to manage responsibly. MSIs have shown limited value for driving movement toward regeneration, and their ability to deliver the Sustainable Development Goals or a world of greater justice and equity is likewise dubious.

International Summits

> The UN Food Systems Summit will launch bold new actions, solutions and strategies to deliver progress on all 17 Sustainable Development Goals (SDGs), each of which relies on healthier, more sustainable and more equitable food systems. The Summit will awaken the world to the fact that we all must work together to transform the way the world produces, consumes and thinks about food.
>
> *(UNFSS 2021, n.p.)*

Implicit Theory of Change

- Actors must cooperate more effectively to beat the polycrisis and meet the Sustainable Development Goals.
- Since multilateral spaces in UN agencies and national governments have not been able to solve global problems on their own and participants have not cooperated sufficiently to build collective solutions, international "summits" are necessary to raise ambition among participants, bring attention to neglected issues, generate commitments to act and raise bilateral and multilateral funds for that action.

Implicit Assumptions

- The people who most need to be part of international summits will participate.
- Summit organizers are fair and impartial in structuring the agenda and inviting speakers, to ensure that the most important issues are addressed by appropriate people.
- Commitments made at summits will be honored.
- Summits are effective at achieving their goals. They have real impacts and go beyond greenwashing.

International summits that include attention to food systems are happening much more frequently than in decades past. For example, the UN Climate Change conferences gave no formal attention to food systems until Glasgow in 2021, despite strong evidence at a much earlier date of greenhouse gas emissions from the food system (Vermeulen et al. 2012; Clark et al. 2020). The conference in 2022 had a "food pavilion" co-sponsored by several organizations concerned about food system impacts and a half-day devoted to discussion of the food system. The 2024 conference had even more of a focus on how the food system can be transformed.

FAO started hosting a World Food Forum in 2021 aimed at youth and introduced the "Hand-in-Hand" initiative in 2022 to introduce aspiring investors to projects designed to accelerate the transformation to sustainable agrifood systems. The 2023 World Food Forum had action tracks on Youth and Education, plus an Innovation Lab. The World Food Forum has taken over World Food Day (October 16) which was once part of the multilateral Committee on World Food Security's annual meeting, and the hullabaloo around it threatens to overshadow the CFS. Civil society organizations fear that this is an intentional effort to draw attention away from the multilateral CFS, where they have voice.

The SDGs are not on track to be met by 2030, and some countries have moved backwards on specific targets including ending hunger. The assumption that summits will be effective is questionable, however: the impacts may be primarily public relations for a company or organization that wants to be perceived as acting in collaboration with others and making progress toward sustainability goals. Summits seldom establish accountability or monitoring mechanisms, and whether countries achieve their goals is based on their own reports. Especially when summits do not include civil society bodies that can provide shadow reports or other authoritative ways to rebut government and business reports, the factual basis of reported "progress" is in doubt.

Summits are being organized in a context of weakening nation-states, changing geopolitical dynamics toward a multipolar world, growing corporate power and inequality, the rise of illegitimate authoritarian governments and shrinking political space for civil society (Unmüßig 2016; Papada et al. 2023). Given that they do not result in binding agreements to which governments can be held accountable, they serve as theater more than as transformative spaces. Civil society participation is a double-edged sword because it can serve to legitimize an event that does not actually advance the interests of civil society. However, summits can help to draw attention to the importance of food systems and impacts of different types of food systems on well-being. They can showcase good practices, and perhaps help shame governments and other actors that are backsliding to move in a more positive direction.

Intergovernmental Guidelines and Treaties

Implicit Theory of Change

- Governmental delegates to international negotiations will set aside the interests of their own governments to find the common good. To protect the public interest, which is shared across countries, governments will support regenerative policies.

Implicit Assumptions

- The public interest in environmental quality, public health and well-being is universal: people and the more-than-human domain in different governmental jurisdictions do not have different basic needs and rights.
- Governmental negotiators understand that regenerative food systems are in the public interest.
- Governmental negotiators will accept responsibility to protect the public interest.
- Once treaties have been agreed upon, they will be respected.

> Ground-breaking, far-reaching global guidelines for governments to help them safeguard the rights of people to own or access land, forests, and fisheries were endorsed five years ago by the Committee on World Food Security (CFS), based at the Food and Agriculture Organization of the United Nations (FAO) in Rome. Today, the Voluntary Guidelines on the Responsible Governance of Tenure (VGGT) are a true global norm of reference in the governance of land tenure. The guidelines are pioneering – outlining principles and practices that governments can refer to when making laws and administering land, fisheries, and forests rights. Ultimately, they aim to promote food security and sustainable development by improving secure access to land, fisheries, and forests, as well as protecting the rights of millions of often very poor people.
>
> *(Muñoz 2017, n.p.)*

Intergovernmental guidelines and treaties, such as the Voluntary Guidelines on Responsible Governance of Tenure, should in theory support regenerative agriculture because governments should be working in the public interest; but in reality, they are subject to the same power dynamics that drive other initiatives. Delegates to international negotiations are bound to put their own countries' interests foremost, or they will be rapidly replaced. Recent negotiations over policy guidelines in the Committee on World Food Security have ridden roughshod over civil society recommendations and given short shrift to recommendations coming from its own High Level Panel of Experts, especially pertaining to agroecology, the global narrative of food system transformation and the roles of youth and women. Chapter 9 will describe these experiences in more detail.

Will governments comply with treaties and agreements? The latter has been an issue for the Committee on World Food Security because there are insufficient mechanisms to translate guidelines and recommendations into national policy, fund their implementation and monitor how well they are being realized. Civil society organizations have led monitoring efforts, but the work of disseminating guidelines and recommendations should be taken up by governments or intergovernmental agencies that have invested the time of their delegates into developing the guidelines.

Trade agreements likewise are not the place to find support for regenerative food systems, although fair terms of trade would go a long way to equalize power imbalances between countries. Trade agreements are negotiated by government representatives and not decided in public forums. Industry lobbyists have considerable power over them and the producers who are heavily affected have little ability to influence decisions. The whole concept of export as a primary function of food systems is counter to regenerative food systems, which focus first on supplying local and regional needs. Yet keeping trade channels open is one of the first things that neoliberal governments stress in a crisis. FAO's publication, *The Future of Food and Agriculture: Drivers and Triggers for Food Systems Transformation* (2022), contains many recommendations that support regenerative food systems, but includes the following:

> International trade is essential for sustainably expanding food availability in countries where the population is expected to increase significantly. Trade has also a role to play in income generation if commercial agreements are set within a solid institutional context that ensures the respect of all stakeholders, including future generations.

The "stakeholder" language here betrays reliance on MSIs rather than human rights to decide what the terms should be, and the allusion to future generations is interesting given that there are no agreements on how or whether to discount the needs of future generations. Trade may well be compatible with regenerative food systems if the trading is done between regions that uphold strong regulations to protect environmental quality, labor and human rights. But the authors admit, "it is not so clear whether countries that adopt more stringent environmental, social and fiscal measures can protect themselves against environmental, social and fiscal dumping by countries with more relaxed legislations" (FAO 2022, 69).

Trade and aid policies of wealthy countries have impoverished the Global South with renewed vigor since World War II through neocolonialism. Olivier De Schutter (2014, 225) cited the Prebisch-Singer thesis of deteriorating terms of trade by which the removal of trade barriers and specialization of each country in areas in which it has presumed comparative advantage does not benefit the least industrialized countries. He wrote, "international trade, replicating the patterns of colonialism, may in fact accentuate the dependency of developing countries on the former colonial powers, and make it impossible for these countries to overcome the obstacles to development."

While wealthier countries subsidized their producers and used both tariff and non-tariff import barriers to protect themselves from foreign competition, developing countries were prohibited from using the same mechanisms. Most of them imposed taxes on producers to finance industrialization and could not afford to provide subsidies (Gonzalez 2014). Numerous multilateral institutions were set up to manage trade and food security, including the International Trade Organization; the UN Conference on Trade and Development; the Global Agreement on Trade and Tariffs (GATT, which did not include agricultural products in trade liberalization plans); the FAO and international commodity agreements (Canfield et al. 2021b). The legal regime set up between the 1980s and 2008 was designed to maximize global trade; in 1986, negotiations were started within the US, EU and other wheat-exporting countries to bring agriculture into formal legal trade agreements. These resulted in the formation of the World Trade Organization Agreement on Agriculture in 1994. The US argued in these negotiations that food security is "best provided through a smooth-functioning world market" (as quoted in Canfield et al. 2021a, 70).

In the 1980s and 1990s, structural adjustment plans were imposed on developing countries by the World Bank and International Monetary Fund, requiring them to limit agricultural subsidies and social safety net spending, drop tariffs, increase interest rates, and shift from food crops to cash crops to repay debts. By the mid-1980s, two-thirds of African countries and almost three-quarters of Latin American countries had agreed to structural adjustment in order to get new loans or restructure existing loans (Peet 2009). These were disastrous for developing countries, leading to riots from food shortages and price spikes in the context of food price speculation and growing effects of climate change. And over just a few decades, developing countries that were once self-sufficient in food turned into net food importers through structural adjustment policies, the Agreement on Agriculture, and bilateral and regional free trade agreements (Gonzalez 2014).

Since the food price spikes of 2006–2008, global value chain proponents and policymakers have focused as much on agribusinesses as on nations. This has been the period in which food industries moved deeper into governance roles by setting numerous private standards on food safety and quality, and voluntary codes of conduct concerning environmental and social impacts (Canfield et al. 2021a). Agribusiness has used its political power to persuade US officials to support biofuels as a solution to climate change, to promote genetic engineering as the solution to food insecurity, and to demand greater access to developing country markets (among other demands). Meanwhile, billions of small-scale farmers in the Majority World have been driven off their land (Gonzalez 2014).

Trade agreements today are often designed by powerful countries to push exports (sometimes below the cost of production) onto other countries to alleviate overproduction in the exporting country or to improve its balance of trade. Although dumping is prohibited by the World Trade Organization if it hurts producers in the importing country, its use by the US has been documented against Mexico (Wise 2023b), and in the guise of humanitarian aid (Murphy and Hansen-Kuhn 2019). Trade liberalization policies promoted by the WTO have contributed to dumping, thus undermining food security and producers' livelihoods in West Africa and other regions (Iloh et al. 2020). And Investor-State Dispute Settlements allow corporations to sue governments that try to protect their own citizens' well-being and environment, if this results in lower than expected profits for foreign investors (UNCTAD 2020).

International guidelines and treaties have limited value for encouraging more regenerative food systems because they are hobbled by national priorities of the wealthiest countries, often those that are exporting significant amounts of commodity crops. Yet ones that strengthen human rights and advance concerns of civil society, such as the Voluntary Guidelines on the Governance of Tenure and the UN Declaration on the Rights of Peasants and Others Living in Rural Areas (UNDROP), have been successful in protecting marginalized people and environmental quality. In these cases, it is the attention to human rights and the work of civil society that have enabled transformation. UNDROP is a notable example; it took decades of steady advocacy from civil society to be approved first by the UN Human Rights Council and then by the UN General Assembly in 2018. UNDROP introduced many rights for peasants that had not been codified previously, such as the right to save seeds, to access land and water bodies, to food sovereignty and to political participation and not to be exposed to hazardous agrichemicals (UNGA 2019). If UNDROP were the basis of new national laws, there would be tremendous changes in power relations, with producers and rural people gaining power vis-à-vis government agencies and corporations. But implementation at the national level will require further years of advocacy. Other international covenants signed by the overwhelming majority of countries also point toward a world of increased attention to human rights in food systems.

In summary, we can hold up each of the notions of how to change global food systems in this chapter to see whether it has potential to disrupt the dominant flows of power. Sustainable intensification, scientific research, technological innovation, MSIs and international summits tend to strengthen the power of the largest food and agrichemical industries. Given the flurry of agreements that FAO has made with industry groups and the enthusiasm for MSIs at the level of the UN Secretary-General, international food summits are much more likely to reinforce industry propaganda than to combat it. International agreements and treaties have a tendency to undercut the public interest because negotiators are more interested in advancing their own countries' interests than the shared public interest, although they may be highly significant if they are enforced.

Scientific reports have the potential to change the dominant narrative supporting industrialized, extractive food systems if they show the value of regenerative food systems and harms of extractive systems, but they cannot change the narrative on their own. Figure 6.1 shows the influence of scientific

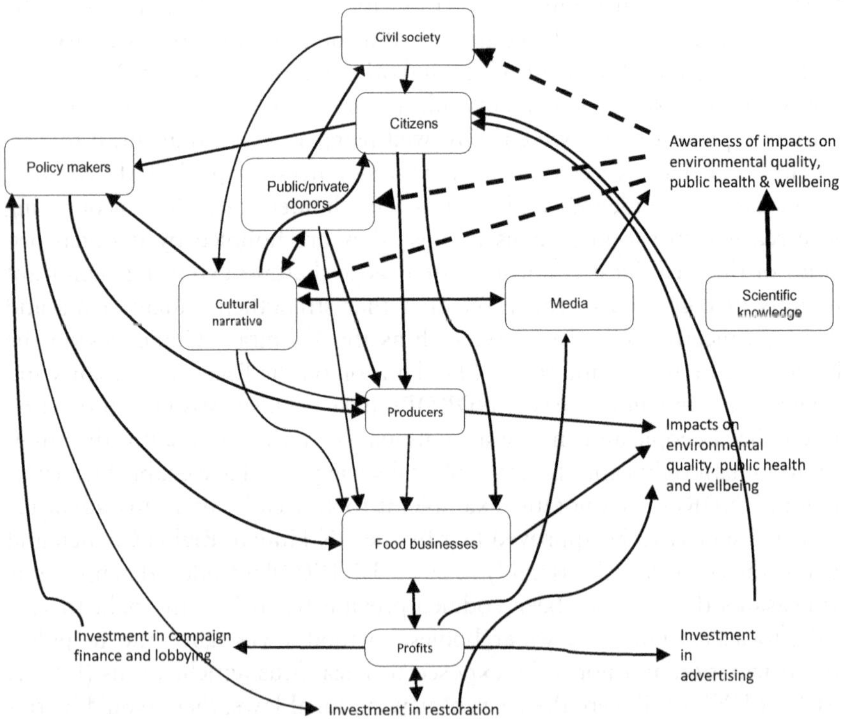

FIGURE 6.1 Impacts of scientific knowledge on the food system.

knowledge *alone* to transform food systems. This diagram assumes that the scientific research is designed to show impacts of the food system on environmental quality, public health and well-being. Although there are secondary influences on civil society, public and private donors and the cultural narrative of building awareness, impacts are quite limited. The research findings would need to be publicized widely by media (counter-acting other influences on media) to have a strong impact. And meanwhile, narratives that elevate the power of the private sector would be active and drowning out scientific findings or messages from civil society.

References

Achan, J, AO Talisuna, A Erhart, A Yeka, JK Tibenderana, FN Baliraine, PJ Rosenthal and U D'Alessandro. 2011. Quinine, an old anti-malarial drug in a modern world: role in the treatment of malaria. *Malar J* 10:144. https://doi.org/10.1186/1475-2875-10-144

Anderson, CR and C Maughan. 2021. "The innovation imperative": the struggle over agroecology in the international food policy arena. *Front Sustain Food Syst* 5:619185. https://doi.org/10.3389/fsufs.2021.619185

Bernard, B and A Lux. 2017. How to feed the world sustainably: an overview of the discourse on agroecology and sustainable intensification. *Reg Env Change* 17:1279–1290. https://doi.org/10.1007/s10113-016-1027-y

Bezner Kerr, R. 2023. Feminist agroecology viewed through the lens of the Plantationocene. *Annals Amer Assoc of Geographers* 0(0):1–8. https://doi.org/10.1080/24694452.2023.2216779

Biovision Foundation for Ecological Development and Global Alliance for the Future of Food (GAFF). 2019. Beacons of Hope: Accelerating Transformations to Sustainable Food Systems. Global Alliance for the Future of Food. https://futureoffood.org/wp-content/uploads/2021/02/BeaconsOfHope_Report_082019.pdf

Birner, R, T Daum and C Pray. 2021. Who drives the digital revolution in agriculture? A review of supply-side trends, players and challenges. *Appl Econ Perspective Policy* 43:1260–1285. https://doi.org/10.1002/aepp.13145

Bradford, J. 2019. *The Future is Rural: Food System Adaptations to the Great Simplification*. Post Carbon Institute. https://www.postcarbon.org/publications/the-future-is-rural/

Buttel, FH. 2005. Ever since Hightower: the politics of agricultural research activism in the molecular age. *Agric Hum Values* 22:275–283. https://doi.org/10.1007/s10460-005-6043-3

Canfield, M, AJ Cohen and M Fakhri. 2021a. Agriculture, law and the state. Pp. 69–72 In: M Valverde, KM Clarke, E Darian Smith and P Kotiswaran (Eds.) *Routledge Handbook of Law and Society*. London: Routledge.

Canfield, MC, J Duncan and P Claeys. 2021b. Reconfiguring food systems governance: the UNFSS and the battle over authority and legitimacy. *Development* 64:181–191. https://doi.org/10.1057/s41301-021-00312-1

Carlile, C. 2023. BBC under fire for doing pesticide giant's PR. *DeSmog*. https://www.desmog.com/2023/07/14/bbc-follow-the-food-corteva-pesticide-giant/

Chandrasekaran, K, S Guttal, M Kumar, L Langner and MA Manahan. 2021. Exposing corporate capture of the UNFSS through multistakeholderism. *Food Systems 4 People.* https://www.foodsystems4people.org/wp-content/uploads/2021/09/UNFSSreport2021.pdf

Clark, AM, NGG Domingo, K Colgan, SK Thakrar, D Tilman, J Lynch, IL Azevedo and JD Hill. 2020. Global food system emissions could preclude achieving the 1.5° and 2°C climate change targets. *Science* 370(6517):705–708. https://doi.org/10.1126/science.aba7357

Conway, G. 2017. Sustainable Intensification could end chronic hunger. *Huffington Post.* https://www.huffingtonpost.co.uk/sir-gordon-conway/sustainable-intensificati-1_b_11603704.html

Cumming, GS and GD Peterson. 2017. Unifying research on social-ecological resilience and collapse. *Trends Ecol Evol* 32(9):695–713. https://doi.org/10.1016/j.tree.2017.06.014

DeLonge, M, A Miles and L Carlisle. 2016. Investing in the transition to sustainable agriculture. *Env Sci Pol* 55(1):266–273. https://doi.org/10.1016/j.envsci.2015.09.013

De Schutter, O. 2014. The reform of the Committee on World Food Security: the quest for coherence in global governance. Pp. 219–238 In: NCS Lambek, P Claeys, A Wong and L Brilmayer (Eds.) *Rethinking Food Systems: Structural Challenges, New Strategies and the Law*. Berlin: Springer.

De Schutter, O and T Dedeurwaerdere. 2022. *Social Innovation in the Service of Social and Ecological Transformation. The Rise of the Enabling State*. London: Routledge.

Donahue, B, J Burke, M Anderson, A Beal, T Kelly, M Lapping, H Ramer, R Libby and L Berlin 2014. *A New England Food Vision.* Durham: Food Solutions New England, University of New Hampshire. https://foodsolutionsne.org/wp-content/uploads/2014/07/LowResNEFV_0.pdf

Duncan, E, A Glaros, DZ Ross and E Nost. 2021. New but for whom? Discourses of innovation in precision agriculture. *Agric Hum Values* 38:1181–1199. https://doi.org/10.1007/s10460-021-10244-8

El Bilali, H. 2019. The multi-level perspective in research on sustainability transitions in agriculture and food systems: a systematic review. *Agriculture* 9:74.

Food and Agriculture Organization (FAO). 2009a. Global agriculture towards 2050. High Level Expert Forum - How to Feed the World in 2050. https://www.fao.org/fileadmin/templates/wsfs/docs/Issues_papers/HLEF2050_Global_Agriculture.pdf

Food and Agriculture Organization (FAO). 2009b. *Strategic Framework 2010–2019.* Rome: FAO.

Food and Agriculture Organization (FAO). 2021. *Strategic Framework 2022–31.* Rome. https://www.fao.org/3/cb7099en/cb7099en.pdf

Food and Agriculture Organization (FAO). 2022. The future of food and agriculture, No. 3. Drivers and triggers for transformation. Rome. https://doi.org/10.4060/cc09592022.

Food Systems 4 People. 2023. Multistakeholderism and the corporate capture of global food governance. What is at risk in 2023? https://www.foodsystems4people.org/wp-content/uploads/2023/05/EN_Analysis-report-2023_FS4P.pdf

Geels, FW. 2002. Technological transitions as evolutionary reconfiguration processes: a multi-level perspective and a case-study. *Res Policy* 31(8/9):1257–1274. https://doi.org/10.1016/S0048-7333(02)00062-8

Geels, FW. 2011. The multi-level perspective on sustainability transitions: responses to seven criticisms. *Environ Innov Societal Trans* 1:24–40. https://doi.org/10.1016/j.eist.2011.02.002

Geels, FW. 2019. Socio-technical transitions to sustainability: a review of criticisms and elaborations of the multi-level perspective. *Curr Opinion Environ Sust* 39:187–201. https://doi.org/10.1016/j.cosust.2019.06.009

Geels, FW and J Schot. 2007. Typology of sociotechnical transition pathways. *Res Policy* 36:499–417. https://doi.org/10.1016/j.respol.2007.01.003

George, S. 1976. *How the Other Half Dies: The Real Reasons for World Hunger*. Harmondsworth, England: Penguin Books.

Ghosh, A. 2022. *The Nutmeg's Curse: Parables for a Planet in Crisis*. Chicago: University of Chicago Press.

Gleckman, H. 2018. *Multistakeholder Governance and Democracy: A Global Challenge*. London: Routledge.

Global Panel on Agriculture and Food Systems for Nutrition (GLOPAN). 2020. *Future Food Systems: For People, our Planet, and Prosperity*. London, UK.

Gonzalez, CG. 2014. International economic law and the right to food. Pp. 165–193 In: NCS Lambek, P Claeys, A Wong and L Brilmeyer (Eds.) *Rethinking Food Systems. Structural Challenges, New Strategies and the Law*. Berlin: Springer.

Hamerschlag, K, A Lappé and S Malkan. 2015. Spinning food: how food industry front groups and covert communications are shaping the story of food. *Friends of the Earth*. https://foe.org/wp-content/uploads/2017/legacy/FOE_SpinningFoodReport_8-15.pdf

Hickel, J and G Kallis. 2020. Is green growth possible? *New Polit Econ* 25(4):469–486. https://doi.org/10.1080/13563467.2019.1598964

High Level Panel of Experts (HLPE). 2018. Multi-stakeholder partnerships to finance and improve food security and nutrition in the framework of the 2030 Agenda. A report by the High Level Panel of Experts on Food Security and Nutrition of the Committee on World Food Security. Rome: FAO.

High Level Panel of Experts (HLPE). 2019. Agroecological and other innovative approaches for sustainable agriculture and food systems that enhance food security and nutrition. A report by the High Level Panel of Experts on Food Security and Nutrition of the Committee on World Food Security. Rome: FAO.

Iloh, EC, M Nwokedi, CF Onyebukwa and Q Ekeeocha. 2020. World Trade Organization's trade liberalization policy on agriculture and food security in West Africa. Pp. 125–144 In: N Edomah (Ed.) *Regional Development in Africa*. London: IntechOpen.

IPES-Food. 2023. Who's tipping the scales? The growing influence of corporations on the governance of food systems, and how to counter it. https://www.ipes-food.org/_img/upload/files/tippingthescales.pdf

Konefal, J, M Hatanaka and DH Constance. 2019. Multi-stakeholder initiatives and the divergent construction and implementation of sustainable agriculture in the USA. *Renew Agric Food Systems* 34:293–303. https://doi.org/10.1017/S1742170517000461

Lipson, M. 1997. *Searching for the "O-word": Analyzing the USA Current Research Information System for Pertinence to Organic Farming*. Santa Cruz, CA: Organic Farming Research Foundation.

McKeon, N. 2017. Are equity and sustainability a likely outcome when foxes and chickens share the same coop? Critiquing the concept of multistakeholder governance of food security. *Globalizations* 14(3):379–398. https://doi.org/10.1080/14747731.2017.1286168

McMichael, P. 2023. Critical agrarian studies and crises of the world-historical present. *J Peasant Stud* 50(2):725–757. https://doi.org/10.1080/03066150.2022.2163630

Monbiot, G. 2022. *Regenesis: Feeding the World without Devouring the Planet*. London: Penguin Books.

Multistakeholder Initiative (MSI) Integrity. 2020. *Not Fit-for-Purpose: The Grand Experiment of Multi-Stakeholder Initiatives in Corporate Accountability, Human Rights and Global Governance*. The Institute for Multistakeholder Initiative Integrity. https://www.msi-integrity.org/wp-content/uploads/2020/07/MSI_Not_Fit_For_Purpose_FORWEBSITE.FINAL_pdf

Muñoz, J. 2017. VGGT: the global guidelines to secure land rights for all. *World Bank Blogs*. https://blogs.worldbank.org/voices/vggt-global-guidelines-ensure-secure-land-rights-for-all

Murphy, S and K Hansen-Kuhn. 2019. The true costs of US agricultural dumping. *Renew Agric Food Systems* 35(4):376–390. https://doi.org/10.1017/S1742170519000097

Papada, E, D Altman, F Angiolillo, L Gastaldi, T Köhler, M Lundstedt, N Natsika, M Nord, Y Sato, F Wiebrecht and SI Lindberg. 2023. *Defiance in the Face of Autocratization*. Democracy Report 2023. University of Gothenburg: Varieties of Democracy Institute (V-Dem Institute).

Peet, R. 2009. *The Unholy Trinity: The IMF, World Bank and WTO*. London: Zed Books.

Plowright, RK, JK Reaser, H Locke, SJ Woodley, JA Patz, DJ Becker, G Oppler, PJ Hudson and GM Tabor. 2021. Land use-induced spillover: a call to action to safeguard environmental, animal, and human health. *The Lancet* 5(4):e237–e245. https://doi.org/10.1016/S2542-5196(21)00031-0

Pretty, JN. 1997. The sustainable intensification of agriculture. *Nat Resources Forum* 21(4):247–256. https://doi.org/10.1111/j.1477-8947.1997.tb00699.x

Rahmann, G, M Reza Ardakani, P Bàrberi, H Boehm, S Canali, M Chaner, D Wahyudi, L Dengel, JW Erisman, AC Galvis-Martinez, U Hamm, J Kahl, U Köpke, S Kühne, SB Lee, A-K Løes, JH Moos, D Neuhof, JT Nuutila, V Olowe, R Oppermann, E Rambialkowska, J Riddle, IA Rasmussen, J Shade, SM Sohn, M Tadesse, S Tashi, A Thatcher, N Uddin, P von Fragstein un Niemsdorff, A Wibe, M Wivstad, W Wenliang and R Zanoli. 2017. Organic Agriculture 3.0 is innovation with research. *Org Agr* 7:169–197. https://doi.org/10.1007/s13165-016-0171-5

Ricciardi, V, Z Mehrabi, H Wittman, D James and N Ramankutty. 2021. Higher yields and more biodiversity on smaller farms. *Nat Sustain* 4:651–657. https://doi.org/10.1038/s41893-021-00699-2

Rip, A and R Kemp. 1998. Technological change. Pp. 327–399 In: S Rayner and EL Malone (Eds.) *Human Choice and Climate Change*. Columbus, OH: Battelle Press.

Rohr, JR. 2021. The atrazine saga and its importance to the future of toxicology, science, and environmental and human health. *Environ Toxic Chem* 40(6):1544–1558. https://doi.org/10.1002/etc.5037

Rose, DC, A Barkemeyer, A de Boon, C Price and D Roche. 2023. The old, the new, or the old made new? Everyday counter-narratives of the so-called fourth agricultural revolution. *Agric Hum Values* 40:423–439. https://doi.org/10.1007/s10460-022-10374-7

Ruysschaert, D and DS Salles. 2014. Towards global voluntary standards: questioning the effectiveness in attaining conservation goals: the case of the Roundtable on Sustainable Palm Oil (RSPO). *Ecol Econ* 107:438–446.

Sachs, J. 2023. From global chaos and danger to understanding and cooperation. *Common Dreams*. https://www.commondreams.org/opinion/multipolar-world-cooperation

Schumpeter, J. 1942. *Capitalism, Socialism and Democracy*. New York: Harper & Brothers.

Sen, A. 1980. *Poverty and Famines. An Essay on Entitlement and Deprivation*. Oxford: Oxford University Press.

Smaje, C. 2023. *Saying NO to a Farm-free Future: The Case for an Ecological Food System and Against Manufactured Foods*. White River Junction, VT: Chelsea Green Publishing.

Stone, GD. 2022. Surveillance agriculture and peasant autonomy. *J Agrar Change* 22(3):608–631. https://doi.org/10.1111/joac.12470

Tilman, D, C Balzer, C., J Hill, J. and BL Befort. 2011. Global food demand and the sustainable intensification of agriculture. *Proc Nat Acad Sci* 108:20260. https://doi.org/10.1073/pnas.1116437108

Union of Concerned Scientists (UCS). 2018. The Disinformation Playbook: How Business Interests Deceive, Misinform, and Buy Influence at the Expense of Public Health and Safety. https://www.ucsusa.org/resources/disinformation-playbook

United Nations. 2021. *Our Common Agenda. Report of the Secretary-General*. New York: United Nations.

United Nations Committee on Trade and Development (UNCTAD). 2021. Highlights: Investor-State Dispute Settlement Cases 2020. https://unctad.org/system/files/official-document/diaepcbinf2021d7_en.pdf

United Nations Food Systems Summit (UNFSS). 2021. About the Summit. https://www.un.org/en/food-systems-summit/about

United Nations General Assembly (UNGA). 2019. Resolution adopted by the General Assembly on 17 December 2018. United Nations Declaration on the Rights of Peasants and Other People Working in Rural Areas. A/Res/73/165. https://www.geneva-academy.ch/joomlatools-files/docman-files/UN%20Declaration%20on%20the%20rights%20of%20peasants.pdf

United Nations High Level Advisory Board on Effective Multilateralism (HLAB). 2023. A Breakthrough for People and Planet. https://highleveladvisoryboard.org/breakthrough/

Unmüßig, B. 2016. Civil society under pressure – shrinking – closing – no space. *Heinrich Böll Stiftung*. https://tn.boell.org/sites/default/files/uploads/2016/03/civil_society_under_pressure_shrinking_spaces_final.pdf

van Dijk, M, T Morley, ML Raul and Y Sagha. 2021. A meta-analysis of projected global food demand and population at risk of hunger for the period 2010–2050. *Nature Food* 2:494–501. https://doi.org/10.1038/s43016-021-00322-9

Van Kerkhoff, L and L Lebel. 2006. Linking knowledge and action for sustainable development. *Ann Rev Environ Resour* 31:445–477. https://doi.org/10.1146/annurev.energy.31.102405.170850

Vermeulen, S, BM Campbell and JSI Ingram. 2012. Climate change and food systems. *Annu Rev Environ Resour* 37:195–222. https://doi.org/10.1146/annurev-environ-020411-130608

von Braun, J, K Afsana, LO Fresco and M Hassan. 2021. Science and innovations for food systems change. P. 2 In: J von Braun, K Afsana, LO Fresco and

M Hassan (Eds.) *Science and Innovations for Food Systems Transformation and Summit Actions: Papers by the Scientific Group and its partners in support of the UN Food Systems Summit.* https://sc-fss2021.org/wp-content/uploads/2021/09/ScGroup_Reader_UNFSS2021.pdf

Wanger, TC, F DeClerck, LA Garibaldi J Ghazoul, D Kleijn, A-M Klein, C Kremen, H Mooney, I Perfecto, LL Powell, J Settele, M Solé, T Tscharntke and W Weisser. 2020. Integrating agroecological production in a robust post-2020 Global Biodiversity Framework. *Nat Ecol Evol* 4:1150–1152. https://doi.org/10.1038/s41559-020-1262-y

Wise, TA. 2023a. Mexico calls U.S. bluff on science of GMO corn restrictions. Institute for Agriculture and Trade Policy. https://www.iatp.org/mexico-calls-us-bluff-science-gmo-corn-restrictions.

Wise, TA. 2023b. Swimming against the tide: Mexico's quest for food sovereignty in the face of US dumping. Institute for Agriculture and Trade Policy. https://www.iatp.org/sites/default/files/2023-06/swimmingagainsttide.3.pdf

World Economic Forum. 2023. Food, Nature and Health Transitions – Repeatable Country Models. Insight Report. https://www.weforum.org/publications/food-nature-and-health-transitions-repeatable-country-models/

Zink, T and R Geyer. 2017. Circular economy rebound. *J Indust Ecol* 21:593–602. https://doi.org/10.1111/jiec.12545

Zuboff, S. 2019. *The Age of Surveillance Capitalism: The Fight for a Human Future at the New Frontier of Power*. New York: PublicAffairs.

7

WHAT DRIVES FOOD SYSTEM TRANSFORMATION TOWARD REGENERATION WITH STRUCTURAL CHANGES IN POWER?

The previous chapter described theories of change and their associated narratives that can be pasted onto the existing food system without making significant changes to the imbalances of power that underlie most food system problems today. Shifting power will not be sufficient to fix all of those problems; for example, climate change is baked in now regardless of who has power because of past failures to act. But reinforcing existing power dynamics will keep citizens from recovering agency so that we can slow down the escalating slide into worsening climatic conditions.

As in the previous chapter, each theory of change includes implicit assumptions and evidence to support or refute it. This chapter is organized from the least contentious to the more contentious narratives; not surprisingly, more contentious narratives are those requiring deep structural changes. The organization of the chapter proceeds from three narratives (government programs and policies, legal strategies and food system governance) that may actually reinforce current power dynamics. However, they are in this chapter rather than the previous one because they also have solid potential to be transformative, if they are accompanied by political will to change who and what holds power in the food system. Transformative change is easier to achieve at devolved levels of governance, so "government policies and programs" ended up in this chapter while "intergovernmental agreements and treaties" was in the previous chapter. Intergovernmental action certainly has the potential to be transformative, as the adoption of UNDROP showed (although bringing UNDROP down to the national and sub-national levels will require more fights). But national and sub-national policies and programs are more likely to have an immediate impact on people's lives.

The first three intervention narratives in this chapter are limited by the power of neoliberalism. Without fair tax policies that restrict wealth

DOI: 10.4324/9781003260264-10

accumulation, restrictions on the exercise of political power by the private sector and anti-trust policies that prevent the growth of market power of industry, inequality and exclusion of poor and marginalized people will continue to be exacerbated. Each of these narratives has real potential to create a more just and sustainable food system, however; and countless people and organizations are pushing each one to its limit. They are achieving tangible improvements in the well-being of poor and marginalized people through their efforts.

Government Policies and Programs

> Changing government policy is critical for wide-spread transition to regenerative agriculture
>
> *(Hsu 2019, n.p.).*

> More than $600 billion per year is spent in agriculture policy support for producers, of which more than 80 percent has been referred by the Organization for Economic Cooperation and Development (OECD) as distorting. **The actions from governments are the most powerful driver of food systems,** and by realigning incentives, the public sector can change the economics that drive change. Governments can focus on repurposing subsidies in their NDCs [Nationally Determined Contributions) to promote more regenerative outcomes, including increasing funding to critical areas.
>
> *(Bora 2022, n.p., emphasis added)*

Implicit Theory of Change

- Governments have powers that exceed those of individual actors or organizations and, in their role as guardians of the public interest, will enact policies and programs that move food systems toward regeneration.

Implicit Assumptions

- Policymakers are motivated more strongly to serve the public interest than to reward their financial contributors and cronies.
- The public elects people to government offices, in fair and open elections, who can best serve the public interest.
- The national government hires and appoints people with appropriate expertise and backgrounds.
- Government policies and programs will institutionalize good ideas that bubble up from community-based organizations, in addition to drawing on the best expertise available nationally.
- Government policies and programs are implemented fairly and without discrimination.

While government programs can be quite beneficial, the theory of change and all of the assumptions above are questionable. In the US, politicians who are not under the thumb of their biggest donors are the exception and the higher up in government that you look, the more money is needed to get office and thus the more potential for corruption. In addition, all too many government officials seem to believe that customary norms of decency and accountability do not apply to them, once they are in office: the US news has daily reports of scandals involving legislators and Supreme Court judges. The Department of Agriculture and other federal agencies have a long and sordid history of discriminating against Black, Indigenous and Hispanic people; only recently have cases been won to give these people compensation.

At their best, government policies and programs can build on scientific evidence of which practices are most effective; but they must be grounded in a solid understanding of what will lead to behavioral change. This is a rich area of research, and sometimes the results are surprising. *Homo economicus,* who looks out for his own self-interest in a rational way, has feet of clay: people often make decisions about what to do or buy based on emotion, advertising, impulse or past experience instead of through reasoned choices.

Federal programs to support farmers' transition to regenerative practices (such as the Organic Transition Initiative of the US Department of Agriculture) are premised on the assumption that farmers want to be good stewards of land and water but they are prevented from adopting conservation practices because they cannot afford to do so. Public support of farmers in the US is strong and has justified billions of dollars in federal expenditures going to farmers; unfortunately, this support has not always been fair, based on actual need. While most farmers may indeed want to be good stewards, they also want to stay in business and will not take risks on using costly practices that they do not believe will work, especially when generous subsidies support monocultures of corn and soy and crop insurance compensates for losses of commodity crops.

An abiding assumption in the US has been that voluntary incentives work best with farmers. However, growing numbers of people question why farms should be exempt from environmental regulations that apply to all other businesses, particularly when evidence mounts of farms' contributions to phosphorus pollution of lakes and waterways with resulting eutrophication, pesticide run-off getting into town drinking water supplies, or nitrate seeping into groundwater. Many farmers believe that the public has no understanding of their realities, and the cost of adhering to environmental regulations will be the last straw for farms that are barely breaking even. Agribusiness fans the flames of farmers' resentment by trying to manipulate the narrative, posing as the farmer's friend and staunchly resisting any moves toward regenerative food systems (Held 2021). In a context of rapidly increasing concentration in all sectors of the food system except farming and small-scale fishing (Howard 2016), farmers have very little control over the prices they receive and do not receive premiums on their products for implementing environmentally beneficial practices, although federal and state programs do support conservation practices.

Other government programs seek to influence consumer behavior and foster more regenerative food systems by reducing food waste or eating healthier diets. For example, the mayor of New York launched a campaign in 2023 to implement plant-based diets in public institutions throughout the city and recounts that he was able to lose weight, regain his eyesight and reverse the course of diabetes-Type 2 by changing his own diet (Krajnc and O'Toole 2023). Scientific evidence is strong that eating a plant-based diet is not only healthier but significantly reduces greenhouse gas emissions; in particular, red meat production has much higher resource use and greenhouse gas emissions than crop or fish production and processed meats are carcinogenic (Springmann et al. 2018; Willett et al. 2019; Project Drawdown 2023; WHO 2023). However, it is important to remember that meat can supply vital nutrients in a dense form to people who are undernourished. Also, for pastoral societies in the Majority World, livestock production is an important part of their culture and they are usually not practicing it at a scale that entails significant damage to the environment. Much of the damage associated with meat-eating is due to the commodity supply chain and its power to extract resources from some places (such as by deforesting the Amazon for soy production or cattle pasture) and oversupply them to others (such as the over-fed Minority World), compromising the ecological base of both (Smaje 2023).

Meat production and consumption have very different consequences depending on how they are being done and by whom. However, there is no question that people in the US eat far more meat than is healthy and the main ways of producing that meat (in confined-animal feeding operations) are environmentally destructive and socially corrosive. Yet the current Dietary Guidelines for Americans do not recommend eating less meat outright, suggesting instead that healthier dietary patterns involve "relatively lower consumption of red and processed meats" (USDA and HHS 2020, 23). Considerations of sustainability (and in some cases health) have been prohibited from the Advisory Council to the Dietary Guidelines by Congress, putting the US outside 49 percent of 195 countries analyzed by FAO that include environmental sustainability in their dietary guidelines, representing approximately 76 percent of the world's population (Bolotnikova 2022; James-Martin et al. 2022).

Food loss and waste have been identified as major sources of greenhouse gas emissions, as well as a waste of land and all of the inputs used to produce the lost or wasted food; they account for half of total greenhouse gas emissions from the food system (Zhu et al. 2023). But government programs to reduce food waste never, to my knowledge, focus on the systemic problem of overproduction; instead, consumers are advised to use leftovers and compost extra food. This is part of neoliberalism's focus on "individual responsibility" rather than systemic dysfunction that vastly overshadows whatever positive actions individual citizens can take.

Overproduction benefits agribusiness because it drives down the price paid to farmers, and surplus often can be exported at a profit. Supply management has been efficacious to keep overproduction in check, but neoliberal policies have almost completed eliminated it under the euphemism of "freedom to farm." The contrast in well-being of dairy farmers in Canada, where dairy is subject to supply management and farmers receive a minimum price, and just over the border in Vermont is striking (Dillon 2018). Canada has a quota system in which quotas can be bought and sold, and farmers can make a decent living with much smaller herds than Vermont farmers need to make a profit, which means that the work-day is not quite as punishing. Meanwhile, dairy farmers in the US are caught on a treadmill and try to avoid bankruptcy by increasing their herd-size or adopting technological innovations such as robotic milkers. The US produces more milk than buyers can accommodate, however, and fluid milk won't keep for long; so some dairy farmers resorted to dumping milk in 2023, as they had to do during COVID when labor shortages closed down processors. The National Family Farm Coalition has been advocating for a Milk from Family Dairies Act that would guarantee farmers a fair price over the cost of production, control imports and exports, strengthen regional dairy infrastructure, break up dairy concentration and balance supply and demand through an annually adjusted production base (NFFC 2023).

Individual programs and policies can have positive environmental, social and health impacts; but the paragraphs above demonstrate that government policies and programs such as the failure to enact supply management for milk may have negative consequences as well by reinforcing extractivism. Referring back to Figure 5.3, industry has a range of tactics for influencing policy that might create programs to reduce their influence. In the US, industry has the upper hand in policies and programs and leads government agencies around with a ring through the nose. I gave a talk for USDA staff about 20 years ago about indicators of whether available food is healthy, fair, "green" and affordable, based on factual and publicly available data. A staff-member who was visibly restless during my presentation asked immediately afterwards, "but when will we hear from business?," implying that factual data was less important than a business-friendly perspective. Under a neoliberal government where politicians with different ideas about how to organize the economy to serve the public interest cannot be elected, it is only to be expected that policies and programs will reinforce extractive food systems and the "food-as-only-a-commodity" narrative. Despite having two parties, the US has an increasingly monolithic government in terms of support for neoliberalism and privatization (Harvey 2005).

Most significantly, individual programs and policies are unlikely to lead to the shift in mindset that is needed to transform food systems. The failures of neoliberalism and the limits on growth that capitalism encounters mean that we need radically new post-capitalist systems and mindsets. Yet behavioral changes may be self-reinforcing and stimulate far-reaching impacts. Not everyone can have an impact on a city of 8.5 million people, like the mayor of New York; but people who have positive experiences of participating in programs to change their behavior may influence peers and family members.

Given all the things that governments *can* do, the reason it is situated at the beginning of this chapter with other narratives that can help or hinder regeneration is that policymakers are constrained by the sociopolitical regime in which they function. In industrialized countries except those that have moved toward democratic socialism, this is neoliberalism. Courageous politicians can put forward policies that are in the public interest, such as Bernie Sanders from Vermont championing healthcare as a human right to fix the abysmally dysfunctional US healthcare system; but these have little chance of succeeding given opposing powers. If we perceive openings, where should we demand that governments focus their policies and programs, in order to accelerate movement toward regenerative food systems? Given that corporate concentration is enabling a stronger political influence fighting regenerative food systems, governments need to enact and implement stronger anti-trust policies, looking at impacts of concentration that go beyond the limited question of whether prices to consumers decrease (the primary consideration in the US). This is a responsibility of governments where agribusinesses are incorporated. Other big topics that need government attention because other entities lack the power to make a real difference include realizing the right to food; addressing wealth and income inequality and inequity; addressing equity in access to education (especially for women and marginalized people); movement away from perpetual growth-ism that fuels resource extraction, especially of fossil fuels; and ensuring that minimum wages are above living wages and regularly updated to reflect the cost of living.

Procurement policies can make a big difference for producers and businesses, by setting clear standards for all foods purchased by school districts, public universities, hospitals and municipal cafeterias. Three US organizations that have worked on food standards, Real Food Generation, Healthcare without Harm and the Center for Good Food Purchasing, came together recently to create a shared framework called the Anchors in Action Alliance (Anchors in Action 2023). The Platform is based on building local and community-based economies, environmental sustainability, a valued workforce, animal welfare and community health and nutrition. It provides guidance on how to procure foods that meet the standards, as well as monitoring purchases by institutions. The framework sends a clear message to producers and businesses of what they must do to sell their products to institutions.

In creating programs and policies, it is important to address the structural barriers to their implementation. Brazil, which enacted a suite of programs and policies under President Luiz Inácio Lula da Silva that halved food insecurity, is again on the "hunger map" of severely food-insecure countries because of reversals that the Bolsanaro government made (Recine 2023). President Lula wants to reinstate these programs and Betta Recine argued that addressing structural inequality will make the reforms lasting this time around. Other specific pro-regenerative policies are included in "Legal Strategies" below.

Legal Strategies

Implicit Theory of Change

- Law upholds the public interest by protecting innocent people, holding culprits accountable for their misdeeds, and supporting policies favorable to a regenerative food system.

Implicit Assumptions

- Lawmakers' motivation to adhere to the law of the land is stronger than any desire for personal gain or giving advantages to friends and colleagues.
- Once laws are made, they will be enacted.
- Laws are enacted fairly, not discriminating against certain groups of people.
- The body of law builds steadily toward greater justice and equity.

> [A]t the heart of the global [food] system lie legal problems: issues of access to land and distribution of property rights over land; competing legal regimes and legal norms; conflicts between the protection of farmers' rights, human rights and intellectual property rights; absent or non-enforced regulation of transnational corporations and transnational investments; unequal multilateral and bilateral trade agreements; failing public institutions and limited access to justice; and a lack of participatory decision making coupled with undemocratic political structures.
>
> *(Claeys and Lambek 2014, 4)*

Like government policies and programs, legal strategies can play a strong positive role or reinforce extractive food systems; but they must be activated to address the problems of the global food system. Strategies that compel entities causing environmental or social damage to desist and create room for alternative less destructive practices or better access to resources for vulnerable people will cause structural changes to ameliorate the conditions leading to environmental and social damage. And as long as courts and lawmakers are not biased toward extractive practices, and as long as the legislature follows the rule of law, legal strategies can be very effective. They have won notable advances for farmworkers (e.g., Migrant Justice's successful suit to allow undocumented Vermont dairy farmworkers to get driver's licenses); farmers (e.g., the Pigford settlement that granted $2.3 billion to Black farmers who had been discriminated against by the US government) and compensation for communities that have been contaminated by agricultural chemicals such as PFAS in soil amendments.

In 2019, following a lawsuit by an environmental group, the top court in the Netherland ordered the government to do more to cut carbon emissions, saying climate change was a threat to human rights. The government estimated that 11,200 farms would have to close and another 17,600 farmers would have to significantly reduce their livestock. Other government proposals included a reduction in intensive farming and the conversion to sustainable "green farms" (Holligan 2022). But when the government ruled that farmers must cut their nitrogen emissions, farmers staged a massive protest and a pro-farmer political party made big wins in provincial elections, raising questions of whether European Union efforts to reduce greenhouse gas emissions from livestock can succeed. This example makes clear that "people power" can override law, even when the laws are designed to protect the public interest. Of course, better advance consultation with Dutch farmers might have resulted in a different outcome and there may still be ways to get around their resistance to changing their way of life.

Lawsuits can protect the most vulnerable people; but they are time-consuming and require legal expertise, usually at a cost. Therefore, they are not available to everyone and often not the first choice of those promoting regenerative food systems. However, legal instruments play a central role in setting norms and structures that respect and protect human rights, allow fair access to resources, ensure accountability and protect land and water from acquisition by foreign entities. They can force public agencies and elected officials to support and enact pro-regenerative policies and practices.

However, law can dig tunnels under the public interest, weakening it to the point of collapse. For example, laws create and protect intellectual property rights and the Investors' Rights that allow industries to sue a country that enacts policies to protect its own people, if this results in investors not receiving their expected pay-out. Law upholds asymmetric trade agreements that hurt communities, smallholders and regenerative food systems. And in countries or states that do not have laws or effective institutions that protect the public interest, where court authorities are corrupt, or where policymakers disregard the law of the land, legal strategies bear little weight unless they can lead to new laws or a favorable reinterpretation of existing law.

What are the priorities for legal reform to enable regenerative food systems? In addition to the points made above under government programs and policies, we need a tax system in which corporations contribute fair taxes to support the government. In the US, the statutory corporate tax rate has been reduced gradually from over 50 percent in the 1950s to its current 21 percent, although the effective tax rate is only 9 percent for large profitable businesses (Tax Foundation 2021; GAO 2022). A decline in corporate tax rates has been the trend across OECD countries since 2000 (OECD 2022), despite growing corporate profits. Another important legal reform in the US would be reversing the *Citizens United* ruling of the Supreme Court, which allowed corporations to donate unlimited amounts of money to electoral campaigns. In 2022, agribusiness donated $58,661,720 to campaigns and an additional $169,483,033 to lobbying (OpenSecrets.org 2023). Restrictions on the "revolving door" whereby government officials go immediately into industry jobs and vice versa also would help to prevent policymakers favoring industry.

Food System Governance

Implicit Theory of Change

- Governance that prioritizes the needs of small-holders, women, Indigenous peoples, youth and other people who have not been well served by domestic or global food systems, and that promotes innovation directed toward sustainability, will transform food systems toward regeneration.

Implicit Assumptions

- Governance over food systems is transparent and can be reconfigured to reflect the needs of the majority of people.
- Although competing interests are at play in food system governance, a balance of power is achieved in modern society by which previous patterns of discrimination are erased.

> We are living in a complex world in which the multiple uncertainties that we face are not amenable to taming via indisputable scientific evidence or audacious technological innovation... In the optic of working towards better governance of better food systems they can only be addressed by political decision-making of the kind that can lead to a new social contract within a human rights framework, based on what is deemed to be most beneficial for the planet and the people who inhabit it—the now vulnerable majority rather than the now privileged few—and endowed with a participatory monitoring capacity that enables adjustments as conditions evolve.
>
> *(McKeon 2021, 179)*

Food system governance refers to

> the institutions, actors, rules and norms that shape how food is produced, distributed, and accessed across borders. It also encompasses the processes by which diverse actors within food systems are incorporated into decision and policymaking at different levels. Food systems governance is constituted by competing and overlapping networks composed of actors including states, civil society, philanthropies and transnational corporations who draw on vastly different resources in exercising power.
>
> *(Canfield et al. 2021, 182)*

Governance occurs at multiple levels, beginning with municipalities that decide on matters such as: where can food businesses be located (e.g., can fast-food restaurants be built near schools?); what kinds of food markets are allowed (e.g., must farmers' markets sell only local products and are they centrally located?) and is funding available to support food system resilience through diversification, building up soils' water-holding capacity and local markets? Other questions with wide-ranging impacts on producers and everyone who purchases food or grows/catches their own are decided by governance bodies at the state, regional and international scales. Food system governance is complex and fragmented, ranging from the Codex Alimentarius at the international scale down to neighborhood associations.

As described earlier, global food regime theorists have distinguished successive periods of food system governance that benefited first Great Britain during the 1870s–1930s, then the US from the 1950s to 1970s, then corporations from the 1970s until the present. According to Nora McKeon (2021, 173):

> Nineteenth century imperialism and the new forms of accumulation it introduced produced much of the foundation for the technical and managerial aspects of global governance as we see it today, aimed particularly at regulating and extending the world market and industrial capitalism and attenuating its social costs.

McKeon identified three milestones of global food governance after World War II: the creation of the UN Food and Agriculture Organization in 1944, the World Food Conference in 1974 and the reform of the UN Committee on World Food Security (CFS) in 2009. This reform enabled civil society and Indigenous peoples, as well as the private sector, to participate in governance as equals to governmental delegates and representatives from other UN agencies, although governments (as duty-bearers for human rights) are the only parties that vote. Chapter 9 deals with the CFS history and current status. Given the overweening power of corporations in the global food system and the harms they are inflicting on the environment and society, we need a new milestone to move into a new era of global food governance.

Keeping vulnerable people at the center of governance is central to rights-based approaches, resting on the logic that governance which includes and protects vulnerable people will serve everyone fairly. Article 20 of the UN Declaration on the Rights of Peasants and Other People Working in Rural Areas (UNGA 2019) states the following:

1 Peasants and other people working in rural areas have the right to active and free participation, directly and/or through their representative organizations, in the preparation and implementation of policies, programs and projects that may affect their lives, land and livelihoods.
2 States shall promote the participation, directly and/or through their representative organizations, of peasants and other people working in rural areas in decision-making processes that may affect their lives, land and livelihoods; this includes respecting the establishment and growth of strong and independent organizations of peasants and other people working in rural areas and promoting their participation in the preparation and implementation of food safety, labor and environmental standards that may affect them.

Article 16. 5 goes on to state:

> States shall formulate, in partnership with peasants and other people working in rural areas, public policies at the local, national, regional and international levels to advance and protect the right to adequate food, food security and food sovereignty and sustainable and equitable food systems.

Governance spaces need to ensure that people who have been marginalized or discriminated against are able to participate openly and fairly; otherwise, outcomes will support those who already have the most political power. Rules for fair and open participation include conflict of interest policies that prevent entities with a financial interest in the outcomes of governance or those that produce and sell harmful products to be part of decision-making. UNICEF created a new policy in 2023 for engagement with food and beverage (F&B) industries, including that UNICEF will continue to advocate for the F&B industry to be excluded from public policymaking and avoid all partnerships with ultra-processed food and beverage industries (UNICEF 2023). This policy responded to the recognition that ultra-processed food is a major contributor to obesity and that partnerships with industry had not resulted in improvements in their practices.

FAO needs a similar policy to exclude corporations that are producing and profiting from synthetic pesticides and fertilizers that destroy insect and bird biodiversity and soil ecosystems from decision-making power, yet it is moving in the opposite direction with several memoranda of agreement with organizations including CropLife, the International Fertilizer Association and the International Chamber of Commerce. These are part of FAO's current strategy for private sector engagement (FAO 2021) and attempts to leverage the financial resources of industry, given FAO's increasing reliance on voluntary commitments. FAO lumps together small-scale farmers, fishers and pastoralists and the largest corporations in the "private sector," however, thus putting people whose human rights are being violated in the same category as those responsible for many of the violations.

What aspects would a more legitimate global food governance system need in order to overcome the obstacles that have blocked past efforts to fight hunger? Nora McKeon has put considerable thought into this, starting with her previous role as civil-society liaison to FAO. More than a decade ago, she described conditions for better governance to ensure food security: it would need to be based on a set of basic values and principles to answer the question of what kind of food future we want. It would require respect for an inclusive, legitimate and democratic political process, giving special attention to meaningful participation by those most directly affected by food insecurity, who are also those in the front line of finding solutions. It would be effective, multisectoral and holistic in its purview. It would be able to access the full range of knowledge necessary to inform its decisions, including that of social actors. And it needs to respect the principle of subsidiarity, building links across different levels of governance to promote participation and accountability at all levels (McKeon 2011). These conditions still seem to hold, and the Committee on World Food Security is the global institution that comes closest to meeting them.

Social Innovation

Implicit Theory of Change

- Regenerative food systems will be created by building new alternatives, changing norms and institutions regarding how people live and work together.

Implicit Assumptions

- Most people want alternatives to the current food system, despite its conveniences and low prices.
- People find enough personal satisfaction from participating in social innovations that they continue to do so, thereby sustaining the innovation.
- Social innovations will grow and network until they overpower the current neoliberal food system.

> The challenge, ultimately, is to rebuild the social capital required … to facilitate collective action and the maximize the potential role of social imagination in bringing about new lifestyles, allowing us to remain within planetary boundaries while at the same time ensuring well-being and, yes, happiness. The ecological transition … can be seen as an opportunity to rethink society in ways that will increase conviviality and solidarity, and that will reduce the pressure from competition and the drive for performance. This is a revolution from which all can gain, and social innovations have a key role to play in making it happen.
>
> *(De Schutter and Dedeurwaerdere 2022, 6)*

Social innovation can be a powerful stimulator of regenerative food systems. Experiments with creating food democracy are examples of social innovation, as are food production systems that spread risk across producers and customers (such as community-supported agriculture); community gardens; pollinator gardens; urban food forests; cooperative markets and farmers' organizations. The common theme is that social innovations entail a different way of organizing and managing social relationships than the dominant pattern in industrialized societies. The European Commission defined social innovation in its 2013 Guide to Social Innovation (p. 6) as "the development and implementation of new ideas (products, services, models) in response to social needs and that create new social relationships or collaborations." In contrast to technological innovation, social innovation has low costs and entry barriers. People participate voluntarily because they receive benefits, often in the form of more interaction with like-minded people or learning new skills, as well as access to healthy food. Social innovation possibilities are unlimited: countless examples are in existence around the world. However, they are often ignored or discounted in recommendations by governments and scientific committees of how to transform the food system.

Social innovations may scale up from citizen-led initiatives through partnerships with corporations or public authorities. Yuna Chiffoleau and Allison Loconto (2018) distinguished three kinds of social innovations: new modalities of governmental intervention (such as food policy councils), development of social enterprises and social entrepreneurs (such as digital tools to help customers find local food in urban areas) and citizen-driven initiatives that fill gaps not satisfied by public policies or markets. Some social innovations may simply be more efficient or effective approaches to extractive food systems: for example, some authors include public-private partnerships as social innovations, even though these are often dominated by the private sector and serve its interests more than the common good (Sundaram 2023).

Social innovations must be driven by a goal to increase well-being to be transformative, not simply changing social relations so that groups and people do things differently. The motivations for corporate partners and public authorities differ from citizens' motivations to participate in social innovations: corporations may want to improve their image, secure a license to operate, or reduce costs (e.g., supermarkets donating food to charities that is close to expiration or of lower quality means that they do not have to pay disposal fees). Public authorities may see partnerships as a way to increase their legitimacy (De Schutter and Dedeurwaerdere 2022).

Bottom-up social innovation has become more prevalent in recent years for a number of reasons. As De Schutter and Dedeurwaerdere (2022, 63) pointed out:

> Classic forms of public action, the millennials intuitively feel, have failed us. There is a need for innovative ways of changing patterns of production and consumption if we want to have a chance, even minimal, to slow down before we reach the cliff.

As COVID-19 spread, many more beyond millennials believed that their best hopes lay with citizen-led initiatives and not with the government. In the US, mutual aid societies in which aid was given and received reciprocally sprang up; and community fridges and other ways to share food became common. The organization Food Not Bombs was founded in 1980 and has been sharing vegan food for free in cities since then. Food-sharing efforts have gotten pushback in conservative states in the US, however, for ostensibly increasing homelessness and vagrancy. For example, the city of Miami outlawed public provision of food to groups larger than 25 in 2020 unless people who are providing the food register with the city in advance and use one of five sites that the city designated. Even with those restrictions, an organization can only get a permit to operate one day per week (Alvarado 2020). This heartlessness is part of the way that the Republican Party has transmuted the successful War on Poverty of an earlier era in the US to a war on poor people.

Other examples of transformative social innovation in the food system include community-supported agriculture, urban food forests, networks of growers trying to introduce new crops to an area and build out appropriate infrastructure, solidarity purchasing groups, seed exchange networks and large organizations including La Via Campesina and the Movimento sim Terra in Brazil (whose members are reclaiming land from large land-owners). Food systems seem to be especially rich areas for social innovations, perhaps because they are at the intersection of social and ecological systems, everyone relies on them in one way or another and their complexity affords multiple places for changing norms and rules. Commoning and social solidarity economies are social innovations that require new forms of governance, as well as new ways of relating to other people, land and other resources. They are efforts to leap beyond the corporate food regime.

> The Solidarity Economy movement focuses on the issues of redistributive justice and alternatives to the neoliberal capitalist model, financialization and the debt-based monetary system: it also builds on the issues of participatory-deliberative democracy and emancipatory processes based on active citizenship and social activism, integrating economic, social, cultural and environmental objectives and the political dimension.
>
> *(Rossi et al. 2021, 548)*

Adanella Rossi and her co-authors (2021) suggested common stages of food system social innovations that arise from solidarity economy principles: first, the development of "pacts" or agreements between producers and customers based on transparent and fair pricing, planning of production and pre-financing. Next, projects move into "food co-production" in which the line between producers and customers blurs, with customers often helping with production. Finally, Participatory Guarantee Systems allow projects to self-certify with teams consisting of producers and customers. The pacts often ensure that profits are only for social utility (perhaps feeding into a fund to help people in emergencies), alternative currencies may be used, and participants in the initiative may join together to resist local land-use planning or other situations that will result in social disadvantage, exclusion or distress. That is, participation in the social innovation may lead to political action on a local or wider scale. These stages seem most applicable to social innovations that produce food; they may not be as relevant to innovations that are focused primarily on distribution or consumption.

In the same article, Adanella Rossi and her co-authors (2021, 548) recognized the connections among social innovation, solidarity economy and a "re-commonification" of food and food systems:

> Solidarity Economy experiences express the willingness of a segment of society to re-signify food value and to rebuild a completely different system … the construction of a new awareness and the systemic diffusion of a different culture around food and food systems among citizens, enterprises and public institutions; a process of "de-colonization" of food as a market commodity and reconstruction of a new social narrative around it.

While social innovations are spaces that attract many people to food system transformation, it is not clear which kinds are effective beyond the discrete aims of individual projects. People may derive great satisfaction and community benefits from their participation, but are these initiatives just fitting into interstices in the extractive food system instead of transforming it? And worse, are they removing the onus from government to meet all people's needs for healthy food, a healthy environment and decent livelihoods? Public policies can play a vital role in enabling social innovation and ensuring that they last beyond initial enthusiasm of founders; without such an enabling environment, social innovations may be limited in their scope and longevity. But to the extent that social innovation rests on Solidarity Economy principles, support from government requires a major leap from neoliberalism:

> It stresses the need to give priority to production-consumption systems that aim at food sovereignty and food justice and, to that end, foster growth of knowledge, shared responsibility, sense of community, citizenship, political awareness, inclusions and social justice around food. This is very far from legitimizing a system based on the domination of private economic interests over those of individuals and communities and, therefore, favors the loss of knowledge and skills, reduction in freedom, individualization of choices and practices, social alienation and denial of rights.
>
> *(Rossi et al. 2021, 548)*

This kind of public support will only come about with participatory deliberative democracy and strong efforts to overcome both power asymmetries between civil society and public institutions, and communication gaps. These steps would go a long way toward overcoming distrust between civil society and public authorities.

Not all social innovations are transformative, but it seems clear that this is a pathway to finding new food systems that truly meet people's needs in ways that the extractive food system cannot. They can re-organize economic exchanges, relationships with other people, and relationships with nature toward regeneration.

Rights-Based Approaches

Implicit Theory of Change

- If all human rights were respected, protected and fulfilled for all people, we would have regenerative food systems.

Implicit Assumptions

- The framework of universal, indivisible, inalienable human rights first articulated in the Universal Declaration of Human Rights in 1948 is the best existing agreement among countries on what every person needs and deserves as a human being.

- Although the Universal Declaration of Human Rights was written by an elite group of government delegates, they apply across all populations.
- The successive refinements of particular rights by the Human Rights Council have built a powerful body of soft law that ensures every person's well-being.
- All countries and people understand human rights in essentially the same ways.
- Soft law is influential in driving countries' legal frameworks.

> Over the past 75 years, the Universal Declaration of Human Rights has guided tremendous progress – helping societies to deal with problems so deep they seemed intractable, and rebuilding new kinds of relationships between social actors, based on greater equality and trust. Many structures that maintained severe racial and gender discrimination were dismantled. Massive advances were made in education and health. The need for governments and institutions that listen to, inform and fully and meaningfully include people in decision-making became clearer. Countries took back their independence. And people were able to exercise their rights. Perhaps most important of all, the Universal Declaration inspired vibrant, creative, powerful activism and solidarity, empowering people to demand their rights and to engage actively in their communities and societies.
>
> *(Türk 2023, n.p.)*

> Human rights are an essential tool to overcome all forms of intersecting discriminations, social exclusion, exploitation, or marginalisation. In particular, a right to food analysis of food access failure must focus on the structural causes and the systemic drivers of their acute and enduring economic, social, and political vulnerabilities.
>
> *(Cohen et al. 2023, 8)*

> [C]alls for individuals to have a legal right to access food can be harnessed as a transitional step towards building the institutions and social infrastructures that will facilitate decommodification, commoning, and empowerment within the food system.
>
> *(Booth 2022, n.p.)*

Strengthening human rights would push governments to protect vulnerable producers, workers and consumers in the food system and protect the environment through domestic legislation and international treaties. Although some of the guidelines addressing human rights are "soft law" and thus not binding on countries, they shape expectations and can be transformed into legally binding obligations at the country level. Rights-based approaches force countries to examine why certain populations are especially vulnerable. Michael Fakhri, UN Special Rapporteur on the Right to Food, emphasized that "human rights law requires scrutinizing how people are made poor, vulnerable or marginalized. How is inequality produced? Structural inequality is not a natural occurrence or anomalous. It is produced by systems, including food systems" (Fakhri 2022, 2).

Almost all countries (with the notable exception of the US) accept the right to food and have become signatories of treaties and conventions that elaborate rights of populations that are vulnerable or oppressed, such as women, children and Indigenous people. The steps that countries should take to respect, protect and fulfill each defined human right are spelled out and apply to human rights generally. Strict adherence to guidelines and recommendations regarding labor rights, the right to food and the right to a healthy environment would force structural changes in the food system: policymakers would have to support the public interest and resist efforts by industry to undermine it; producers and businesses would have to pay labor fair wages and producers and businesses would have to internalize the costs of managing whatever waste they produce instead of dumping it into the environment.

The interpretation of human rights is constantly evolving, generally in the direction of regenerative communities. However, this is not a given. In the US, the right to bear arms guaranteed in the US Constitution has been manipulated to weaken any efforts at gun control, even though the US has the highest homicide rate among industrialized nations of 7.8 deaths per 100,000 per year (Chamie 2023). The right to own and use a gun is not an internationally recognized human right, fortunately. But new international human rights are being recognized regularly, with the right to a healthy environment one of the most recent. Recognition of this right was prompted by the toll of climate change.

Human rights are a cross-cutting theme in all UN policies and programs that deal with peace and security, development, humanitarian assistance and economic and social affairs. As a result, virtually every UN body and specialized agency is involved to some degree in the protection of human rights. Human rights are indivisible and interdependent: strengthening human rights in one domain often makes it easier to exercise human rights in another domain. For example, upholding the right to food, considered to be an economic and social right, is essential for upholding civil and political rights: malnourished and starving people cannot participate meaningfully in governance.

Although the unanimous signatures to the UN Declaration of Human Rights in 1948 was a major victory, not all countries have signed and ratified follow-up conventions and treaties that specified what these rights are, including the 1966 Covenant on Civil & Political Rights and Covenant on Economic, Social & Cultural Rights. Not all countries recognize the same set of human rights and religious or cultural law may supersede human rights in authoritarian regions. For example, some people have claimed that human rights impose "Western" ideals of private property or freedom of expression on other countries, leave out collective rights of communities and suffer from ambiguities of interpretation. A major weakness of the framework of human rights is that not all are legally binding and justiciable (that is, people cannot always turn to courts for redress if their rights are violated). Another line of criticism advanced by Samuel Moyn is that human rights fail to challenge inequality and have done nothing to shrink widening gaps between the very rich and the very poor:

> The real trouble about human rights, when historically correlated with market fundamentalism, is not that they promote it but that they are unambitious in theory and ineffectual in practice in the face of market fundamentalism's success. Neoliberalism has changed the world, while the human rights movement has posed no threat to it... Human rights have been the signature morality of a neoliberal age because they merely call for it to be more humane.
>
> *(Moyn 2018, 216–217)*

Yet despite these criticisms, the fight for human rights and their articulation in different UN documents have prevented countless abuses against people's security and freedoms. The UN Declaration of Human Rights has inspired several legally binding international human rights treaties and all countries have created laws to enforce human rights as part of their social contract with their populations. Human rights are not a perfect system, but they are the best expression we have of global agreement on what every person needs and deserves to be a full participant in society. If human rights were respected, protected and fulfilled everywhere, the world would be transformed for the better.

The right to food deserves particular attention as a transformative narrative. The ability to nourish people by providing healthy food without destroying the means of producing it is a core requirement for a regenerative food system. This right was included in the UN Declaration on Human Rights as part of the right to an adequate standard of living (Article 25) then included in the 1966 International Covenant on Economic, Social and Cultural Rights. However, articulation of states' obligations under the right to food did not happen until 1996 with General Comment 12 of the Committee on Economic, Social and Cultural Rights. This explained that states must respect, protect and fulfill this right by not engaging in activities that would interfere with the ability of populations to grow or purchase food (respect), protect their people from interference by any third parties, and ensure that no one goes hungry, even in times of emergency (fulfill). The right to food is elaborated and refined in several additions to the UN Declaration on Human Rights and the Covenant on Economic, Social and Cultural Rights and in the *Voluntary Guidelines to support the progressive realization of the right to adequate food in the context of national food security* (FAO 2005; OHCHR 2023).

Several countries have taken steps to operationalize the right to food through constitutional amendments or law: over twenty countries have amended their constitutions to include the right to food and most Latin American countries have adopted or proposed right to food framework laws. Notable cases in which the right to food has been achieved through judicial action and court rulings include India, which recognized a constitutional right to food, determined a basic nutritional floor, set up accountability mechanisms to monitor noncompliance and gave directives to provide mid-day meals in schools (Claeys and Lambek 2014). Creating judicial recourse mechanisms when the right to food is violated was a major achievement in India; and violations of the right to food have been brought to courts in Canada, Switzerland, Fiji, Germany, Ireland, Moldava, Russia and a large number of other countries in Asia, Africa and Latin America (De Schutter 2010; IDLO and Irish Aid 2015).

FAO's Right to Food office, Special Rapporteurs for the Right to Food and civil society organizations have advanced right to food concepts and framework laws. Chapter 10 on local struggles describes work in the US to implement the right to food at the state level in the absence of national acceptance of this right. Their work, and the work around the globe to advance human rights, is tremendously impactful in creating a more just and sustainable world.

Food Democracy

Implicit Theory of Change

- Food democracy will advance regenerative food systems, which have greater benefits for the whole, if all people who are affected by food system decisions can participate in decision-making.

Implicit Assumptions

- If free from coercion, people will decide what is best for society as a whole, rather than choosing alternatives that further their own self-interests.
- People are sufficiently well-informed to make good choices about food systems.
- Food democracy sets up mechanisms for eliciting the opinions of all affected people.

- People are able to disregard advertisements and silver-tongued politicians who urge them to "vote" against choices that advance public health, environmental quality and universal well-being.

> Simply put, food democracy emphasizes fulfillment of the human right to safe, nutritious food that has been justly produced. It means ordinary people getting together to establish rules that encourage safeguarding the soil, water, and wildlife on which we all depend. It is also pragmatic politics built around the difficult lesson that food is too important to leave to market forces—that we all have a right and responsibility to participate in decisions that determine our access to safe, nutritious food.
>
> *(PANNA 2015, as quoted in Norwood 2015, 1)*

> Throughout the world, peoples are asserting control over their territories, strengthening their ability to govern themselves, and developing ways of negotiating with "the powers that be," taking advantage of a new recognition of their rights and abilities. These communities are moving beyond the tired calls for (representative) democracy, private property, and individual rights; they are forging a renewed form of participatory democracy and collective control of their communal patrimony.
>
> *(Barkin 2014, n.p.)*

Food democracy allows everyone affected by policies to contribute to decision-making and flows from rights-based governance. The idea is rather utopian, in that it assumes that people will not make decisions based solely on their own self-interest but also consider the common good. However, neoliberalism has elevated selfishness as a justifiable goal: society lauds billionaires as successes, even if they made money through unscrupulous means. In addition, masses of people can be manipulated by charismatic politicians and disinformation to act against their own interests. The allure of consumerism prevents many people recognizing the dangers of resource-extractive systems, which have well exceeded the planet's capacity to regenerate ecosystems and absorb waste. The Republican party in the US has taken advantage of this weakness since the 1980s, especially in the election of Donald Trump, to become the party of disgruntled working-class people. Their loyalty has not been shaken by Republican policies that have consistently redistributed wealth upwards.

In Anderson (2023), I argued that food democracy is not possible where civic democracy is eroding. Political democracies are decreasing in number, giving way to authoritarian regimes (Papada et al. 2023). Three of the ways that authoritarian governments control their populations are by cracking down on independent media, promulgating disinformation and doubts about the veracity of information available, and restricting activities of civil society. Such tactics result in fewer people having the means to ascertain truth in information they receive. In the current context of a polycrisis, accurate information is essential to make good policy choices and to elect public figures who will work for the common good. Enabling conditions for food democracy include the creation of alternative spaces where people can meet their needs, genuine inclusion of underprivileged people in food system governance, and public forums for deliberation about the food system that are active and respected by public institutions.

Some might argue that food democracy is a wedge into creating civic democracy among citizens who are estranged from politics. Food choices elicit strong feelings, and lack of food or the kinds of food that people want motivates them to act. For example, food shortages and high prices spurred protests against authoritarian governments during Arab Spring in the 2010s (Soffiantini 2020). Although people in many Middle Eastern and North African countries demanded changes in food policies and overthrew the president of Tunisia, results of the uprising were mixed and it is not possible to say that democracies have spread in the Middle East due to Arab Spring (Hubbard and Kirkpatrick 2021).

Although evidence suggests that protests focused on food supply do not lead to civic democracy, greater public participation in food policies may have more limited positive impacts. Food policy councils (FPCs) have proliferated in the US and Canada, with their growth documented by the Food Policy Network at Johns Hopkins Center for a Livable Future. The Network created a "policy wheel" in 2016, 2018, 2019, 2020 and 2021 showing notable achievements (Center for a Livable Future 2023). The 2021 wheel included many ways that city FPCs contributed to partnerships, policies and programs to improve food access and racial equity during COVID-19 and beyond. Another model of public participation is the Brazilian CONSEA, in which food and nutrition policy councils at the municipal and state levels are nested within a national council. President Jair Bolsonaro disbanded the CONSEAs in 2019, but one of President Luiz Inácio Lula da Silva's first actions was to reinstate the national CONSEA (Secretaria de Comunicaçao Social 2023, n.p.), stressing the need to combat hunger and encourage family farming: "We're going to try to hold a big discussion with small and medium-sized food producers so that we can increase production of healthy food in Brazil."

Food policy councils always include actors across the food system, but they tend to be dominated by people who work within government agencies and civil society. There is often explicit attention to sharing power; for example, racial equity and including voices of low-income people who experience hunger are cross-cutting themes for several FPCs in the US now in the wake of the Black Lives Matter movement and growing inequality. This is a meaningful use of the concept of "inclusion" to advance the common good and the wellbeing of disadvantaged people.

Agroecology

Implicit Theory of Change

- When agroecology is the dominant practice in food production, marketing and consumption, we will have regenerative food systems.

Implicit Assumptions

- As more producers recognize the financial, nutritional and environmental benefits of agroecology and are able to take advantage of financial incentives, they will change their production practices to agroecology.
- Agroecology can restore degraded land through practices such as agroforestry, cover cropping and mulching.
- Shifting to agroecological production will not demand more arable land than is available.
- Producers are willing to use more labor-intensive practices.
- Agroecology is context specific, so its practices and policies will differ from place to place. However, all agroecology is congruent with defined sets of elements and principles.
- Increasing numbers of scientists will help to build the evidence base for benefits of agroecology.
- Social movements are vital to build momentum for this transformation.
- Extractive food systems will give way to agroecological systems.

> Agroecology is a truly transformational pathway to address all the structural changes needed in our food system in a systemic and integrated way. Agroecology has catalysed the agency of those most affected by insecurity and marginalization to become the architects and drivers of socio-economic justice in their food systems.
>
> *(CSM 2019, 1)*

> Agroecological practices improve food security, nutrition, and health, while adapting to and mitigating climate change, without compromising the ecosystems. Furthermore, these practices support equality and social justice from production to consumption of food. There is strong evidence showing that agroecological approaches can achieve high productivity and profitability without the environmental externalities of conventional agriculture. Introducing processes typical of natural ecosystems, agroecology

> also enhances system complexity in producing, distributing, and consuming food and thereby enhances system resilience against climate change beyond what would be possible with production measures alone.
>
> *(Bezner Kerr et al. 2023, 5)*

> Agroecology is the transformation needed for LDC food sovereignty.
>
> *(AFSA 2023, n.p.)*

Agroecology has been defined famously as a science, a set of practices and a movement (Wezel et al. 2009). Laura Silici (2014, 6) described these facets of agroecology:

> As a science, it studies how different components of the agro-ecosystem interact. As a set of practices, it seeks sustainable farming systems that optimize and stabilize yields. As a movement, it pursues food sovereignty and new, multifunctional roles for agriculture.

Rachel Bezner Kerr et al. (2023, 1) drew from multiple sources to define agroecology as:

> a transdisciplinary science applying ecological concepts and principles to agri-food systems at multiple scales through individual and collective action, which explicitly considers political, economic, social and environmental aspects, drawing on Indigenous and local knowledge. Agroecology uses ecological and humanistic principles to farm with minimal degradation of soil, water, and ecosystem services while providing sufficient, healthy diverse foods for consumption and livelihoods.

Agroecology is based on a set of principles which differ markedly from the principles of extractive agriculture; for example, agroecology uses recycling and synergies between different components of the system rather than inputs of synthetic pesticides and fertilizers to deal with pests, diseases and nutrient needs. The extent to which it can transform a food system depends largely on supporting infrastructure and policy, such as markets for agroecological products and the elimination of subsidies to industrialized agriculture. Colin Anderson and his co-authors from the Center on Agroecology, Water and Resilience at Coventry University (2021) made a careful distinction between transformative agroecology, the form promoted by La Via Campesina and civil society organizations allied with them, and weaker variants promoted by governments or businesses. They argued that the transformation of political institutions through agroecology entails making changes in realizing human rights and access to nature, knowledge and culture, systems of economic exchange, networks, equity and discourse. As agroecology has grown in popularity, it has been co-opted by industries and governments in a weak variant that consists only of selected practices encouraged by subsidies and extension staff, stifling peasant initiative and leadership (Giraldo and Rosset 2023). Given the threats to agroecology, Omar Giraldo and Peter Rosset proposed seven principles of an "emancipatory" agroecology that builds on their field research with peasants in Latin America, the Caribbean, Mozambique and India. These principles work together to support an anti-capitalist, anti-productivist food system that promotes farmer autonomy and knowledge and local control.

Agroecology is a holistic and emancipatory approach to food systems. Jessica Milgroom (2021, n.p.) claimed that agroecology, food sovereignty and feminism are "intertwined emancipatory movements and political projects that fight for autonomy, self-determination, egalitarianism, epistemic reconstitution and social justice." But emancipation from patriarchal, colonial and exploitative structures is not a given in agroecology: it requires the participation of women, Indigenous and marginalized people, and the embrace of feminism. Scholars who examine the connections between agroecology and feminism have found close congruence. Diana Lilia Trevilla Espinal and her co-authors from Latin America and the Caribbean (2021) called on agroecology to give as much attention to social inequality and all forms of oppression as it does to ecological violence. They highlighted four key actions that agroecology needs to incorporate: recognize women's work and knowledge in food systems, distribute care work equally between men and women, strengthen the social fabric and defend the commons. Haley Zaremba et al. (2021) emphasized that agroecology is about self-determination and reclaiming control of one's own food, land and body in addition to lowering chemical inputs and increasing sustainability. They examined the 13 agroecological principles introduced in the 2019 High Level Panel of Experts report through a feminist lens and argued that social inequality must be considered at every stage of implementing agroecology. Their view of agroecology overlaps with food sovereignty in their examination of control and self-determination; the two approaches to food system transformation often go hand-in-hand and both have highlighted women's rights and participation as necessary to transform food systems. In the introductory article of the 2019 Right to Food and Nutrition Watch (Andrews et al. 2019, 7), Donna Andrews and her co-authors stated:

> Women are, and have always been, central to the creation of radical food politics that have the power to reconnect us with nature, remake social relations and prioritize intersectional justice.

The evidence for agroecology's benefits to food security, nutrition, livelihoods, environment and resilience in the face of perturbations is strong (e.g., HLPE 2019; Bezner Kerr et al. 2021; Gliessman et al. 2023). The Global Alliance for the Future of Food supported a project to create a compendium of evidence for agroecology's benefits from teams in different regions of the world (GAFF 2021). The project was instigated by the refusal of some governments to accept agroecology as superior to industrialized agriculture, despite its robust evidence. This refusal to accept the evidence is politically motivated and especially strong from governments such as the US where agribusiness corporations that profit from the sale of agricultural inputs carry outsized influence with government agencies. The US Ambassador to the United Nations Agencies for Food and Agriculture, and chief of the US Mission to the UN from 2019 to 2021, Kip Tom, made infamous allegations about agroecology's inferiority to industrialized agriculture at a USDA Agricultural Outlook Forum dinner speech (Tom 2020). Tom's own farm operation, one of the largest in Indiana, is a major seed supplier to Monsanto, creating a clear conflict of interest in his ability to speak objectively about industrialized agriculture. His outspoken contempt for agroecology may be due to the threat it poses to agribusiness, although his lack of understanding of its benefits also contributed. Current US efforts to promote "climate-smart" agriculture bypass agroecology, focusing on the capacity of selected practices to increase carbon-sequestration of soil. Yet agroecology is not only climate-smart but also biodiversity-smart, nutrition-smart and livelihood-smart, while allowing farmers increased autonomy and independence from external inputs.

The contrasting narratives of agroecology and industrialized food systems were very clear as the International Assessment of Agricultural Knowledge, Science and Technology for Development (IAASTD) headed to publication, which coincided with the 2008 World Development Report. The latter claimed that it was time to put agriculture at the center of the development agenda, where it would be "led by private entrepreneurs in extensive value chains linking producers to consumers" with the private sector driving

> the organization of value chains that bring the market to smallholders and commercial farms. The state—through enhanced capacity and new forms of governance—corrects market failures, regulates competition, and engages strategically in public-private partnerships to promote competitiveness in the agribusiness sector and support the greater inclusion of smallholders and rural workers.
>
> *(World Bank 2008, 7)*

While both reports emphasized the importance of small-scale farmers, their positions could hardly have been more different. The IAASTD pointed to agroecological food systems with greater autonomy, greater respect for farmer knowledge and less dependence on external inputs, while the WDR anticipated farmers in "value chains" led by corporate agribusiness (World Bank 2008; IAASTD 2009). The idea that smallholders need to be linked to global markets to improve their well-being has persisted, even though this puts vulnerable producers from low-income countries that cannot subsidize agricultural production in competition with large-scale producers in the Minority World who receive generous subsidies.

One of the big questions about agroecology is how quickly it can scale up to involve more producers and feed more people, and what the enabling conditions are for this growth. Mateo Mier y Terán Giménez Cacho and his co-authors (2018) examined this in Central America, Mexico, Cuba, India and Brazil and concluded that eight drivers are key to "massification": (1) recognition of a crisis that motivates the search for alternatives, (2) presence of facilitating social organization(s), (3) constructivist learning processes, (4) effective agroecological practices, (5) mobilizing discourses, (6) external allies, (7) favorable markets and (8) favorable policies. Their work points to the factors that other groups seeking to scale up agroecology need to consider. Haley Zaremba and her co-authors (2021) cautioned that initiatives trying to scale up agroecology may lock out women and assign disproportionate labor to them, unless there are active efforts to remain focused on social equality.

Given the complexity of agroecology and its enablers, the challenge of scaling up may seem formidable. If enablers of industrialized extractive agriculture (e.g., subsidies, propaganda, lobbyists and conservative front groups such as the American Farm Bureau Federation) were removed, however, agroecology would have a much better chance of becoming dominant because of its many advantages. So the work for advocates is not only to create enabling conditions but also to subvert disabling conditions.

Food Sovereignty

Implicit Theory of Change

- With greater control at the community level, people will choose regenerative food systems that protect public health, environmental quality and universal well-being.

Implicit Assumptions

- "People power" is stronger than financial power.
- Food movements mobilize effectively at the community level.
- The power of corporate agriculture must be steadily resisted by peoples' movements to achieve control over food systems.

- Extractive industrialized food systems within neoliberalism will give way to food sovereignty.

> Food sovereignty policies must be promoted, so as to reverse corporate concentration, and dismantle corporations' power in food systems. Governments must regulate prices, limit opportunities for corporations to dominate global food markets, and introduce and enforce legal instruments to ban financial speculation in commodities. They should insist on reduction or elimination of foreign debt, and raise taxes on corporate profits to redistribute funds. The concentration of private grain reserves must be over-turned; instead, public food reserves must be supported to protect people from shocks. Economic sanctions that turn food into a political weapon must be withdrawn. Neoliberal trade agreements and finance and investment rules have severely undermined people's food sovereignty. Trade and investment must be reoriented to serve people and societies, not corporations. Free Trade Agreements (FTAs) should be halted, and existing WTO agreements must be dismantled. Governments must be accountable to their citizens for trade, investment and finance policies.
>
> *(CSIPM 2022, 17)*

> Only food sovereignty can offer long-term, sustainable, equitable and just solutions to the urgent food and climate crises.
>
> *(IPC 2008, n.p.)*

Food sovereignty was defined by La Via Campesina in (LVC 1996) as "the right of each nation to maintain and develop its own capacity to produce its basic foods respecting cultural and productive diversity". The 2007 Nyéléni Declaration on Food Sovereignty, created by more than 500 representatives from peasants, Indigenous peoples, landless peoples, rural workers, migrants, pastoralists, forest communities, women, youth, consumers, environmental and urban movements around the world, defines it as:

> the right of peoples to healthy and culturally appropriate food produced through ecologically sound and sustainable methods, and their right to define their own food and agriculture systems. It puts those who produce, distribute and consume food at the heart of food systems and policies rather than the demands of markets and corporations. It defends the interests and inclusion of the next generation. It offers a strategy to resist and dismantle the current corporate trade and food regime, and directions for food, farming, pastoral and fisheries systems determined by local producers. Food sovereignty prioritises local and national economies and markets

and empowers peasant and family farmer-driven agriculture, artisanal fishing, pastoralist-led grazing, and food production, distribution and consumption based on environmental, social and economic sustainability.
(Nyéléni 2007, n.p.)

Core principles of food sovereignty are that it:

- puts the right to sufficient, healthy and culturally appropriate food for all people at the center of food, agriculture, livestock and fisheries policies;
- values food providers;
- localizes food systems;
- puts control locally;
- builds knowledge and skills and
- works with nature through agroecology (European Coordination Via Campesina 2018, n.p.).

Additional principles came from the 2007 Nyéléni Declaration: agrarian reform, reorganizing global trade so that it is transparent and guarantees a just income to all peoples and ensuring social peace and rights of women and other marginalized populations. Many of the principles of food sovereignty are included in the UN Declaration on the Rights of Peasants and Other People Working in Rural Areas, which brought it into international human rights soft law. At the national level, many countries have recognized the right to food sovereignty through constitutional amendments (Ecuador, Bolivia, Nepal, Venezuela, Mali) or legal frameworks. Legal recognition and the approval of UNDROP does not lead immediately to new national laws and policies; these require long-term advocacy by peasant organizations (Claeys and Lambek 2014; Wittman 2023).

Food sovereignty drives greater local and community control of the food system and, of the interventions described in this chapter, is the one focusing most clearly on power. In addition, it is the only intervention of the ones examined here that specifies scale as a key principle. By emphasizing local control of the food system, it places control over food system decisions in the hands of those who are most directly affected by the decisions. This is in marked contrast with some of the other narratives of what will drive transformation, such as government programs, MSIs or intergovernmental summits, in which decisions are made by people who do not necessarily have any contact with what is happening on the ground. Food democracy allows direct communication by members of the public with policymakers, but it allows the general public to make the decisions and does not prioritize producers and other local food system participants, as food sovereignty does.

There are numerous debates about the locus of control in food sovereignty (Edelman et al. 2014; Iles and Montenegro 2015; Alonso-Fradejas et al. 2017). The way civil society organizations have advocated for it makes clear that producers must have a central place and that foreign governments must never be responsible for decisions that affect what people can eat and how it is produced, such as by dumping or by exporting genetically engineered foods under the guise of humanitarian aid. Other actors have a necessary role, however, of supporting producers, purchasing their food, and fighting for policies that keep control over food systems local and ensure fair compensation for labor. Food sovereignty is somewhat less clear when a government sets policies that disadvantage its own small-scale agroecological producers. How it can be institutionalized, especially in countries where only a small percentage of the population is producing food, is still an open question.

Food sovereignty is the most transformative of the narratives considered in this chapter because, along with the changes in governance described above, it also calls for agroecology, feminism, human rights and radical changes in how society values nature. By establishing food sovereignty as a human right, responsibilities of governments are explicit. And by demanding an end to oppression of all forms, including violence against nature, food sovereignty goes to the deepest levels that lead to dysfunction in the food system. Food sovereignty, like agroecology, is closely connected with feminism and women's rights (Calvário and Desmarais 2023). La Via Campesina's "Manifesto for the Future of the Planet" (LVC 2021, n.p.) stated that:

> Peasant women and other oppressed gender minorities must find equal space in the leadership of our movement at all levels. We must sow the seeds of solidarity in our communities and address all forms of discrimination that keep rural societies divided.
>
> Food sovereignty offers a manifesto for the future, a feminist vision that embraces diversity. It is an idea that unites humanity and puts us at the service of Mother Earth that feeds us and nourishes us.

Food sovereignty stresses that government should serve peoples' needs for regenerative food systems, not respond first to what industry wants to gain higher profits. It aims to guarantee and protect people's territory, ability, and right to define their own models of production, food distribution, and consumption patterns. It seeks to reverse the socially inequitable and ecologically destructive nature of industrial farming, fisheries, forestry and livestock management, and the wider food systems of which they are a part. Food sovereignty is aimed at recreating the democratic realm and regenerating a diversity of autonomous food systems based on equity, social justice and ecological sustainability. This transformation with, by, and for people implies radical changes in ecological, political, social, technological and economic domains (Pimbert 2009).

Many of the narratives included in this chapter (social innovation, strengthening human rights, inclusive governance grounded in human rights, food democracy, agroecology and food sovereignty) are complementary and need to work together to transform food systems toward regeneration. These narratives require—but also facilitate—a change in the dominant narrative and they need government action and legal strategies to succeed. That is, the narrative will change because social movements and NGOs work together with independent media and government to reinforce the messages that the extractive food system under neoliberalism is killing us but healthy, inclusive alternatives are available. It is only the combined influence of citizens, civil society, independent media and courageous policymakers that can enact this narrative change and overcome the influences of extractive food industries. The roots in human rights ensure a moral economy or an ethos of governance that attends to the public good, going beyond nationalism or industry interests. The experiments in alternative post-capitalist food systems that are underway as social innovations show people that transformation is feasible and in reach, not just a matter of rhetoric.

In Chapter 5, Figure 5.4 showed the many ways that the cultural narrative influences other components of the food system. Figure 7.1 shows the impacts of changing the cultural narrative on other actors in the food system.

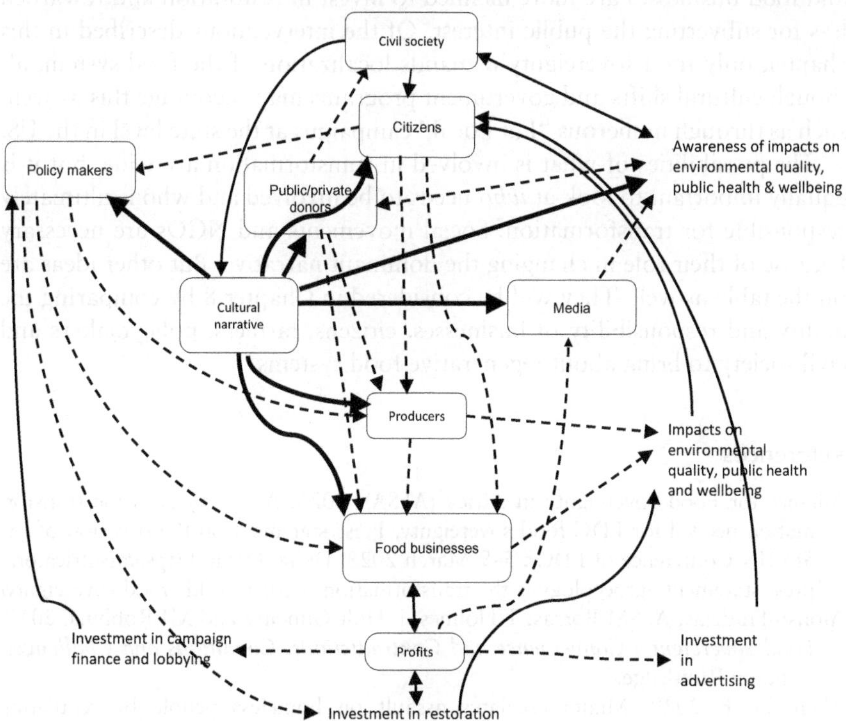

FIGURE 7.1 Impacts of changing the cultural narrative.

Since the cultural narrative has such broad influence, changing it has wide-spreading direct and indirect effects. Direct effects are shown in this diagram with bold lines; indirect with dashed lines. A pro-regenerative narrative leads to the expectation that policymakers will act in the public interest, strengthens independent media, strengthens citizen engagement directly by making this the norm and indirectly through encouraging civil society, strengthens civil society because engaged citizens want to improve their food system, influences public and private donors to support regenerative food systems and strengthens producers and businesses using regenerative practices because citizens come to expect this and avoid producers and businesses that are not regenerative. They know how to tell regenerative from extractive producers and businesses because they educate themselves about the impacts of food systems through independent media, and they interact directly with the producers and businesses. This is possible in a localized food system; if products come from far away, customers must depend on proxies such as organic or fair trade certification. Note that many private standards lack legitimacy because they were created by multistakeholder initiatives dominated by industry, so it is not always possible to discern which foods are best. As producers and food businesses move toward regenerative practices, there are impacts on environmental quality, public health and well-being; and food businesses are more inclined to invest in restoration and rewarded less for subverting the public interest. Of the interventions described in this chapter, only food sovereignty demands localization of the food system, although cultural shifts and government programs may encourage this as well, such as through numerous "Eat Local" campaigns at the state level in the US.

The possibilities of what is involved in transformation are wide, but it is equally important to look at *who* needs to be involved and who is ultimately responsible for transformation. Social movements and NGOs are necessary because of their role in changing the dominant narrative. But other ideas are on the table as well. They will be considered in Chapter 8 by comparing the ability and responsibility of businesses, citizens, farmers, policymakers and civil society to bring about regenerative food systems.

References

Alliance for Food Sovereignty in Africa (AFSA). 2023. Agroecology is the transformation needed for LDC food sovereignty. Press statement on the occasion of the 5th UN Conference of LDCs, 5–9 March 2023, Doha, Qatar. https://afsafrica.org/press-statement-agroecology-is-the-transformation-needed-for-ldc-food-sovereignty/

Alonso-Fradejas, A, SM Borras, T Holmes, E Holt-Gimenez and MJ Robbins. 2017. *Food Sovereignty: Convergence and Contradictions, Conditions and Challenges*. London: Routledge.

Alvarado, F. 2020. Miami escalates assault on homeless people by regulating public feedings. *Miami New Times*. https://www.miaminewtimes.com/news/miami-ordinance-limits-public-feeding-of-homeless-11665011

Anchors in Action. 2023. Alliance responds to growing demand for values-based food. https://www.anchorsinaction.org/press-room

Anderson, CR, J Bruil, MJ Chappell, C Kiss and MP Pimbert. 2021. *Agroecology Now! Transformations Towards More Just and Sustainable Food Systems*. Cham: Springer Nature.

Anderson, MD. 2023. Expanding food democracy: a perspective from the United States. *Front Sustain Food Syst* 7:1144090. https://doi.org/10.3389/fsufs.2023.1144090

Andrews, D, K Smith and MA Morena. 2019. Enraged: women and nature. *Right to Food and Nutrition Watch*. Global Network for the Right to Food and Nutrition https://www.righttofoodandnutrition.org/enraged-women-and-nature

Barkin, D. 2014. Contribution to Great Transition Initiative forum on radical ecological democracy. https://www.greattransition.org/commentary/david-barkin-radical-ecological-democracy-ashish-kothari

Bezner Kerr, R, S Madsen, M Stüber, J Liebert, S Enloe, N Borghino, P Parros, DM Mutyambai, M Prudhon and A Wezel. 2021. Can agroecology improve food security and nutrition? A review. *Glob Food Secur* 29:100540. https://doi.org/10.1016/j.gfs.2021.100540

Bezner Kerr, R, JC Postigo, P Smith, A Cowie, PK Singh, M Rivera-Ferre, MC Tirado-von der Pahlen, D Campbell and H Neufeldt. 2023. Agroecology as a transformative approach to tackle climatic, food, and ecosystemic crises. *Curr Opinion Env Sust* 62:101275. https://doi.org/10.1016/j.cosust.2023.101275

Bolotnikova, M. 2022. How US government diet guidelines ignore the climate crisis. *The Guardian* (26 August). https://www.theguardian.com/environment/2022/aug/26/usda-diet-guide-myplate-climate-crisis

Booth, R. 2022. Beyond the right to food? *New Socialist* (9 April). https://newsocialist.org.uk/transmissions/beyond-right-food/

Bora, S. 2022. Food systems should be central to slimate and biodiversity solutions. The Nature Conservancy. https://www.nature.org/en-us/what-we-do/our-insights/perspectives/climate-health-energy-food-crisis-intersectionality/

Calvário, R and AA Desmarais. 2023. The feminist dimensions of food sovereignty: insights from La Via Campesina's politics. *J Peasant Studies* 50(2):640–664. https://doi.org/10.1080/03066150.2022.2153042

Canfield, MC, J Duncan and P Claeys. 2021. Reconfiguring food systems governance: the UNFSS and the battle over authority and legitimacy. *Development* 64:181–191. https://doi.org/10.1057/s41301-021-00312

Center for a Livable Future. 2023. Food policy councils achievements. https://publichealth.jhu.edu/sites/default/files/2023-06/food-policy-council-achievements-2021.jpeg

Chamie, J. 2023. America's high homicide rate. https://www.niussp.org/health-and-mortality/americas-high-homicide-rate/

Chiffoleau, Y and A Loconto. 2018. Social innovation in agriculture and food: old wine in new bottles? *Int J Soc Agri Food* 24(3):306–317. https://doi.org/10.48416/ijsaf.v24i3.13

Civil Society and Indigenous Peoples Mechanism of the Committee on World Food Security (CSIPM). 2022. Voices from the ground 2: transformative solutions to the global systemic food crises. Popular consultation on grassroots impacts of COVID-19, conflicts and crises on the right to food and food sovereignty. https://www.csm4cfs.org/wp-content/uploads/2022/09/layout-CSIPM-report-EN.pdf

Civil Society Mechanism (CSM). 2019. CSM Inputs for the CFS policy convergence process on "Agroecological and other innovative approaches for sustainable agriculture and food systems that enhance food security and nutrition". https://www.csm4cfs.org/csm-written/

Claeys, P and NCS Lambek. 2014. Introduction: in search of better options: food sovereignty, the right to food and legal tools for transforming food systems. Pp. 1–16 In: NCS Lambek, P Claeys, A Wong and L Brilmeyer (Eds). *Rethinking Food Systems. Structural Challenges, New Strategies and the Law*. Berlin: Springer.

Cohen, A, K Garthwaite, J Lohnes and M Wolpold-Bosien. 2023. Rights, not charity. A human rights perspective on corporate food aid. Global Solidarity Alliance for Food, Health and Social Justice; Global Network on the Right to Food and Nutrition FIAN International. https://www.fian.org/en/publication/article/rights-not-charity-a-human-rights-perspective-on-corporate-backed-charitable-food-aid-3188

De Schutter, O. 2010. Countries tackling hunger with a right to food approach. Briefing Note 1. https://www2.ohchr.org/english/issues/food/docs/briefing_note_01_may_2010_en.pdf

De Schutter, O and T Dedeurwaerdere. 2022. *Social Innovation in the Service of Social and Ecological Transformation. The Rise of the Enabling State*. London: Routledge.

Dillon, J. 2018. As Vermont's milk industry continues to free-fall, Canadian dairies are thriving. *National Public Radio*. https://www.npr.org/sections/thesalt/2018/04/06/599434624/as-vermonts-milk-industry-continues-to-free-fall-canadian-dairies-are-thriving

Edelman, M, T Weis, A Baviskar, SM Borras Jr, E Holt-Giménez, D Kandiyoti and W Wolford. 2014. Introduction: critical perspectives on food sovereignty. *J Peasant Studies* 41(6):911–931. https://doi.org/10.1080/03066150.2014.963568

European Commission. 2013. Guide to Social Innovation. https://ec.europa.eu/regional_policy/en/information/publications/guides/2013/guide-to-social-innovation

European Coordination Via Campesina. 2018. Food Sovereignty Now: a Guide to Food Sovereignty. https://viacampesina.org/en/wp-content/uploads/sites/2/2018/02/Food-Sovereignty-A-guide-Low-Res-Vresion.pdf

Fakhri, M. 2022. *Conflict and the right to food - Report of the Special Rapporteur on the right to food, Michael Fakhri*. A/HRC/52/40. Geneva: Human Rights Council.

Food and Agriculture Organization (FAO). 2005. Voluntary Guidelines to Support the Progressive Realization of the Right to Adequate Food in the Context of National Food Security. https://www.fao.org/publications/card/en/c/cceef08f-0627-5ec9-a8e2-63d7c0b608c2/

Food and Agriculture Organization (FAO). 2021. FAO Strategy for Private Sector Engagement, 2021–2025. Rome. https://doi.org/10.4060/cb3352en

Giraldo, OF and PM Rosset. 2023. Emancipatory agroecologies: social and political principles. *J Peasant Studies* 50(3):820–850. https://doi.org/10.1080/03066150.2022.2120808

Gliessman, SR, VE Méndez, VM Izzo and EW Engles. 2023. *Agroecology Leading the Transformation to a Just and Sustainable Food System*, 4th Edition. London: Routledge.

Global Alliance for the Future of Food (GAFF). 2021. The Politics of Knowledge: Understanding the Evidence for Agroecology, Regenerative Approaches, and

Indigenous Foodways. https://futureoffood.org/wp-content/uploads/2022/03/GA-Politics-of-Knowledge.pdf

Government Accountability Office (GAO). 2022. *Corporate Income Tax: Effective Rates Before and After 2017 Law Change.* GAO-23–105384. Washington, DC.

Harvey, D. 2005. *A Brief History of Neoliberalism.* Oxford, UK: Oxford University Press.

Held, L. 2021. At an annual sustainability gathering, Big Ag describes its efforts to control the narrative. *Civil Eats.* https://civileats.com/2021/12/09/at-an-annual-sustainability-gathering-big-ag-describes-its-efforts-to-control-the-narrative/

High Level Panel of Experts (HLPE). 2019. Agroecological and other innovative approaches for sustainable agriculture and food systems that enhance food security and nutrition. A report by the High Level Panel of Experts on Food Security and Nutrition of the Committee on World Food Security. Rome: FAO.

Holligan, A. 2022. Why Dutch farmers are protesting over emissions cuts. *British Broadcasting Company* (29 July). https://www.bbc.com/news/world-europe-62335287

Howard, PH. 2016. *Concentration and Power in the Food System: Who Controls What We Eat?* London: Bloomsbury.

Hubbard, B and DD Kirkpatrick. 2021. A decade after the Arab Spring, autocrats still rule the Mideast. *New York Times* (14 February). https://www.nytimes.com/2021/02/14/world/middleeast/arab-spring-mideast-autocrats.html

Hsu, E. 2019. Policy changes needed for the regenerative agriculture in the US food system. *Medium.* https://medium.com/@elainewhsu/policy-changes-needed-for-the-regenerative-agriculture-in-the-us-food-system-37c1774c5562

Iles, A and M Montenegro de Wit. 2015. Sovereignty at what scale? An inquiry into multiple dimensions of food sovereignty. *Globalizations* 12(4):481–497. https://doi.org/10.1080/14747731.2014.957587

International Assessment of Agricultural Knowledge, Science & Technology for Development (IAASTD). 2009. Agriculture at a Crossroads. http://www.fao.org/fileadmin/templates/est/Investment/Agriculture_at_a_Crossroads_Global_Report_IAASTD.pdf

International Development Law Organization (IDLO) and Irish Aid. 2015. Realizing the Right to Food: Legal Strategies and Approaches. https://www.idlo.int/publications/realizing-right-food-legal-strategies-and-approaches

International Planning Committee for Food Sovereignty (IPC). 2008. Statement at the 2008 World Food Summit, as cited on pg. 730 in P. McMichael. 2023. Critical agrarian studies and crises of the world-historical present. *J Peasant Studies* 50(2):725–757. https://doi.org/10.1080/03066150.2022.2163630

James-Martin, G, DL Baird, GA Hendrie, J Bogard, K Anastasiou, PG Brooker, B Wiggins, G Williams, M Herrero, M Lawrence, AJ Lee, MD Riley. 2022. Environmental sustainability in national food-based dietary guidelines: a global review. *Lancet Planet Health* 6:e977–86. https://doi.org/10.1016/S2542–5196(22)00246-7

Krajnc, A and J O'Toole. 2023. 8 ways NYC Mayor Eric Adams is creating a plant-based city. https://plantbasedtreaty.org/eric-adams-plant-based-city/?mc_cid=37e7323fa5&mc_eid=8ca07679cf

La Via Campesina (LVC). 1996. The right to produce and access to land. Food sovereignty: a future without hunger. Statement on the occasion of the World Food Summit, Rome, Italy, November 11.

La Via Campesina (LVC). 2021. A manifesto for the future of our planet. Official statement from La Via Campesina, as we mark 25 years of our collective struggles for food sovereignty. https://viacampesina.org/en/food-sovereignty-a-manifesto-for-the-future-of-our-planet-la-via-campesina/

McKeon, N. 2011. *Global Governance for World Food Security: A Scorecard Four Years after the Eruption of the "Food Crisis"*. Berlin: Heinrich-Böll-Stiftung.

McKeon, N. 2021. Global food governance. *Development* 64:172–180. https://doi.org/10.1057/s41301-021-00326-9

Mier y Terán Giménez Cacho, M, OF Giraldo, M Aldasoro, H Morales, BG Ferguson, P Rosset, A Kahse and C Campos. 2018. Bringing agroecology to scale: key drivers and emblematic cases. *Agroecol Sust Food Systs* 42(6):637–665. https://doi.org/10.1080/21683565.2018.1443313

Milgroom, J. 2021. Linking food and feminisms: learning from decolonial movements. Agroecology Now! Centre for Agroecology, Water and Resilience, Coventry, UK. https://www.resilience.org/stories/2021-03-08/linking-food-and-feminisms-learning-from-decolonial-movements/

Moyn, S. 2018. *Not Enough. Human Rights in an Unequal World*. Cambridge, MA: Harvard University Press.

National Family Farm Coalition (NFFC). 2023. Milk from Family Dairies Act. https://nffc.net/what-we-do/dairy/

Norwood, FB. 2015. Understanding the food democracy movement. *Choices* 30(4):1–5.

Nyéléni. 2007. Nyéléni Declaration of Nyéléni. https://nyeleni.org/IMG/pdf/DeclNyeleni-en.pdf

Office of the High Commissioner on Human Rights. 2023. About the right to food and human rights. https://www.ohchr.org/en/special-procedures/sr-food/about-right-food-and-human-rights

OpenSecrets.org. 2023. Agribusiness Lobbying and Money to Congress. https://www.opensecrets.org/industries/summary.php?cycle=2022&ind=A

Organization for Economic Cooperation and Development (OECD). 2022. *Corporate Tax Statistics*, 4th Edition. https://www.oecd.org/tax/tax-policy/corporate-tax-statistics-fourth-edition.pdf

Papada, E, D Altman, F Angiolillo, L Gastaldi, T Köhler, M Lundstedt, N Natsika, M Nord, Y Sato, F Wiebrecht and SI Lindberg. 2023. Defiance in the Face of Autocratization. Democracy Report 2023. University of Gothenburg: Varieties of Democracy Institute (V-Dem Institute).

Pimbert, M. 2009. *Towards Food Sovereignty: Reclaiming Autonomous Food Systems*. London: IIED.

Project Drawdown. 2023. Plant-rich diets. https://drawdown.org/solutions/plant-rich-diets and

Recine, E. 2023. This time around Brazil can and must do the anti-hunger fight right. *Al Jazeera* (26 September). https://www.aljazeera.com/opinions/2023/9/26/this-time-around-brazil-can-and-must-do-the-anti-hunger-fight-right

Rossi, A, M Coscarello and D Biolghini. 2021. (Re)commoning food and food systems: the contribution of social innovation from solidarity economy. *Agriculture* 11(6):548. https://doi.org/10.3390/agriculture11060548

Secretaria de Comunicaçao Social. 2023. President Lula reinstates national food council and makes combating hunger a priority. https://www.gov.br/secom/

en/latest-news/president-lula-reinstates-national-food-council-and-makes-combating-hunger-a-priority

Silici, L. 2014. *Agroecology. What it is and What it Has to Offer*. IIED Issue Brief. London: IIED.

Smaje, C. 2023. *Saying NO to a Farm-free Future: The Case for an Ecological Food System and Against Manufactured Foods*. White River Junction, VT: Chelsea Green Publishing.

Soffiantini, G. 2020. Food insecurity and political instability during the Arab Spring. *Glob Food Secur* 26:100400. https://doi.org/10.1016/j.gfs.2020.100400

Springmann, M, M Clark, D Mason D'Croz, K Wiebe, BL Bodirsky and L Lassalette. 2018. Options for keeping the food system within environmental limits. *Nature* 562(7728). https://doi.org/10.1038/s41586-018-0594-0

Sundaram, JK. 2023. PPPs fiscal hoax is a blank financial silver bullet. *Inter Press News Agency* (8 November). https://www.ipsnews.net/2023/11/ppps-fiscal-hoax-blank-financial-silver-bullet/

Tax Foundation. 2021. Historical U.S. Federal Corporate Income Tax Rates & Brackets, 1909–2020. https://taxfoundation.org/data/all/federal/historical-corporate-tax-rates-brackets/

Tom, K. 2020. Dinner speech at Agricultural Outlook Forum Program: The Innovation Imperative: Shaping the Future of Agriculture. https://www.usda.gov/oce/ag-outlook-forum/past-programs#2020aof

Trevilla Espinal, DL, ML Soto Pinto, H Morales and EIJ Estrada-Lugo. 2021. Feminist agroecology: analyzing power relationships in food systems. *Agroecol Sust Food Systems* 45(7):1029–1049. https://doi.org/10.1080/21683565.2021.1888842

Türk, V. 2023. Statement by UN Human Rights Chief on human rights economy (20 April 2023). Office of the High Commissioner for Human Rights. https://www.ohchr.org/en/statements-and-speeches/2023/04/statement-un-human-rights-chief-human-rights-economy

United Nations Children's Fund (UNICEF). 2023. *Engaging with the Food and Beverage Industry*. New York: UNICEF Programme Guidance.

United States Department of Agriculture (USDA) and United States Department of Health and Human Services (HHS). 2020. *Dietary Guidelines for Americans, 2020–2025*. 9th Edition. Washington, DC: USDA and HHS.

United Nations General Assembly (UNGA). 2019. Resolution adopted by the General Assembly on 17 December 2018. United Nations Declaration on the Rights of Peasants and Other People Working in Rural Areas. A/Res/73/165. https://www.geneva-academy.ch/joomlatools-files/docman-files/UN percent20Declaration percent20on percent20the percent20rights percent20of percent20peasants.pdf

Wezel, A, S Bellon, T Doré, C Francis, D Vallod and C David. 2009. Agroecology as a science, a movement and a practice. A review. *Agron Sustain Dev* 29:503–515.

Willett, W, J Rockström, B Loken, M Springmann, S Vermeulen, T Garnett, D Tilman, F DeClerck, AWood, M Jonell, M Clark, LJ Gordon, J Fanzo, C Hawkes, R Zurayk, JA Rivera, W De Vries, L Majele Sibanda, A Afshin, A Chaudhary, M Herrero, R Agustina, F Branca, A Lartey, S Fan, B Crona, E Fox, V Bignet, MTroell, T Lindahl, S Singh, SE Cornell, K Srinath Reddy, S Narain, S Nishtar and CJL Murray. 2019. Food in the anthropocene: the EAT–*Lancet* Commission on healthy diets from sustainable food systems. *The Lancet* 393(10170):447–492. https://doi.org/10.1016/S0140-6736(18)31788-4

Wittman, H. 2023. Food sovereignty: an inclusive model for feeding the world and cooling the planet. *One Earth* 6:474–478.

World Bank. 2008. *World Development Report 2008: Agriculture for Development.* Washington, DC: World Bank.

World Health Organization. 2023. Red and processed meat in the context of health and the environment: many shades of red and green. *Information Brief*. https://iris.who.int/bitstream/handle/10665/370775/9789240074828eng.pdf?sequence=1

Zaremba, H, M Elias, A Rietveld and N Bergamini. 2021. Toward a feminist agroecology. *Sustainability* 13:11244. https://doi.org/10.3390/su132011244

Zhu, J, Z Luo, T Sun, W Li, W Zhou, X Wang, X Fei, H Ton and K Yei. 2023. Cradle-to-grave emissions from food loss and waste represent half of total greenhouse gas emissions from food systems. *Nat Food* 4:247–256. https://doi.org/10.1038/s43016-023-00710-3

8

WHO WILL LEAD TRANSFORMATION?

A frequently heard call to action is that all of us are necessary for food system transformation. "Whether as a consumer, producer, retailer, distributor, investor or innovator—we all have a role to play in delivering the deep transformational change that's so urgently needed—and so long overdue" surmised Lesley Mitchell when she directed global food systems practice at Forum for the Future (Mitchell 2021, n.p.). And Amina Mohammed, Deputy UN Secretary-General, tweeted after the UN Food Systems Summit+2 in 2023: "The time for #FoodSystems transformation is now and depends on each of us working collectively and in solidarity." But whose behavior needs to change most? Aren't some actors already using transformative practices? Could some behavioral changes exert leverage that would compel other changes? Who has agency to change and who doesn't? Who is ultimately responsible and accountable? This chapter explores the different capacities of actors who are part of the food system.

Although this chapter echoes some of the material in Chapters 6 and 7, the focus here is on the actors who will actually carry out food system transformation. For each actor, we look at the implicit theory of change (i.e., why this actor is particularly important), assumptions about how they will support regeneration and necessary pre-conditions to allow this to happen.

Large Businesses as Change Agents

> Businessmen and businesses are best placed to save the world
>
> *(Bill Gates in BER 2019, n.p.)*

DOI: 10.4324/9781003260264-11

Implicit Theory of Change

- If the largest food businesses switch to regenerative practices and donate to regeneration, we will have regenerative food systems.

Implicit Assumptions

- Companies have sufficient incentives to improve their ecological and social footprints.
- Companies will follow the leaders in sustainability programs, instead of "racing to the bottom."
- Companies will continue their efforts to become more sustainable, not plateau after making modest improvements.

Several large agribusinesses, including some that produce the products that are most harmful to public health, biodiversity and a stable climate, have tried to jump on the sustainability or regenerative bandwagon. Large corporate retailers have followed suit. Every company posts regular sustainability reports with glowing assessments of its progress and commitments. For example, in July 2023, PepsiCo and Walmart announced a 7-year collaboration to invest $120 million in US and Canadian farmers who are trying to improve soil health and water quality (Walmart 2023, n.p.). They aim to enable and accelerate the adoption of regenerative agriculture practices on more than 2 million acres of farmland and deliver approximately 4 million metric tons of greenhouse gas (GHG) emission reductions and removals by 2030 (Walmart 2023). Walmart's website describes the collaboration as a "voluntary, flexible approach to regenerative agriculture that gives farmers a seat at the table, recognizes the diversity of agriculture and that one size does not fit all." Jane Ewing, Senior Vice President for Sustainability at Walmart, claimed that "our sustainability strategy is built to make the everyday choice the sustainable choice for our customers." PepsiCo's goals (with the sprightly name of "pep+" for PepsiCo Positive) include driving the adoption of regenerative agriculture practices across 7 million acres by 2030 and reducing absolute GHG emissions by more than 40 percent across its entire value chain by 2030 (against a 2015 baseline) while striving toward net-zero emissions by 2040. Walmart's goal is to "restore or more sustainably manage 50 million acres of land and 1 million square miles of ocean by 2030 along with the Walmart Foundation."

The announcement about this commitment is full of inspiring language: supporting farming communities, empowering farmers, working "very hard" to gain farmers' trust, investment, profitability, transforming farming in a way that benefits the planet and people. What's not to like? The catch is what they mean by regenerative agriculture, whether the practices they will reward will actually result in the intended results and how they will be validated, how decisions about the program will be made and by whom. Regenerative agriculture is notoriously vague and encompasses a broad range of practices (IDS and IPES-Food 2022; Gordon et al. 2023). Although it includes many worthwhile practices that increase soil fertility and thereby sequester carbon in the soil, it does not have an internationally recognized definition that puts clear boundaries on what is in and what is out. And the bigger questions for this example are about the products that PepsiCo and Walmart produce and market. Does the world really need Pepsi and Fritos? And how much does Walmart contribute to excessive consumption, waste and non-recyclable products with planned obsolescence? These businesses might not make the cut of "essential" and "life-promoting" by degrowth criteria.

Numerous business coalitions have formed to advance more sustainable food systems, with examples including the Sustainable Agricultural Initiative Platform in the EU and Sustainable Food Lab (US-based). Several business coalitions deal with food systems as part of their repertoire, although they also consider many other issues and systems, e.g., the World Economic Forum and the World Business Council for Sustainable Development. Like MSIs, many coalitions have strong business membership but also include UN or government agencies and foundations. Some examples are the Sustainable Productivity Coalition, Scaling Up Nutrition and the Global Alliance for Improved Nutrition. Many businesses work independently or in partnership with government agencies or NGOs on more sustainable food systems. Finding out the extent to which food and agricultural industries support various coalitions or how much they contribute to partnerships is often difficult; the admonition to "follow the money" is impossible to follow because budgets are not public.

Why is the private sector involved in food system transformation, especially since the largest food businesses are benefiting handsomely from the current food system? The top 25 companies in the food and beverage sector, led by Nestlé, Anheuser-Busch InBev and PepsiCo, generated $1.8 trillion in revenue in 2022, while profits for the sector increased that year to more than $160 billion (Popli 2023; Sorvino 2023). Large pesticide and fertilizer companies are extremely profitable, especially in crisis years like 2022. Two investment firms, Blackrock Inc. and Vanguard Group, Inc., accounted for most of the shareholding in eight of the largest publicly traded pesticide and fertilizer companies (Mousseau 2022). Overall *profits* from fertilizer sales alone for 2021 and 2022 amounted to $84 billion or more than 30 times what US farmers were projected to pay for fertilizer imports in 2022 ($1.9 billion). Nine of the biggest fertilizer companies were projected to rake in $57 billion in profit in 2022, a fourfold increase from two years prior. In 2020, Nutrien, Yara, Mosaic, ICL Group, CF Industries, PhosAgro, OCI, K+S and OCP reported combined profits just under $13 billion dollars (Swann 2023).

Some of the increase was precipitated by the ways that Russia's invasion of Ukraine disrupted fertilizer and natural gas sales, but claims of price gouging are prevalent.

Perhaps because of this cornucopia of profits amid ongoing crises that gobble up public funds, the private sector is being asked or told with increasing frequency to contribute to sustainability, nutrition and food security initiatives (Haddad and Smaller 2021). An online survey by the media platform Devex found that 91 percent of development professionals believe that increased private sector engagement is critical to achieving the SDGs (Verizon and Devex 2021). Additional reasons why the private sector, especially the largest food and agribusiness companies, are targets for initiatives to increase sustainability are that even incremental changes in a very large business may have big impacts (much larger than a host of changes in small farms or businesses). In addition, changes in the private sector are essential to create regenerative food systems, given that companies are most responsible for extractive food systems. Companies are eager to back the perception that they care about sustainability, as evidenced by their efforts to produce Corporate Social Responsibility reports and to advertise their achievements on their own websites.

In fact, "doing good" can be a competitive advantage for a business. The "business case" for investing in solutions to hunger includes the following:

- new market and product development that is or has potential to become commercially viable with market expansion and economies of scale
- stimulating innovation in the company
- reputation management and building positive brand value
- motivating employees directly through volunteering or indirectly through association with a company addressing social issues
- strengthening government and community relations, especially in poor countries
- developing a healthy and productive labor force in low-income countries
- contributing to economic development and building long-term markets
- enacting corporate values

The solution most favored by the private sector for overcoming malnutrition in a survey conducted by GAIN was biofortification, an example of the first incentive above (Nelson 2007). While this tactic may address specific nutrient or micronutrient deficiencies, it is not a solution that will increase autonomy or agency of undernourished people or address malnutrition in the long term. The private sector has many other opportunities for reducing hunger and improving nutrition, including sourcing from small-scale producers in low-income countries, developing and supporting small and medium-scale enterprises for processing and distribution, investing in innovations to help small-scale producers and businesses, extending essential services and infrastructure, educating women and girls and partnering with governments and NGOs to increase their capacity.

The final item on this list, public-private partnerships (PPP), has come under increased scrutiny by civil society over the last few years, although PPPs may bring funds to specific worthwhile projects (Smyth et al. 2021). Public funding of research and development has declined by one-third over the last two decades in the US, at the same time that investment in R&D by food and agrochemical input industries has increased (Fuglie and Nelson 2022). The need for additional financing to solve food system problems and implement national pathways was emphasized at the UN Food Systems Summit "stocktaking" in 2023 by the Director General of FAO, Qu Dongyu. At the event's closing, Amina Mohammed, the Deputy Secretary General of the UN, announced a new "Joint SDG Fund's Food Systems Window" to serve as a mechanism to mobilize financing and expertise and "leverage broader investments through blended financing and partnership with the private sector" (Mohammed 2023, n.p.).

While many studies point to the potential of PPPs, examples that have advanced regenerative agriculture, even in part, are acknowledged to be hard to find (HLPE 2018; Kennedy et al. 2021). This may be due to constraints pointed out by Spielman and Grebmer (2006): fundamentally different incentive structures, prohibitive direct and indirect costs, mutually negative perceptions between the sectors, and high levels of competition and risk associated with valuable assets and resources. Or it may be due to the reasons why civil society has been so critical of multistakeholder initiatives generally: business interests tend to dominate the partnership and activities are focused on whatever has potential profits to the business rather than needs expressed by the community that is ostensibly being served. Other drawbacks of PPPs included in the HLPE (2018) report are that they can:

- increase corporate influence on political discourse and agenda-setting and weaken representative democracy;
- contribute to focus attention on issues where technical solutions can bring immediate benefits at the expense of, instead of addressing the needs of, the most vulnerable;
- contribute to the fragmentation of global food governance, raising new challenges in terms of accountability, coherence and efficiency and
- threaten the stable delivery of public goods and services when funding relies more on private sources and becomes increasingly expensive and unpredictable—as has occurred in some cases of PPPs delivering water utilities (such as in Cochabamba, Bolivia, and Flint, Michigan in the US).

There are additional limitations imposed by industry on NGOs trying to work with them on food system issues. Irit Tamir, Director of Oxfam America's Private Sector Department, noted (2023):

> Companies will engage us when we are talking about policies around the edges. And what I mean by that is sort of the floor, the most basic of compliance when it comes to things like forced labor, child labor, or even when it comes to land issues. Where we can never penetrate is when we're going directly at their business model. So when you start talking about, you know, distribution of value, who's getting the money, raising prices, the conversation stops quite quickly. Companies are not willing to engage on those kinds of topics in a robust way.

While many governmental and intergovernmental officials are turning to partnerships with the private sector, are food and agricultural businesses trustworthy partners? Given the weakness of Corporate Social Responsibility, failures to disclose conflicts of interest in policymaking forums such as the UN Food Systems Summit and backsliding on voluntary commitments to improve outcomes such as the nutritional value of products or reductions in plastic use, some are dubious. Yates et al. (2021, 5) argue:

> Big Food's track record ... demonstrate[s] a lack of responsibility that, in turn, fails to engender trust. Given this track record, we ask: is it reasonable to expect researchers, practitioners and government policy-makers to engage with such companies in processes of evidence generation, policy agenda-setting or determining solutions for food systems transformation? And if so, where should the onus for such engagement lie?... [P]owerful transnational companies must demonstrate clear adherence to the principle of "do no harm" and make significant, independently verifiable progress in improving food environments and impacts along product life-cycles before mutual engagement and collaboration can be expected.

Food industries are worried about slippage in their reputations. A study conducted for the Food Marketing Institute and Grocery Manufacturers Association (Deloitte 2016, 1) noted:

> According to interviews with retail and manufacturing executives, consumers have an unprecedented ability to access information about products and share this information via social media, making it more challenging than ever for companies to manage messaging. In addition, many consumers have signaled a distrust of the established food industry in spite of retailers' and manufacturers' traditional efforts to keep consumers positively

engaged with their brands. These consumer-led disruptions represent an opportunity, even an imperative, for manufacturers and retailers to reset and reposition themselves with consumers and shoppers.

Béné (2022) posited that the concentration of resources in the hands of "Big Food" (the largest seed, agrichemical, agrifood and retail corporations) is the first of three major barriers to food system transformation due to visible and hidden influences that allow Big Food to maintain its power and the status quo. Lack of transparency on the part of food industry about activities is a formidable obstacle, as is double-dealing such that a corporation will agree to progressive policies with partners but lobby against them at the same time (or be part of trade associations that lobby against these policies). In *Who's Tipping the Scales?* (IPES-Food 2023), authors argued that the concentration and dominance of food industries are damaging processes, outcomes and accountability of global food system governance, resulting in weak governance tilted toward industry interests.

Given that new funds are needed to implement most of the ideas for transforming the food system, what will be their source? We might calculate the costs to the public interest of private sector activities (e.g., health costs borne by governments and individuals of obesity and diet-related disease, pollinator declines due to pesticides, water contamination by pesticides and fertilizer runoff) and bill the responsible parties. The full cost of the US food system, including health costs of diet-related diseases, environmental costs of greenhouse gas emissions and biodiversity loss and social costs to marginalized, underpaid workers and producers is more than three times the direct cost of food expenditures: approximately USD $3.2 trillion (Rockefeller Foundation 2021). The latest State of Food and Agriculture report from FAO included a first attempt to identify hidden costs of environmental and social damage caused by the global food system (Lord 2023). The expected damage to global gross domestic product (GDP) at purchasing power parity (PPP) in 2023 from the hidden costs of agrifood systems was around 13 trillion in 2020 PPP dollars and trending upwards. At present, those costs are being absorbed by people who are alive now (mainly those in low-income countries), future generations and the environment.

The "polluter pays" approach seems to be gaining popularity among civil society actors in the US with respect to the damages caused by climate change and the clear evidence that fossil fuel companies knew about the dangers well before they became evident to the public. A similar argument could be brought against food and agrichemical companies which have consistently externalized health, environmental and social costs and profited from damaging the commons and public health, even when they knew about risks. For example, Monsanto was aware of studies showing links between glyphosate and cancer for years, yet tried to cover them up (Gillam 2021; Seralini et al. 2021).

Other approaches to finding funds to transform food systems that would not require PPPs or direct engagement with the private sector include fair taxation and closing tax loopholes, legislation forcing industry to internalize their costs so that less external money is needed for repair and restoration and re-directing subsidies that now benefit the private sector to benefit the public interest. A stunning majority (87 percent) of the $540 billion that goes to agricultural producers each year supports practices that are inefficient and inequitable, distort food prices, hurt people's health, and degrade the environment (FAO, UNDP and UNEP 2021). None of these approaches is politically palatable or feasible in the current neoliberal food system. Even modest measures, such as asking beverage industries to cover the costs of recycling bottles, are met with strident resistance from industry. Especially in the current context of increasing rifts in the US between far-right and left politicians and a disengaged public, imposing restrictions on US business to make it more transparent and accountable seems virtually impossible. That is, the most likely future scenario is a continuation or even escalation of the influences of industry shown in Figure 5.3.

In sum, large businesses are not likely change agents for regenerative food systems despite professed support and financial commitments. They are often the source of environmental or social degradation, or products that undermine public health and well-being. Their primary motivation is earning profits, not benefiting the public interest; so they cannot justify to their shareholders distributing profits more equitably to producers, using more environmentally sound practices, investing in land and water restoration or switching to healthier products unless these efforts result in higher profits. A business that is truly supporting regenerative food systems might source preferentially from disadvantaged producers, provide technical assistance so that the poorest producers can improve the quality of their harvests, provide transparent information about public health risks of products that they sell and have low-income or disadvantaged producers on their boards instead of wealthy patrons from other corporations, banks or investment firms. Such actions would demonstrate commitment to the public interest. But big businesses are deeply entrenched in the current neoliberal food system, which is already tilted in their favor. At the most, we can hope that they will desist from their most destructive activities to protect their brands.

Philanthropists as Change Agents

Implicit Theory of Change

- The wealthiest people in the world will act on incentives to invest in making food systems regenerative.

Implicit Assumptions

- People who have mastered profit maximization understand how to act in the public interest.
- Billionaires want to invest in regenerative food systems, following the lead of community organizations that understand local needs.
- Regenerative food systems are held back primarily by a lack of funding.

> The successful initiatives of the Gates Foundation have been hailed as proof that market is king and that privatization of philanthropy is the most efficient approach to creating change.
>
> (*BER 2019, n.p.*)

> Philanthropy aimed at promoting rights and empowerment has an outsized role to play in [the food system transformation] field… [P]hilanthropy plays a pivotal role in supporting narrative change and building a collective vision for change that is largely missing nowadays. In the United States, the USFRA [US Farmers and Ranchers in Action] has produced a compelling vision for the Decade [of] Ag, along with supporting powerful storytelling pieces, all of which can only be done through philanthropic capital.
>
> (*Bellone 2021, n.p.*)

Financial investment by private donors obviously can serve many agendas. Rockefeller Foundation and Bill & Melinda Gates Foundation donations to AGRA have supported extractive food systems, despite its rhetoric of serving hundreds of millions with nourishing food, improving smallholder productivity and preserving the environment (Rockefeller Foundation 2023). These US-based foundations have gained extraordinary wealth and power because of the US tax system which favors wealthy people and the Republican Party's eagerness to reduce taxes on wealth and income. Philanthropists operate outside the political system to a large extent; their charitable giving must comply with law (e.g., in the US, private foundations are required to distribute at least 5 percent of their net investment assets annually in the form of charitable donations); but otherwise they are free agents and investment in the foundation is tax-exempt other than a small excise tax. They can spend money on programs that are not accountable to the public interest or public officials nor subject to unbiased evaluations.

Foundation assets total $1.5 trillion US dollars, heavily concentrated in the United States (60 percent) and Europe (37 percent) (Johnson 2018). The growth of foundations has been very recent; out of approximately 80,000 foundations from Hong Kong and 19 countries included in a global report cohort, 44 percent were established in this century and almost three quarters (72 percent) were established since 1992 (Johnson 2018). This reflects the rise in inequality that accompanied neoliberalism; income inequality has risen in most advanced economies and major emerging economies, which together account for about two-thirds of the world's population and 85 percent of global GDP. The increase has been especially large in the United States, China, India, and Russia (Qureshi 2023). Peter Turchin, a historian who has studied cycles of societal collapse, wrote that the "over-production" of elites (billionaires, trillionaires) combined with the immiseration of the masses of people are the factors most likely to trigger civil wars and eventual breakdown of a functioning government (Turchin 2023).

Philanthrocapitalism is a capitalist, for-profit, market-based approach to solving problems made possible by the increase in billionaires and incentives they have for charitable giving. Investments can be used to promote models of profit maximization from the private sector that allowed the philanthrocapitalist to accumulate the wealth they are looking to "redistribute" in the public sector. Such market-based "solutions" are often inappropriate for improving social welfare and may hurt the people they are designed to help. Yet many philanthrocapitalists are greatly admired for their charitable largesse (which does not cut into their own lifestyles), and they get a political platform to make pronouncements on issues about which they have little experience, yet which can affect the well-being of millions of people. This greatly extends the power that they are already exerting by their financial investments (Schwab 2023). As an example, Bill Gates, the wealthiest philanthrocapitalist, is frequently invited to keynote college graduations and international events, at a price-tag of $100,000-$200,000 per event (All American Entertainment 2023).

The lack of public accountability and transparency is a serious shortcoming of private donor giving, but many donors are providing invaluable support to regenerative food systems. For example, the Global Alliance for the Future of Food (GAFF 2019), a strategic alliance of 27 foundations, is knit together by 7 principles which apply to regenerative food systems: renewable, resilient, equitable, diverse, healthy, inclusive and interconnected. GAFF members came together to fund the *Beacons of Hope* initiative, which showcased case studies of communities around the world that are successfully addressing climate change, migration, urbanization, the need for healthier diets, and other challenges (Biovision and Global Alliance for the Future of Food 2019). Recently they worked with contributors from every region of the globe to identify the evidence behind agroecology, regenerative agriculture and Indigenous food systems and why detractors have refuted that evidence (Global Alliance for the Future of Food 2021).

Regenerative food systems are dramatically underfunded, compared with industrialized and extractive systems (e.g., DeLonge et al. 2016; Pimbert and Moeller 2018; Biovision and IPES-Food 2020). Non-governmental organizations and social movements that are spearheading regenerative food systems spend inordinate amounts of time trying to get grants and crafting their aims in ways that private donors will support. Governments should be supporting these programs with research, development and implementation, rather than continuing to subsidize and stand behind extractive agriculture. NGOs can expand the reach of government to create regenerative food systems if government at all scales is in an enabling rather than controlling or obstructing mode.

Increasing numbers and wealth of private donors can usurp the responsibilities of governments to provide for their people's needs by funding adequate social protection networks, research and programs to protect and restore goods and services that are in the public interest. Without fair tax policies, which most wealthy people resist, billionaires will continue to proliferate and dominate charitable giving with market-based programs. This creates a vicious circle, and the dominant narrative tends to support it by fawning on billionaires who donate to charity and failing to question whether neoliberal policies and politicians supporting them are truly in the public interest. Given the exigencies imposed by climate change, pandemics and biodiversity loss, we need an alternative that can break the strangle-hold of neoliberalism on international and domestic food policies.

Consumers as Change Agents

Implicit Theory of Change

- If every person chose to buy foods from regenerative food systems, demand for these foods would increase, more producers and businesses would start using regenerative practices and prices would go down.

Implicit Assumptions

- Everyone has the agency to purchase foods with low environmental and social impacts.
- Food from regenerative food systems is affordable, accessible and widely available.
- Consumers are sufficiently aware of problems associated with extractive food systems and care enough that they will preferentially purchase food from regenerative food systems.
- Food from regenerative food systems is identifiable in marketplaces.
- Food from regenerative food systems can outcompete food from extractive systems in terms of price, convenience and the organoleptic properties such as flavor that drive consumer purchases.

> Food is different. You can simply stop participating in a system that abuses animals or poisons the water or squanders jet fuel flying asparagus around the world. You can vote with your fork, in other words, and you can do it three times a day.
>
> *(Pollan 2006, n.p.)*

At least some consumers have the power to "vote with their forks"; but all too many people either don't have food at all, or have no choice over what they will eat. Relatively wealthy people do have agency to select foods that are raised in regenerative ways. This potential excites many academicians and people working in NGOs and foundations: if consumer power could be harnessed, then producers and businesses would have strong encouragement to change their practices to be regenerative. Countless campaigns have been launched to encourage people to eat less meat, for example, in the face of considerable evidence that red meat production is a primary contributor to greenhouse gas emissions from the food system (and over-use of water and other resources) and its overconsumption is linked with several kinds of cancer.

The consumer-driven theory of change is a lovely virtuous circle, but how realistic is it? In support of the assumptions behind it is the growing market share of organic food in the US (a proxy for food from regenerative food systems) from $26.9 billion in 2010 (inflation adjusted to 2021 dollars) to $61.7 billion in 2022 (OTA 2023). The organic food sector is growing faster than other food sectors. A study from the Organic Trade Association using data from a large, nationally representative sample found that more than 80 percent of US households purchased organic food in 2016. Customers who were born between 1981 and 1986/87 (millennials) were more likely to purchase organic food than older generations (ERS 2023a; OTA 2023). Organic food sales have risen even more dramatically in other countries, as has organic food production (Willer et al. 2023).

But how good a proxy is organic sales for regenerative food system abundance? The primary motivation for purchasing organic food in the US is concerns about personal health or family members' health, although awareness of environmental impacts, level of education, availability, price differentials and perceived norms also play a role (Gundala and Singh 2021). Producers may be looking at price premiums more than environmental impacts as they switch to organic production systems. Several studies have demonstrated that organic producers do not always have better labor practices than others, and organic standards do not always reflect the best environmental practices. For example, organic farms may have soil erosion and some approved organic products have higher toxicity that synthetic products. Furthermore, organic food is available from the mainstream retailers where most customers buy their food. The food may be healthier and entail lower environmental risks, but supporting concentrated retail outlets is not a way to further regenerative food systems which share the value of food purchases equitably with small-scale producers and distributors. That said, eliminating or reducing synthetic agrochemicals does have solid environmental benefits for soil and water quality and health benefits for farmers, farmworkers and communities that otherwise would be subjected to pesticide drift from industrialized farms. And organic farmers often use direct marketing such as farmers' markets or community-supported agriculture, or sell through food cooperatives, rather than selling through superstores or concentrated retail chains.

We need to consider the "vote with your fork" narrative in the context of the extant neoliberal food system, where industry and governments that are closely aligned with industry continue to support extractive food systems and encourage customers to buy their products. "Vote with your fork" messages may be barely audible above the blaring cacophony of advertising and sales messages. And "choice" among products is often illusory, given the concentration of food companies. Customers may think that they are supporting independent progressive companies, even when they are all owned by the same industry. For example, PepsiCo controls 88 percent of the chips market in the US, because it owns five of the most popular brands including Tostitos, Lay's and Fritos. Ninety-three percent of the sodas sold in the US are owned by just three companies, and three companies own 73 percent of our breakfast cereals despite the variety stocking the shelves in supermarkets (Lakhani et al. 2021). Amanda Starbuck from Food & Water Watch described monopolization in the US food system (in Lakhani et al. 2021, n.p.):

> It's a system designed to funnel money into the hands of corporate shareholders and executives while exploiting farmers and workers and deceiving consumers about choice, abundance and efficiency.

The main factors that US consumers have taken into account over the last few decades as they make food purchases are price, taste and convenience (Deloitte 2016). Brand recognition has also been important. But customer preferences have shifted, especially as a result of the COVID pandemic. As restaurants closed, people started eating at home more and buying food online. Pre-existing health conditions including obesity and diet-related diseases were demonstrated to be strong predictors of hospitalization and mortality from COVID; but it is not clear whether customers have started eating healthier diets with more fruits and vegetables and less red meat, fats, salt and sugar as a consequence. Similarly, the flood of recent events caused by global warming may have induced more people to look for products from regenerative food systems; but this has not been shown in the scientific literature yet.

Customer preferences for foods from regenerative food systems would be much easier to gauge if there were markets in all regions that limited sales to such foods. These have appeared in Mexico, Colombia, Mozambique and several other countries (Loconto et al. 2018). They often use Participatory Guarantee Systems (PGS) to verify that products are grown without synthetic inputs. PGS involves producers along with customers or other people who are knowledgeable about local agriculture visiting each other's farms to ascertain production practices. Territorial markets that are scaled to a locale or region and sell products from small- to medium-scale farms are also appearing or being revived; buying from these markets supports smallholders, although production methods may vary.

In the US, farmers' markets that sell local products are quite common; but there are no agroecological markets labeled as such. Customers can buy products in supermarkets, food cooperatives and other stores that bear the USDA organic label, meaning that they are certified to follow a set of standards developed by a national advisory board. However, establishing a comparable agroecological label is not a popular option among producers; many people do not want to give the US government control over defining agroecology, given that the government has ignored or been hostile to agroecology previously. And some people believe that the organic "brand" has been watered down since it came under USDA control, no longer adhering to the principles that attracted producers and consumers originally. These original principles came much closer to regenerative food systems. The International Federation of Organic Agriculture Movements has responded by proposing a new "Organic 3.0" for "truly sustainable production and consumption" (IFOAM 2017). Its core principles (4) are:

- a culture of innovation;
- continuous improvement toward best practices;
- diversity of ways to ensure transparent integrity beyond 3rd-party certification;
- inclusion of wider sustainability interests via alliances with organizations that have similar values;
- empowerment from the farm to the final consumer with special attention to small-scale farmers, gender equality and fair trade and
- true value and cost accounting by internalizing costs and benefits, encouraging transparency and empowering farmers as partners with rights.

Meanwhile, the "Real Organic Project" has sprung up in the US to distinguish products that are soil-grown and pasture-raised from USDA-organic certified. But the extent to which customers are looking for alternative food labels and certification schemes that come closer to regenerative food systems than organic is not clear.

In sum, consumers are not likely candidates to lead food system transformation even though some do seek out products from regenerative food systems and support them through advocacy and other means. Only relatively wealthy and well-educated consumers have real agency to buy selectively and food from regenerative food systems may be neither available, affordable nor accessible to poor or disadvantaged customers. Most consumers have too many distractions to pay attention to messages from regenerative food systems, are usually not sufficiently well informed to make good choices (because finding objective information about food system impacts and alternatives requires active work) and have difficulties distinguishing products from regenerative food systems where they buy food.

If we return to Figure 5.4 and impose consumer choice on our diagram, we see that the most we can achieve is to move a greater proportion of sales into the regenerative food system category, thereby encouraging more production by producers aligned with these values. But toggling to a larger proportion of sales does nothing to change the dominant narrative nor the underlying power dynamics unless the number of customers demanding food from regenerative food systems reaches a tipping point such that extractive food systems are outcompeted. Given that 95 percent of food purchases in the US now come from concentrated supermarket chains and government support is tilted to extractive industry, we are not even close to that tipping point.

In Figure 8.1, the heavy lines from citizens to producers and food businesses reflect changed purchasing preferences in the direction of more regenerative practices. These benefit producers and businesses using these practices. There are secondary impacts on improving environmental quality, public health and well-being as less food from extractive systems is purchased. But at best

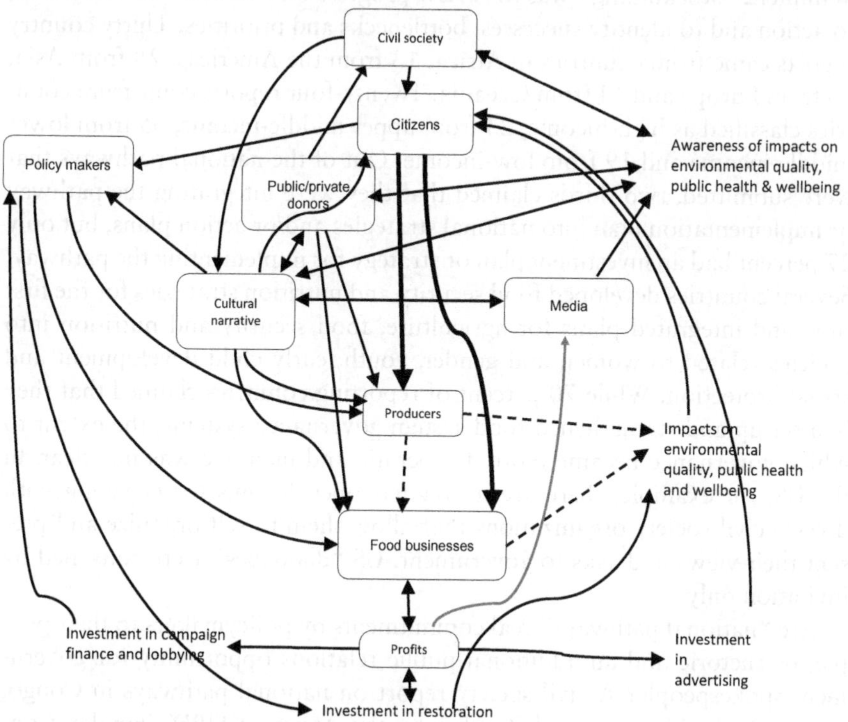

FIGURE 8.1 Effects of "voting with your fork."

we have tertiary impacts on the cultural narrative, as impacts of the extractive food system diminish, because other forces that affect the narrative continue unabated.

Government Policymakers as Change Agents

(N.B. The theory of change and implicit assumptions regarding government policymakers are the same as those regarding government programs and policies in the preceding chapter.)

International cooperation on food policy faces many challenges, some of which are examined in the next chapter about the Committee on World Food Security. Partly because of the difficulties of getting countries with vastly different levels of resources, types of government, geopolitical dynamics, and needs to work together, the UN Food Systems Summit in 2021 tasked each country with developing a "national pathway" for transformation and appointing a "national convenor" who would organize "dialogues" and create the national pathway. As of the 2023 "stocktaking," 126 countries had adopted national pathways and 155 had identified "national convenors" (UN Secretary-General 2023). One of the objectives of the UN Food Systems Summit+2 "stocktaking" was to review progress on countries' commitments to action and to identify successes, bottlenecks and priorities. Thirty country reports came from countries in Africa, 13 from the Americas, 28 from Asia, 16 from Europe and 14 from Oceania. Twenty-four reports come from countries classified as high-income, 23 from upper middle-income, 35 from lower middle-income and 19 from low-income. Out of the national pathways that were submitted, two-thirds claimed that they were integrating the pathway or implementation plan into national strategies and/or action plans, but only 27 percent had an investment plan or strategy for implementing the pathway. Several countries developed food security and nutrition strategies for the first time and integrated plans for agriculture, food security and nutrition into policies related to women and gender, youth, early child development and social protection. While 70 percent of reporting countries claimed that they had set up and strengthened food system governance systems, the extent to which governance became more democratic and inclusive was not clear. In the US, for example, there are no regular open forums for engaging with diverse civil society organizations that allow them to self-organize and present their views and asks to government. US "dialogues" were convened by invitation only.

Are "national pathways" real commitments by policymakers to their people, or rhetoric and an additional public relations opportunity for government spokespeople? A civil society report on national pathways in Congo, Kenya, Mali, Morocco and Zambia by the African CSIPM Popular Consultation Space (2023) found that Peasant Organizations and civil-society organizations (POs/CSOs) were recognized as key players, were invited to participate and contributed to the drafting of the pathway, but were excluded afterwards; POs/CSOs with a legitimate mandate to represent the views of people's organizations working in food systems were excluded while other CSOs without such a mandate were invited instead; and POs/CSO were invited and participated in the process, but their concerns were ignored in the final document and in the follow-up. In all of the cases studied, except for Mali and Congo Brazzaville, POs/CSOs advocating a rights-based approach were completely omitted from the section of the national pathway action plan regarding monitoring and evaluation systems, with governments foreseeing no role for them in the implementation of the pathway despite the fact that monitoring is a recognized role for civil society. Most governments, while mentioning agroecology and occasionally food sovereignty, drafted documents rooted in a technology-oriented Green Revolution model of production. Their documents lacked reference to a rights-based approach (except for Morocco, Kenya and Mauritania) and emphasized the corporate private sector as a key actor in food system transformation. In addition, the civil society report pointed to problems in ways that gender equity and youth's access to opportunities were addressed in all of the countries studied.

The statements from the US Secretary of Agriculture on the US pathway were brief and general, applauding a recent commitment of funds by the US President which would be divided 50:50 between domestic and international work. Given that there is no mechanism for holding governments accountable to their "national pathways," we might discount the "dialogues" and "national pathways" that came out of the UN Food Systems Summit as hot air. But clearly there were good intentions behind many of the efforts and the exercises may have brought greater attention at the national level to food system issues. Astonishingly, only half of the countries recognized the urgency of adapting food systems to climate change and promoting environmental resilience in their national pathways: this is guaranteed to become a pressing issue in the near future, if not already a priority.

Although international collaboration is essential, some international policymakers and advisors have become disheartened by the obstacles in the way and believe that solutions lie at the national level instead. Government policymakers have the power to set in place transformative policies and programs, unless they are impeded by factions within their own countries. And accountability is far more direct for national policies than those agreed in international forums. Figure 5.3 shows some of the ways that industry blocks policy upholding regenerative food systems; but corruption, ideology, path dependence and incompetence also stand in the way. Corruption is apparent in campaign contributions and records of disproportionate numbers of meetings of government officials with lobbyists or other industry representatives, compared to meetings with civil society or independent citizens.

Since the *Citizens United vs. Federal Election Commission* ruling in 2010, corporations, non-profits, labor unions and other associations can give unlimited contributions to elections. This has created conditions in which public offices are bought by the person able to solicit the most money. In 2022, 93 percent of elections in the House of Representatives and 82 percent of elections in the Senate were won by the candidate who spent the most money. Agribusiness spent a total of $124,484,142 in 2022 to influence elections and legislation, with 71 percent of spending on government candidates going to the conservative Republican Party (Open Secrets 2023). Congressional candidates raise most of their money from individual donors and political action committees (PACs) formed for the purpose of fundraising to support candidates or legislation. The 10 most generous donors and their spouses donated $1.2 billion to federal candidates over the last decade and *Citizens United* opened the door to "dark money" (undisclosed spending). Groups that don't disclose their donors poured in $963 million in outside spending between 2010 and 2020, compared to just $129 million over the previous decade (Evers-Hillstrom 2020). This influx of funds from dark money groups and wealthy individuals has resulted in more conservative legislators winning elections and more conservative policies being enacted since 2010 (Harvey and Mattia 2022).

In summary, government policymakers can be powerful change agents, and people with deep integrity and commitment to transforming the food system do achieve public office at times. What they can actually accomplish is mixed, however. Given the many ways that industry and wealthy individuals who support extractive systems can block legislation, progressive legislators fight unending battles under neoliberalism. Policymakers are caught like flies in a spiderweb in the dominant cultural narrative and existing institutions. At best, their proposals can open space for changing that narrative so that people begin to consider that the current neoliberal system isn't inevitable and "the only alternative," as Margaret Thatcher famously said.

Farmers as Change Agents

Implicit Theory of Change

- If farmers adopt regenerative practices, we will achieve regenerative food systems.

Implicit Assumptions

- Farmers want to use regenerative practices and the barriers to their adoption can be overcome with financial incentives and education.
- Farmers understand how to implement regenerative practices.

- Sufficient arable land exists to convert to regenerative practices and it is available for use by farmers.
- Farmers are willing to use more labor-intensive practices and forego labor-saving technology such as synthetic pesticides and fertilizers.
- Sufficient labor is available to work on regenerative farms.

> Equipped with the right training, tools, and guidance, young people can build successful agribusiness ventures and lead a new generation of agricultural innovation when it's most needed to feed a growing population.
> *(Franzel et al. 2022b, n.p.)*

> The very realization of future generations' food security, the sustainable transformation of food systems and the combat against unemployment all depend upon an increased attractiveness of the agri-food sector for the youth.
> *(FAO n.d., n.p.)*

> Small farmers have the answer to feeding the world.
> *(Mpofu and Hobbelink 2021)*

Most farmers have considerable agency in deciding among production options, input prices allowing, even though what they sell and how much they earn are likely to be determined by the markets available to them. The World Economic Forum, UN agencies and agricultural economists encourage farmers, especially African youth, to become "agripreneurs" and adopt new technology (Juma and Spielman 2014; Franzel et al. 2022a). This theme was clear in the UN Food Summit. The connotations of agripreneurship are that farmers learn business skills to manage their farms more profitably and efficiently. Recommendations include developing leadership and managerial skills such as negotiation, self-confidence, record-keeping and accounting. Steven Franzel and his co-authors at IFPRI and FAO (2022a, 6) noted that,

> Public-private partnerships are particularly effective in fostering agripreneurship, as in the case involving Mars Incorporated, the International Fund for Agricultural Development (IFAD) and the Government of Indonesia providing training to smallholder cocoa growers.

In other words, agripreneurs are being groomed to aspire to agribusiness management or partnerships with large businesses. Civil society organizations that work together in the Civil Society and Indigenous Peoples' Mechanism of the Committee on World Food Security (CSIPM) strongly resist the push toward entrepreneurism by farmers:

> [M]any governments have bought into the "modernization" narrative and think of support to small-scale food producers in terms of connecting

> them to agribusiness value chains and transforming them into individual entrepreneurs, in deep contrast with what these producers themselves demand.
>
> *(CSIPM 2022, 13)*

The World Farmers' Organization (WFO) might be considered as an international organizing space for agripreneurs. Its Wikipedia entry claims that it is especially focused on agroecology, Indigenous farmers and small-holders; and it describes itself as a member-based network of farmers' organizations and cooperatives from around the world. But it lists as "partners" Bayer, CropLife International, the International Dairy Federation and the International Seed Federation, in addition to numerous research institutes, academic institutions, and international agencies, developmental agencies and civil society organizations. The extent to which "partners" direct WFO's policies or fund its activities is not clear from its website, but it seems to be quite comfortable with multistakeholderism.

A few years ago, WFO argued that it needed to be officially recognized by the Committee on World Food Security's Advisory Group, and that neither the Private Sector Mechanism (PSM) nor the Civil Society and Indigenous People's Mechanism (CSIPM) were appropriate spaces for it. These are the two large mechanisms that aggregate diverse non-governmental organizations and social movements for interventions in the CSM, and distinguishing WFO outside these would be an unusual move. In terms of how WFO operates, it seems closer to the PSM than the self-organized CSIPM, where food-insecure people have primacy (Schramm 2017). Since small-holders, Indigenous people and agroecology are all directly represented in the CSIPM, recognizing WFO as a legitimate spokesperson would upset the careful balance of representation established in the 2009 reform of the Committee on World Food Security (see Chapter 9 for more on the CFS and the significance of its reform). WFO was not recognized as "the farmers representative" in the CFS Advisory Group, but it holds an *ad hoc* seat.

Most farmers are quite resourceful: they must be to adapt to unpredictable weather events, poor crop yields and prices, unreliable machinery, labor shortages and more. But many resist being labeled as "agripreneurs" because farming is much more to them than just a business: it is a way of life and an identity. In this group with a broader view of farming is La Via Campesina (LVC), the largest social movement in the world. It is considered here as part of civil society and has far more potential than agripreneurs to lead a transformation to regenerative food systems, for reasons that will be explained below.

If farmers are indeed leaders toward regenerative food systems, several conditions must be met. First, sufficient land and labor must be available.

Regenerative food systems are more land-extensive and labor-intensive because they use much fewer fossil fuel and chemical inputs to replace land and labor. But finding sufficient land and labor for people who want to farm now is difficult; finding and affording farmland on a farm income was the top barrier for people wanting to start farming in the US in a national survey of 94 organizations by the National Young Farmers Coalition (NYFC 2017). The number of hired farmworkers in the US increased six percent between 2010 and 2022 but only 56 percent were US citizens (ERS 2023b). Farm and food-processing labor in industrialized countries often consists of undocumented workers from poor countries, and immigration crackdowns have hurt farms as well as the people who want to immigrate. Labor availability is intimately connected with immigration policy, which is in the domain of national policymakers. Policymakers are also responsible, under the terms of the human right to food and nutrition, for facilitating access to land and other resources for people to grow their own food (OHCHR 2010). This right was reiterated in the UN Declaration on the Rights of Peasants and Other People Working in Rural Areas.

Will farmers lead food system transformation? That all depends on their goals and alliances. Small-scale farmers produce most of the food that is consumed in the world. Farmers and other food producers have direct connections to land and oceans and thus are able to transform food production so that it regenerates resources instead of degrading them. Their livelihoods and the health of their children and communities depend in the long term on protecting ecosystems, so they have abundant motivation to use regenerative practices. Yet many farmers are unable or unwilling to use regenerative practices; they are the people who are destroying land and contaminating the ocean with their practices. Where this is happening, however, it is because of external pressures or incentives that either make regenerative agricultural systems costly to implement or opposed to the technical advice and support coming from governmental agents and the private sector.

This section began with the claim that farmers have considerable agency to choose among production options; and while this is true, that agency can be easily undermined by agricultural extensionists or private consultants promoting extractive practices as "modern" farming or government hand-outs of synthetic fertilizer and seeds. Farmers who join organizations that help them use transformative practices, such as the Alliance for Food Sovereignty in Africa or La Via Campesina, can find help in using regenerative practices and fighting the forces that push extractive agriculture. But the private sector is eagerly seeking "poster-farmers" willing to use their products and proclaim how beneficial they are, in their attempts to control the narrative of good farming.

Civil Society as Change Agents

Implicit Theory of Change

- Social movements and NGOs promoting regenerative food systems will attract growing numbers of people who are disabused of the benefits of extractive food systems and frustrated by the lack of effective actions by governments and the private sector to address the polycrisis of climate chaos, hunger, biodiversity loss, inequality and poverty.
- As they grow, these civil society organizations will gain power and policymakers will respond to their demands.

Implicit Assumptions

- The public can be mobilized to demand regenerative food systems.
- Civil society organizations can organize public protest effectively and make citizens' needs known to policymakers.
- Actors behind extractive food systems will not be able to keep their grip on policy, policymakers and the dominant cultural narrative as the polycrisis worsens.

> When I look at the private sector, or the government, they are moving toward each other in a way, which is very hard to stop. And the only one that can really make a change here is civil society. So when I look at what we want from the state, and what we want from corporations, it's really from seeing them as generally, being not sympathetic. And even hostile. I want them to do what they're told ... We've got to convince them and make them do it. They are willing to be made to do it, but we're gonna have to push them all along the way ... They can't ignore us because we're too dangerous ... We have to be able to show them that we actually have the muscle to make their lives very hard if they don't pay attention.
>
> *(Mooney 2023)*

> [C]ivil society-led food system transformation could shift USD 4 trillion from the industrial food chain to food sovereignty and agroecology, cut 75 percent of food systems' GHG emissions, and deliver incalculable benefits to the lives and livelihoods of billions of people over the next 25 years.
>
> *(IPES-Food and ETC Group 2021, 13)*

> For an answer to global hunger, look to peasants, not multinational corporations.
>
> *(NFFC 2023, n.p.)*

La Via Campesina (LVC) brings together millions of peasants, landless workers, Indigenous people, pastoralists, fishers, migrant farmworkers, small and medium-size farmers, rural women and peasant youth. It is made up of 182 local and national organizations in 81 countries from Africa, Asia, Europe and the Americas and represents about 200 million small-scale food producers (LVC 2023).

Food sovereignty is the rallying cry for LVC, along with peasant agroecology and feminism. LVC proudly embraces the nomenclature of "peasant," defined in the UN Declaration on the Rights as Peasants and Others Working in Rural Areas as:

> any person who engages or who seeks to engage, alone, or in association with others or as a community, in small-scale agricultural production for subsistence and/or for the market, and who relies significantly, though not necessarily exclusively, on family or household labour and other non-monetized ways of organizing labour, and who has a special dependency on and attachment to the land. (Article 1)

LVC offers grassroots solutions to global warming, hunger, malnutrition and distress migration from rural areas. It defends peasants' rights to lands, seed, water and forests. It consists of the people who actually feed the world: 70 percent of the food consumed in the world comes from small-scale farmers and peasants (ETC Group 2022a). This point was contested recently and downsized to one-third; but ETC Group's careful analysis shows that the 70 percent estimate is accurate, and the International Fund for Agricultural Development claims that peasants provide up to 80 percent of the food consumed in some regions (IFAD and UNEP 2013). This is an excellent example of narrative sparring and its consequences: if indeed small-holders are responsible for providing only one-third of the food consumed in the world, it is easier to defend claims that agribusiness corporations and large-scale farms are essential. But the accurate figure lends considerable weight to calls to invest more in small-holders if the concern is food security and nutrition.

There is more to civil society than peasant farmers, although they are recognized to hold a unique role because their lives and livelihoods depend on agriculture; they grow most of the food consumed in the world, often using traditional and agroecological practices passed down for generations that are regenerative; and they constitute the largest group of food-insecure people in the world. Small-scale fishers, pastoralists and Indigenous peoples are other important groups of producers. Numerous non-governmental organizations support producers and small-scale food businesses in their quest for food sovereignty. The Civil Society and Indigenous Peoples' Mechanism (CSIPM) of the Committee on World Food Security brings together more than 380 million affiliated members (Autonomous People's Response to the UNFSS+2 2023).

Many in civil society anticipate that food systems will become more localized and self-sufficient with greater use of territorial markets, stronger urban-rural linkages and reduced dependencies for food, fertilizer or fuel as the polycrisis continues. This will happen in part because of the inherent vulnerability of overly complex supply chains that support cities now and their complete dependence on fossil fuels, which cannot continue to be used at the same rate because they are destroying the habitability of many regions through climate change. A strong element within civil society anticipates a radical decentralization of society that will accompany an "unraveling" of social structures and ecological integrity (e.g., Bradford 2019; Heinberg and Miller 2023). Current institutions and urban centers are completely reliant on fossil fuels, and there is no substitute with equal energy density. That is, even if governments ramp up their investment in renewable energy generation significantly, energy use must decline. This is aligned with the urgent call to action from the degrowth movement to resist consumerism and reckless resource consumption to soften the impacts of unraveling (see Hickel 2020).

There is an underlying assumption within civil society that localized food systems are more resilient, or better able to withstand perturbations while maintaining core functions. The relative stability of the global food system versus local and regional food systems is a subject of debate. During the COVID pandemic, national and global food and grocery supply chains broke down at critical points, often because of labor shortages, leaving retail shelves bare. In the US, meat-packers at the five largest companies run by JBS, Tyson, Smithfield, Cargill and National Beef Packing Company were forced to come to work, even when they were sick and had no personal protective equipment, with the threat of losing their jobs hanging over them if they failed to show up (Philpott 2021). But not all national and global supply chains were willing to use such brutal coercive measures. Global and national supply chains for meat-packing and every other food system activity are dominated by a very small number of companies, with harmful consequences to farmer autonomy and income, the scope of innovation, control over information, well-being of labor, public health, environmental quality and global decision-making over policies (IPES-Food 2017; ETC Group 2022b). The impacts of that degree of domination on workers' autonomy were horrifyingly evident during the worst of the pandemic. A regenerative food system would increase the diversity of producers and distributors to increase equity and diminish the harmful impacts of excessive concentration.

Local and regional food systems are less complex with fewer interconnections that are susceptible to collapse; yet labor shortages, lockdowns and mobility restrictions imposed by national governments affected local and regional food systems as well and resulted in worsening food security. Labor shortages have continued through 2023. In an examination of local food system resilience in lower and middle-income countries, Christophe Béné (2020) observed that small-scale producers and food suppliers in local and regional food systems are extremely vulnerable because of lack of infrastructure such as roads, markets and power; lack of business opportunities; lack of services; and high dependence on weather conditions. This means that they have extreme difficulty responding to shocks and stressors. In addition, national governments tend to protect the largest agro-food businesses more than the smallest. That is, small-scale actors and local food systems may encounter the greatest barriers to resilience, and most need support from local and national governments. Extreme weather events due to climate change can wipe out local supply quickly, and even more disruptions are foreseen in the future. The vulnerability of local food systems is a major reason that many people call for regional food systems now, with food coming first from the local area but from adjacent regions if local food supply is disrupted.

Diversifying distribution networks can improve the stability of food availability when disruptions occur. Increasing emphasis on local and regional food systems could foster more rapid innovation and the ability to adapt to global-change forces (Schipanski et al. 2016). Regional and local food systems also create social embeddedness between producers and consumers, fostering greater attention to social inequities and agroecosystem management. Interest in local food (or growing food oneself) increased during COVID, in part because customers trusted its quality more than food from national supply chains. The impulse to help, especially when children are going without food that they need, is stronger when people know each other and live in proximity; people understand needs better at the local level as well. During COVID, local and regional systems were bolstered by mutual aid networks and community organizations that stepped in to help harvest and distribute produce or cooked food to people who couldn't access it (e.g., Sanderson Bellamy et al. 2021 in the UK, Thilmany et al. 2021 in the US, and Carstensen et al. 2021 in Kenya, occupied Palestine territory, the Philippines, and Sudan). Recognizing the role of community-based organizations and providing funds to them would increase resilience during disruptions of food supply. With local support, sometimes local food systems are more resilient than national and global.

Figure 8.2 depicts schematically what happens when civil society is powerful enough to change the dominant cultural narrative to support regenerative food systems. There are secondary impacts on citizens, producers and food businesses because more people are purchasing healthy food produced in agroecological, sustainable ways. But changing the cultural narrative also affects donors' preferences, policymakers' willingness and ability to instate policies that will intervene in corporate power, and the way that media depicts food system futures. Compared with Figure 8.1, this is a much wider scope of impact, involving far more people. A changed cultural narrative is a compass for food system transformation, ensuring that it remains on track despite challenges.

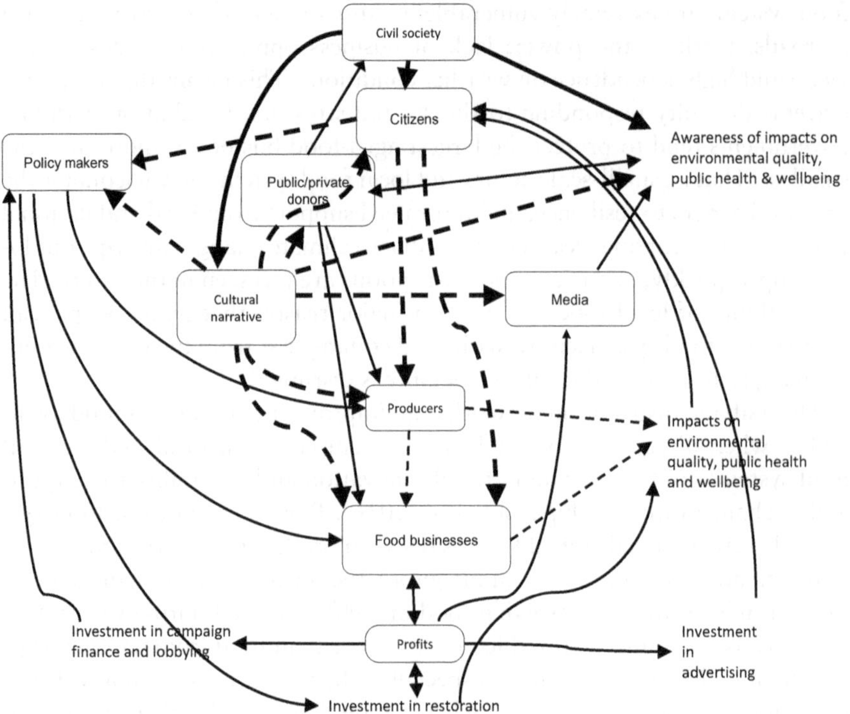

FIGURE 8.2 Impacts of civil society on the food system.

Food security is the central role and goal of food systems: a food system that isn't nourishing people is worth little. The small-scale producers and organizations aligned with food sovereignty are not only nourishing their households and territories, but also protecting women's rights and youth opportunities in agriculture. In addition, they protect biodiversity, water quality and soil fertility by using agroecology (LVC 2021). They are clear winners in the debate of who is most capable of transforming food systems in the direction of regeneration. They can lead the charge, if other contenders will get out of their way.

References

African CSIPM Popular Consultation Space. 2023. *African Civil Society Assessment of the UNFSS National Pathways*. https://www.csm4cfs.org/policy-brief-african-civil-society-assessment-of-the-unfss-national-pathways/

All American Entertainment. 2023. Bill Gates. https://www.allamericanspeakers.com/speakers/386891/Bill-Gates

Autonomous People's Response to the UNFSS+2. 2023. Social movements and Indigenous Peoples oppose the UN Food Systems Summit and call for true food systems change. https://www.csm4cfs.org/to-overcome-the-global-food-crisis-we-need-real-food-systems-change-for-people-and-the-planet/

Bellone, F. 2021. Food systems philanthropy: hope for a regenerative future. Shifting Systems Initiative. *Medium*. https://medium.com/@shiftingsystems/food-systems-philanthropy-hope-for-a-regenerative-future-e2cf360b70bc

Béné, C. 2020. Resilience of local food systems and links to food security – A review of some important concepts in the context of COVID-19 and other shocks. *Food Sec* 12:805–822. https://doi.org/10.1007/s12571-020-01076-1

Béné, C. 2022. Why the Great Food Transformation may not happen – A deep-dive into our food systems' political economy, controversies and politics of evidence. *World Develop* 154:105881. https://doi.org/10.1016/j.worlddev.2022.105881

Berkeley Economic Review (BER). 2019. The merits and drawbacks of philanthrocapitalism. https://econreview.berkeley.edu/the-merits-and-drawbacks-of-philanthrocapitalism/

Biovision Foundation for Ecological Development and Global Alliance for the Future of Food (GAFF). 2019. *Beacons of Hope: Accelerating Transformations to Sustainable Food Systems*. Global Alliance for the Future of Food. https://futureoffood.org/wp-content/uploads/2021/02/BeaconsOfHope_Report_082019.pdf

Biovision Foundation for Ecological Development & IPES-Food. 2020. Money Flows: *What Is Holding Back Investment in Agroecological Research for Africa?* https://www.ipes-food.org/_img/upload/files/Money percent20Flows_Full percent20report.pdf

Bradford, J. 2019. *The Future is Rural: Food System Adaptations to the Great Simplification*. Post Carbon Institute. https://www.postcarbon.org/publications/the-future-is-rural/

Carstensen, N, M Mudhar and F Schurmann Munksgaard. 2021 'Let communities do their work': the role of mutual aid and self-help groups in the Covid-19 pandemic response. *Disasters* 45(S1):S146–S173. https://doi.org/10.1111/disa.12515

Civil Society and Indigenous Peoples Mechanism of the Committee on World Food Security (CSIPM). 2022. Voices from the ground 2: transformative solutions to the global systemic food crises. Popular consultation on grassroots impacts of COVID-19, conflicts and crises on the right to food and food sovereignty. https://www.csm4cfs.org/wp-content/uploads/2022/09/layout-CSIPM-report-EN.pdf

Deloitte. 2016. Capitalizing on the shifting consumer food value equation. *Food Marketing Institute and Grocery Manufacturers of America*. https://www2.deloitte.com/content/dam/Deloitte/us/Documents/consumer-business/us-fmi-gma-report.pdf

DeLonge, MS, A Miles and L Carlisle. 2016. Investing in the transition to sustainable agriculture. *Env Sci Policy* 55:266–273. https://doi.org/10.1016/j.envsci.2015.09.013

Economic Research Service (ERS). 2023a. Organic agriculture. https://www.ers.usda.gov/topics/natural-resources-environment/organic-agriculture/

Economic Research Service (ERS). 2023b. Farm labor. https://www.ers.usda.gov/topics/farm-economy/farm-labor/

ETC Group. 2022a. *Backgrounder: Small Scale Farmers and Peasants Still Feed the World*. https://www.etcgroup.org/sites/www.etcgroup.org/files/files/31-01-2022_small-scale_farmers_and_peasants_still_feed_the_world.pdf

ETC Group. 2022b. *Food Barons: Crisis Profiteering, Digitalization and Shifting Power*. https://www.etcgroup.org/content/food-barons-2022

Evers-Hillstrom, K. 2020. More money, less transparency: a decade under Citizens United. *Open Secrets*. https://www.opensecrets.org/news/reports/a-decade-under-citizens-united?year=2023

Food and Agriculture Organization (FAO) of the UN. N.d. Empowering young agri-entrepreneurs to invest in agriculture and food systems. https://sdgs.un.org/partnerships/empowering-young-agri-entrepreneurs-invest-agriculture-and-food-systems

Food and Agriculture Organization (FAO), United Nations Development Program (UNDP) and United Nations Environmental Program (UNEP). 2021. A multibillion-dollar opportunity – Repurposing agricultural support to transform food systems. Rome: FAO. https://www.fao.org/3/cb6562en/cb6562en.pdf

Franzel, S, K Davis, J Gammelgaard and J Preissing. 2022a. Investing in young agripreneurs: why and how? FAO and IFPRI. https://www.fao.org/3/cc2747en/cc2747en.pdf

Franzel, S, K Davis, J Gammelgaard and J Preissing. 2022b. Unleashing the power of young agripreneurs: why and how? *IFPRI*. https://www.ifpri.org/blog/unleashing-power-young-agripreneurs

Fuglie, K and KP Nelson. 2022. *Agricultural and Food Research and Development Expenditures in the United States*. USDA, Economic Research Service. https://www.ers.usda.gov/data-products/agricultural-and-food-research-and-development-expenditures-in-the-united-states/

Gillam, C. 2021. *The Monsanto Papers: Deadly Secrets, Corporate Corruption, and One Man's Search for Justice*. Washington, DC: Island Press.

Global Alliance for the Future of Food (GAFF). 2021. *The Politics of Knowledge: Understanding the Evidence for Agroecology, Regenerative Approaches, and Indigenous Foodways*. https://futureoffood.org/insights/the-politics-of-knowledge-compendium/

Gordon, E, F Davila and C Riedy. 2023. Regenerative agriculture: a potentially transformative storyline shared by nine discourses. *Sustainability Science* 18:1833–1849. https://doi.org/10.1007/s11625-022-01281-1

Gundala, RR and A Singh. 2021. What motivates consumers to buy organic foods? Results of an empirical study in the United States. *PLoS One* 16(9):e0257288. https://doi.org/10.1371/journal.pone.0257288

Haddad, L and C Smaller. 2021. How big companies can help end hunger. International Food Policy Research Institute. https://www.ifpri.org/blog/how-big-companies-can-help-end-hunger

Harvey, A and T Mattia. 2022. Does money have a conservative bias? Estimating the causal impact of *Citizens United* on state legislative preferences. *Public Choice* 191:417–441.

Heinberg, R and A Miller. 2023. *Welcome to the Great Unraveling: Navigating the Polycrisis of Environmental and Social Breakdown*. https://www.postcarbon.org/publications/welcome-to-the-great-unraveling/

Hickel, J. 2020. *Less is More: How Degrowth will Save the World*. London: William Heinemann.

High Level Panel of Experts (HLPE). 2018. Multi-stakeholder partnerships to finance and improve food security and nutrition in the framework of the 2030 Agenda. A report by the High Level Panel of Experts on Food Security and Nutrition of the Committee on World Food Security, Rome.

International Federation of Organic Agriculture Movements (IFOAM). 2017. Organic 3.0 for Truly Sustainable Farming and Consumption, IFOAM - Organics International. https://www.ifoam.bio/sites/default/files/2020-03/summary_organic3.0_web_1.pdf

International Fund for Agricultural Development (IFAD) and United Nations Environment Program (UNEP). 2013. *Smallholders, Food Security and the Environment.* https://www.ifad.org/documents/38714170/39135645/smallholders_report.pdf/133e8903-0204-4e7d-a780-bca847933f2e

Institute for Development Studies (IDS) and International Panel of Experts on Sustainable Food Systems (IPES-Food). 2022. Smoke & Mirrors. Examining Competing Framings of Food System Sustainability: *Agroecology, Regenerative Agriculture, and Nature-based Solutions.* https://ipes-food.org/_img/upload/files/SmokeAndMirrors.pdf

International Panel of Experts on Sustainable Food Systems (IPES-Food). 2017. *Too Big to Feed: Exploring the Impacts of Mega-mergers, Consolidation and Concentration of Power in the Agri-food Sector.* https://www.ipes-food.org/_img/upload/files/Concentration_FullReport.pdf

International Panel of Experts on Sustainable Food Systems (IPES-Food). 2023. *Who's Tipping the Scales? The Growing Influence of Corporations on the Governance of Food Systems, and How to Counter it.* http://www.ipes-food.org/pages/tippingthescales

International Panel of Experts on Sustainable Food Systems (IPES-Food) and ETC Group. 2021. *The Long Food Movement. Transforming Food Systems by 2045.* https://www.ipes-food.org/_img/upload/files/LongFoodMovementEN.pdf

Johnson, PD. 2018. Global Philanthropy Report. *Perspectives on the Global Foundation Sector.* Hauser Institute for Civil Society, Harvard University. https://cpl.hks.harvard.edu/files/cpl/files/global_philanthropy_report_final_april_2018.pdf

Juma, C and D Spielman. 2014. Farmers as entrepreneurs: sources of agricultural innovation in Africa. Pp. 355–374 In: PBR Hazell and A Rahman (Eds.) *New Directions for Smallholder Agriculture.* Oxford: Oxford University Press. https://doi.org/10.1093/acprof:oso/9780199689347.003.0012

Kennedy, E, P Webb, S Block, T Griffin, D Mozaffarian, and R Kyte. 2021. Transforming food systems: the missing pieces needed to make them work. *Curr Dev Nutr* 5(1):NZAA177. https://doi.org/10.1093/cdn/nzaa177

Lakhani, N, A Uteuova and A Chang. 2021. Revealed: the true extent of America's food monopolies and who pays the price. *The Guardian* (14 July). https://www.theguardian.com/environment/ng-interactive/2021/jul/14/food-monopoly-meals-profits-data-investigation

La Via Campesina (LVC). 2021. La Via Campesina. The Global Voice of Peasants! https://viacampesina.org/en/international-peasants-voice/

La Via Campesina (LVC). 2023. From Mons to the world: La Via Campesina celebrates 30 years of globalizing peasant struggle and solidarity. *Press Release.* https://viacampesina.org/en/from-mons-to-the-world-la-via-campesina-celebrates-30-years-of-peasant-struggle-and-solidarity/

Loconto, A, A Jimenez and E Vandecandelaere. 2018. *Constructing Markets for Agroecology. An Analysis of Diverse Options for Marketing Products from Agroecology.* FAO and INRA. https://www.fao.org/3/I8605EN/i8605en.pdf

Lord, S. 2023. Hidden costs of agrifood systems and recent trends from 2016 to 2023 – Background paper for The State of Food and Agriculture 2023. FAO Agricultural Development Economics Technical Study, No. 31. Rome, FAO. https://doi.org/10.4060/cc8581en

Mitchell, L. 2021. Food systems transformation: what shifts are needed and how do we get there? *Forum for the Future.* https://www.forumforthefuture.org/blog/food-systems-transformation-what-shifts-are-needed-and-how-do-we-get-there

Mohammed, A. 2023. Deputy Secretary-General's remarks at UN Food Systems Summit Stocktake: Catalysing Food Systems Transformations [as delivered]. https://www.un.org/sg/en/content/dsg/statement/2023-07-26/deputy-secretary-generals-remarks-un-food-systems-summit-stocktake-catalysing-food-systems-transformations-delivered

Mooney, P. 2023. Former Executive Director of ETC Group. Personal communication (used by permission).

Mousseau, F. 2022. 38 Billion Dollar Question – *Who is Driving the Destructive Industrial Agriculture Model?* Oakland Institute. https://www.oaklandinstitute.org/blog/vanguard-blackrock-driving-destructive-industrial-agriculture-model

Mpofu, E and H Hobbelink. 2021. Small farmers have the answer to feeding the world. Why isn't the UN listening? *The Guardian* (23 September). https://www.theguardian.com/global-development/2021/sep/23/small-farmers-have-the-answer-to-feeding-the-world-why-isnt-the-un-listening

National Family Farm Coalition (NFFC). 2023. For an answer to Global Hunger, look to Peasants, not Multinational Corporations. https://nffc.net/for-an-answer-to-global-hunger-look-to-peasants-not-multinational-corporations/

National Young Farmers Coalition. 2017. *Building a Future with Farmers. Results and Recommendation of the 2017 National Young Farmer Survey.* https://www.youngfarmers.org/wp-content/uploads/2019/03/NYFC-Report-2017_LoRes_Revised.pdf

Nelson, J. 2007. Business as a Partner in Overcoming Malnutrition: An Agenda for Action. Kennedy School of Government, the Conference Board and International Business Leaders Forum. Harvard University. https://www.hks.harvard.edu/sites/default/files/centers/mrcbg/programs/cri/files/report_14_NUTRITION%2BFINAL.pdf

Office of the High Commissioner of Human Rights (OHCHR). 2010. The Right to Adequate Food. Fact Sheet 34. Published jointly with FAO. https://www.ohchr.org/en/publications/fact-sheets/fact-sheet-no-34-right-adequate-food

Organic Trade Association (OTA). 2023. Organic food sales break through $60 billion in 2022. *Press Release.* https://ota.com/news/press-releases/22820

Philpott, T. 2021. Meatpackers "prioritized profits" over worker safety during the pandemic. A new bill would force them to change. *Mother Jones* (3 December). https://www.motherjones.com/food/2021/12/meatpackers-prioritized-profits-over-worker-safety-during-the-pandemic-a-new-bill-would-force-them-to-change/

Pimbert, MP and NI Moeller. 2018. Absent agroecology aid: on UK agricultural development assistance since 2010. *Sustainability* 10(2):505. doi:10.3390/su10020505

Pollan, M. 2006. Voting with your fork. *The New York Times* "On the Table" Blog (7 May). https://michaelpollan.com/articles-archive/voting-with-your-fork/

Popli, N. 2023. How food companies' massive profits are making your groceries more expensive. *Time Magazine* https://time.com/6269366/food-company-profits-make-groceries-expensive/

Qureshi, Zia, 2023. Rising inequality: A major issue of our time. Brookings Institution. https://www.brookings.edu/articles/rising-inequality-a-major-issue-of-our-time/

Rockefeller Foundation. 2021. *True Cost of Food: Measuring What Matters to Transform the U.S. Food System.* New York. https://www.rockefellerfoundation.org/wp-content/uploads/2021/07/True-Cost-of-Food-Full-Report-Final.pdf

Rockefeller Foundation. 2023. Alliance for a Green Revolution in Africa. https://www.rockefellerfoundation.org/initiative/alliance-for-a-green-revolution-in-africa/

Sanderson Bellamy, A, E Furness, P Nicol, H Pitt and ATaherzadeh. 2021. Shaping more resilient and just food systems: Lessons from the COVID-19 Pandemic. *Ambio* 50:782–793.

Schipanski, ME, GK MacDonald, S Rosenzweig, MJ Chappell, EM Bennett, R Bezner Kerr, J Blesh, T Crews, L Drinkwater, JC Lundgren and C Schnarr. 2016. Realizing resilient food systems. *BioScience* 66(7):600–610. https://doi.org/10.1093/biosci/biw052

Schramm, A. 2017. Who is the "real" farmer? Contestation in the Committee on World Food Security. *Resources and Conflict.* http://resources-and-conflict.org/2017/06/who-is-the-real-farmer/

Schwab, T. 2023. *The Bill Gates Problem: Reckoning with the Myth of the Good Billionaire.* New York: MacMillan Publishers.

Seralini, G-É, J Douzelet and V Shiva. 2021. *The Monsanto Papers: Corruption of Science and Grievous Harm to Public Health.* New York: Skyhorse.

Smyth, SJ, SR Webb, PWB Phillips. 2021. The role of public-private partnerships in improving global food security. *Glob Food Sec* 31:100588.

Sorvino, C. 2023. What's the world's largest food company? *Forbes Magazine.* https://www.forbes.com/sites/chloesorvino/2023/06/08/whats-the-worlds-largest-food-company/?sh=36f228857979

Spielman, DJ, K von Grebmer. 2006. Public–private partnerships in international agricultural research: an analysis of constraints. *J Tech Transfer* 31:291–300.

Swann, C. 2023. Fertilizer industry booms with $57 billion in profits despite struggles from farmers and governments. *Chem Analyst.* https://www.chemanalyst.com/NewsAndDeals/NewsDetails/fertilizer-industry-booms-with-57-billion-in-profits-despite-struggles-from-governments-14245

Tamir, I. 2023. Director of Oxfam America's Private Sector Department. Personal Communication (used by permission).

Thilmany, D, E Canales, SA Low and K Boys. 2021. Local food supply chain dynamics and resilience during COVID-19. *Applied Econ Perspect Policy* 43(1):86–104.

Turchin, Peter. 2023. *Elites, Counter-elites, and the Path of Political Disintegration.* London: Penguin Press.

United Nations Secretary-General. 2023. Making food systems work for people and planet. Report. Report of the Secretary General to UN Food Systems Summit +2. https://www.unfoodsystemshub.org/docs/unfoodsystemslibraries/stocktaking-moment/un-secretary-general/unfss2-secretary-general-report.pdf?sfvrsn=560b6fa6_19

Verizon and Devex. 2021. Leading the charge on the SDGs: best practices for CEOs and corporate leaders. https://pages.devex.com/leading-sdgs

Walmart. 2023. PepsiCo and Walmart aim to support regenerative agriculture across more than 2 million acres of farmland. https://corporate.walmart.com/newsroom/2023/07/26/pepsico-and-walmart-aim-to-support-regenerative-agriculture-across-more-than-2-million-acres-of-farmland

Willer, H, B Schlatter, J Trávníček. 2023. The World of Organic Agriculture. *Statistics and Emerging Trends*. FiBL and IFOAM. https://www.fibl.org/en/shop-en/1254-organic-world-2023

Yates, J, S Gillespie, N Savona, M Deeney, and S Kadiyala. 2021.Trust and responsibility in food systems transformation. Engaging with Big Food: marriage or mirage? *BMJ Glob Health* 6:e007350. https://doi.org/10.1136/bmjgh-2021-007350

SECTION 4

Case Studies

International and Local

9

INTERNATIONAL FORUMS

The CFS and the UNFSS

Competing narratives of the pathway to food system transformation are rife in existing global governance spaces, and also in the creation of new bodies such as the High Level Task Force on Global Food and Nutrition Security in April 2008 to respond to problems in the food system. The UN Secretary-General also set up a Global Crisis Response Group in May 2022 to advise on interlinked problems of food, fuel and finance. Whether new groups are deemed to be necessary and who should be represented on them reflects the narratives that influential policymakers and governments hold. This chapter looks in more depth at two forums that have been set up to deal with food security and food crises, the Committee on World Food Security and the UN Food Systems Summit.

UN Committee on World Food Security

The Committee on World Food Security (CFS) stands out as the "foremost inclusive international and intergovernmental platform for all stakeholders to work together to ensure food security and nutrition for all." After its reform in 2009, it was considered to be a model of inclusiveness. This chapter examines the significance of that reform; the clashing narratives that are evident in the CFS and how these affect its ability to meet its lofty goals; and what it needs to enable people holding very different narratives to work together. Several excellent articles and books have been written to describe the CFS and especially its reform; the intention here is to focus on narratives and not to reiterate what has already been written about the CFS except when that is necessary to understand competing narratives.

DOI: 10.4324/9781003260264-13

Despite challenges that CFS has encountered since the 2009 reform, it has had important achievements relevant to regenerative food systems. It shifted global attention away from increasing productivity as the answer to hunger, to understand the importance of small-holders and territorial markets (Lambek 2014). Reports from its High Level Panel of Experts and civil society successfully reframed "investment" as primarily by small-scale producers, countering the belief that large-scale farmers feed the world. CFS influenced narratives about land and tenure rights for smallholders through the Voluntary Guidelines on the Responsible Governance of Tenure of Land, Fisheries and Forest (VGGT), which have been picked up in several other governance spaces. CFS products such as voluntary guidelines on the right to food, approved in 2004, and the VGGT have helped to shape international human rights instruments including UNDROP (McKeon 2015a, b; Duncan et al. 2021).

Since 2009, I have attended most of the civil society forums that occur each year before the CFS plenary meetings in October and the plenary as well. I also joined several civil society working groups and participated in calls. The people who engage with CFS from social movements and non-profit organizations turn over regularly, but the core concerns of the group are very consistent: violations and abuses of the right to food and how these can be rectified, which is the central mandate of the CFS. I have observed that civil society participants in CFS are often better informed and more articulate about issues in food system governance than government delegates. They draw from the decades that social movements and NGOs have been involved in food security issues and governance forums, including the 1996 World Food Summit, the World Food Summit +5, development of the IPC, and the development and adoption of the Voluntary Guidelines for Progressive Realization of the Right to Food (McKeon 2009). CFS is a lively, rich and sometimes frustrating space where narratives about how the food system should be transformed clash and debate. Duncan and Barling (2022, 157) observed that the civil society participants in CFS are "committed predominantly to deconstructing and contesting the logic of embedded neoliberalism as it appears in food security policy, most notably through the advancement of a food sovereignty framework." This fundamental commitment is at the root of most of the narrative clashes between civil society and government delegates, especially those from the major exporters of commodity crops (e.g., US, Australia, Argentina, Russia). But other clashes are due to differing perspectives on human rights, gender, production systems, where coordinated governance is needed and how that governance should be implemented. In this chapter, I will draw from participant observation and the wealth of analysis produced by scholars and civil society organizations.

The CFS was established by the World Food Conference in 1974 as an intergovernmental body housed in FAO to serve as a forum for review and follow-up of food security policies. It supports country-led processes toward the elimination of hunger and ensuring food security and nutrition for everyone. It provides a platform for global coordination on food security and nutrition, promotes policy convergence, shares lessons and experiences and reviews global progress toward achieving food security. It monitors decisions, promotes accountability and develops its own policy guidelines. Having a global committee to deal with food security is vital because actions taken by individual countries cannot be sufficient; many of the contributors to hunger are either global themselves (such as climate change and pandemics) or in the interactions of countries (such as conflict). A progressive, civil society-pushed development within the CFS led first to the inclusion in the 1996 Plan of Action of a commitment to develop Voluntary Guidelines on the Governance of Tenure and subsequently to the negotiation of these guidelines in the CFS, with steadily increasing civil society participation. But overall the CFS was still a "talk show" when the food crisis broke out in 2007 (McKeon 2009). Until 2009, the most significant accomplishment of the CFS was negotiating the Voluntary Guidelines to Support the Progressive Realization of the Right to Adequate Food in the Context of National Food Security in 2003–2004. But it was largely ineffectual in ensuring food security or detecting threats, which became shockingly obvious to the world when food prices shot up in 2007–2008 and led to food riots in 30 countries and political upheavals in several regions (Patel and McMichael 2009). This set the stage for the reform which was finalized in 2009.

According to the reform text (CFS 2009), the CFS has a mandate to work toward realization of the right to food. All Member States of the UN were invited to join at the Ministerial level. In addition, representatives of UN agencies and bodies with a specific mandate related to food security and nutrition and the right to food were invited to engage with CFS and attend annual meetings as Participants: the Special Rapporteur on the Right to Food, the Office of the High Commissioner on Human Rights, the World Health Organization, the UN Children's Fund, the UN Development Programme and the Standing Committee on Nutrition. Additional Participants include civil society, international agricultural research centers, the World Bank, the International Monetary Fund, regional development banks, the WTO, the private sector and philanthropic organizations active on food security. Others may attend as Observers. The aim of creating such an inclusive body was to give greater coherence to food system policy.

Member States are the only decision-making participants in the CFS, which means that accountability for following through on CFS decisions rests with governments; this is congruent with governmental responsibility for realizing the right to food, spelled out in documents of the Human Rights Council. The CFS reform document also stressed the principle of subsidiarity and the need to build links between policy forums and action at all levels.

CFS was assigned the task of developing a Global Strategic Framework "in order to improve coordination and guide synchronized action by a wide range of stakeholders" (CFS 2009). A High Level Panel of Experts (HLPE) was established to provide scientific and knowledge-based analysis and advice on specific issues relevant to food security and nutrition. The Panel is made up of a Steering Committee and *ad hoc* project teams of experts working on specific issues. CFS also has a Bureau, which serves executive functions and is made up of the Chair and representatives from 12 member countries, an Advisory Group and a Secretariat to help with logistics.

The reformed CFS is a governance entity like nothing else in the UN system. The reform happened because of two decades of networking and capacity building, particularly by the International Planning Committee for Food Sovereignty (McKeon 2015a), which was able to act in the face of governmental and intergovernmental incapacities during the 2007–2008 food price crisis. Civil society had slowly assumed a more active role in food security governance over the previous decades, with the support of some member states and sympathetic CFS Chairs (Duncan and Barling 2012). The Civil Society Mechanism (CSM, since renamed CSIPM in recognition that Indigenous Peoples cannot be assimilated into civil society) is the permanent autonomous coordinating body for civil society in the CFS. The CFS through the CSIPM allows direct interaction of people whose right to food has been violated or abused with delegates from their governments, responsible for ensuring their right to food, and with businesses or others that have perpetrated violations. Although representatives from other UN agencies have commented on how CFS discussions are substantive and lively because of its inclusion of civil society, no other agency has adopted its model. According to the former Secretary of the CSIPM, this is because many governments think the CFS went too far in "opening the door" to civil society and want governments to retain full control of international forums. Of course, civil society does not vote in the CFS; but evidently their presence and interventions make some government delegates uncomfortable.

The CSM created a Secretariat and a Coordinating Committee made up of 41 members representing 11 constituencies of civil society and 17 subregions. The constituencies are people whose right to food is threatened globally and who face criminalization or violence for defending their territories: smallholder farmers, pastoralists, fisherfolk, Indigenous peoples, agricultural and food workers, landless, women, youth, consumers, urban food insecure and NGOs. Smallholder farmers have twice as many seats in the Coordinating Committee as other constituencies, in recognition of their greater numbers compared with other constituencies and their importance in nourishing the world. Although they produce most of the food consumed in the world, they are the population that is most impoverished and most food insecure. Since they work in agriculture, their practices have a tremendous impact on sustainability (ETC Group 2022; Bread for the World 2023; FAO et al. 2023). Civil society and in particular small-scale food producers should logically be the central focus of CFS in its efforts to combat food insecurity and malnutrition. Their participation in the CFS is what gives it legitimacy, allows linkages between civil society in home countries and internationally, and ensures that CFS guidelines and policies will be monitored (De Schutter 2014).

The CSIPM meets for two days in October before each annual CSM meeting to decide on priorities, clear messages and spokespeople. However, working groups operate year-round to develop and defend positions on thematic issues on the CFS agenda. The CSIPM meetings attract people from over 250 non-governmental organizations and social movements around the world, ranging from peasant cooperatives to small women's fishing organizations to international NGOs. Many make the trip to Rome without external funding (only the Coordinating Committee members' expenses are paid) and are taking time away from their normal work. Participants have very different perspectives that occasionally lead to heated debates; but there is a strong commitment to presenting unified positions, as a former CFS Chair asked them to do (Duncan and Barling 2012). The 2009 reform document states that every effort will be made to reach consensus in the CFS; but where there is not consensus different views need to be represented, with priority given to those of organizations of people most affected.

The private sector also has a coordinating mechanism, as encouraged in Paragraph 17 of the CFS reform document. The International Agri-Food Network set up the Private Sector Mechanism with open membership to for-profit enterprises across the agri-food value chain, from farmers to input providers, cooperatives, processors and food companies (IAFN 2011). While some CFS participants see the CSIPM and PSM as being comparable, they are qualitatively different in that CSIPM members are rights-holders defending their right to food and PSM members represent their businesses. The first CFS meetings after the reform attracted few PSM members, but their numbers have grown with each successive year.

The CFS50 plenary session ended on 13 October 2022 without agreement on how to address the global food crisis, despite hours of negotiation and interpretation wasted on trying to find a compromise between Russia, whose delegates were intent on including wording on sanctions in the final resolution, and the US, whose delegates wanted wording on the impacts of Russia's invasion of Ukraine. Both sides refused to compromise, ignoring the proposals from the CSIPM and the Special Rapporteur on the Right to Food for a coordinated global response to the food crisis. Many people believed that bringing this dispute into the CFS was an intentional effort to weaken the CFS and the Chair, Gabriel Ferrero (Schuftan 2022; CSIPM 2022a). For years, powerful governments have tried to weaken the CFS by slowing down policymaking processes through obstructionist interventions, reducing the CFS's program of work, and then criticizing it for moving at a slow pace (Canfield et al. 2021). Yet this was the first time in history that the CFS was suspended because of failure to agree on negotiated text. It reconvened in December and finally agreed to the Chair's proposal that CFS leverage its convening power to strengthen coordinated policy responses to the ongoing food crises. The CSIPM proposal to strengthen the CFS response to the new layer of global food crisis, by outreach to Member States in many countries, received appreciation by countries from Latin America, Africa and Europe. However, it was not adopted (CSIPM 2022a).

The inability to find a satisfactory resolution during CFS50 reflects a very basic narrative conflict: what is the purpose and importance of the CFS? These are defined clearly in the 2009 Reform documents but not fully accepted by all countries. For some, CFS is just a multistakeholder forum for sharing information and boasting about one's own successes. From this perspective, it is important to uphold one's own country's status and compel other countries to agree to one's positions. Furthermore, since civil society has become so insistent in voicing its views in the CFS, which sometimes conflict with government accounts, these countries would like to minimize attention to the CFS by "forum shifting" (evading contentious issues by assigning them to other spaces) and insisting that trade, health and human rights are the purview of other UN agencies even when they affect food security and nutrition.

For other participants, CFS is a forum for finding shared solutions to problems regarding failures to respect, protect and fulfill the right to food, based on the best evidence available. This group is likely to give considerable credence to the reports and other products of the HLPE; delegates from Member States in the first group have few compunctions about ignoring its evidence or recommendations if they do not align with their country's positions. For other participants, including many in CSIPM, CFS is not only a space for seeking shared solutions but also where people whose human rights have been violated or abused can make these problems visible and seek redress. For others, including many in the PSM, it is a place to further consolidate control over food systems and influence the narrative of who is essential in food systems transformation. PSM members who belong to the World Economic Forum may believe in the need for a "great reset" based on the "Global Redesign Initiative" by which corporations would take control for global governance from nation-states, which corporations argue are too weak for the job and not sufficiently efficient (WEF 2010; see Gleckman 2012). This is a classic "Shock Doctrine" move, by which the private sector moves in to capitalize and consolidate its power during crises (Klein 2008). Many of these differences in narratives can be boiled down to whether Member States and other participants want to protect or transform the status quo of existing power relations in the food system.

Narrative conflicts in CFS reveal fundamentally different views on how the food system should be transformed and by whom. A recurring disagreement is whether international human rights instruments are relevant to CFS policy recommendations. Negotiations over guidelines and policy recommendations take place in Open-ended Working Groups that convene throughout the year between CFS plenary meetings (although formerly they occurred in plenary). Questions over human rights came up during negotiation of the "Agroecology and Other Innovations" policy recommendations, regarding CSIPM's proposal to include a reference to UNDROP, the UN Declaration on the Rights of Peasants and Others working in Rural Areas (CSIPM 2021a). The US is opposed to any suggestions that CFS policy guidelines must be congruent with language on human rights from other international agreements that it did not vote to support and, when they are mentioned, always enters the reservation: "as far as each of these instruments are [sic] relevant and applicable and as far as they have been agreed, acknowledged and/or endorsed by respective Member States."

The US is unusual in not having ratified most of the major international human rights agreements and resolutions including the International Covenant on Economic, Social and Cultural Rights; Convention on the Elimination of All Forms of Discrimination Against Women; Convention on Rights of the Child; Convention on the Protection of the Rights of All Migrant Workers and Members of Their Families; and Convention on the Rights of Persons with Disabilities (OHCHR n.d.). In addition, the US did not vote in favor of UNDROP or UNDRIP, the Declaration on the Rights of Indigenous Peoples (however, since the approval of UNDRIP, the US has said it will comply with its provisions). Therefore, through its reservations in CFS documents, US delegates may be following instructions from their home offices to avoid any hint that the US accepts these international agreements. Yet "relevant and applicable" is misleading, in that States are legally bound to adhere to these agreements, if they have signed and ratified them. It should be noted that other countries, such as Russia, also raise objections to human rights language in negotiations. Russian delegates have said that the discussion of human rights should take place in the HRC, not the CFS. But CFS is in no position to undermine the UNDROP, which was passed by the Human Rights Council (HRC) and the UN General Assembly (UNGA). States that did not vote in favor of UNDROP cannot object that it is not valid and applicable to food security issues, after it was supported by a strong majority in the UNGA and HRC.

Another small but important point of dispute relevant to the transformation of food systems is whether the term "peasant" can be included in policy recommendations, with the US again objecting to this despite widespread use of the term for self-identification by small-scale farmers around the world. Their objection may be based on concern that accepting the term peasant might be construed as accepting the UNDROP. Yet it is important to many people that policy recommendations specify that they apply to peasants, since these are the primary food producers in the world and also the most food-insecure group.

Also related to how human rights will be incorporated in CFS policy recommendations, disputes have centered on whether women's "empowerment" or women's "rights" and autonomy is the appropriate goal. For some people, empowerment has paternalistic connotations and involves an instrumentalist approach to gender equality. Programs that promote empowerment often do not tackle structural issues that prevent gender equality, but simply try to bring women into existing economic systems or add them to decision-making forums. Language may be shifting to "rights," however and toward a broader acceptance of states' obligations to protect rural women's rights in the CFS, as a strategy to re-politicize the issue of women's equality (Collins 2022). Narrative conflicts arose in negotiations over the Gender Equality and Women's Empowerment Guidelines because some delegates thought that the Zero Draft and First Draft did not sufficiently recognize that the patriarchal structures of inequality in dominant food systems have been designed to intentionally exclude and marginalize women, non-binary and LGBTIQ+ people (MacInnis et al. 2022). Questions about the meaning of "empowerment" came up in these negotiations as well.

The negotiations over Voluntary Guidelines on Food Systems and Nutrition (VGFSyN; CFS 2021a) were a critical missed opportunity for CFS to describe how food systems should operate to ensure food security and healthy food for all. The negotiations were frustrating and disappointing for the CSIPM, which was not able to approve the final guidelines. They had drafted their own vision of Food Systems and Nutrition (CSIPM 2021b), which was substantively different from the adopted Guidelines. The clash between upholding the status quo of neoliberal governance of food systems and a different vision, in which food and nutrition were addressed as global public goods that belong in the commons, is clear in a comparison of the final guidelines with the CFS Vision on Food Systems and Nutrition (CSIPM 2021b, 8).

> Transitioning from food systems with an understanding of food as a commodity towards a food commons regime for healthy, sustainable and just food systems should be based on sustainable agricultural practices (agroecology), and open-source knowledge (creative commons licenses) through the assumption of knowledge (cuisine recipes, agrarian practices, public research), material items (land, water, seeds, fish stocks) and abstract entities (transboundary food safety regulations, public nutrition) as global commons, governed in a polycentric and democratic manner, valuing the different dimensions of food.

Additional ways in which the CSIPM narrative differed from the CFS guidelines included recognition of the rights of Mother Earth; interconnections between ecosystem health and human health; interrelations of human rights including the right to food, UNDROP, UNDRIP and women's rights; and an emphasis on agency, participation and autonomy. None of these principles made their way into the negotiated Guidelines (CFS 2021a) including, remarkably, the centrality of the right to food, which is the core mandate of CFS. (The VGFSyN were intended to "build upon and complement" the Voluntary Guidelines on the Progressive Realization of the Right to Food, as well as a large number of other policy guidelines and recommendations "as far as each of these instruments are relevant and applicable and as far as they have been agreed, acknowledged and/or endorsed by respective Member States").

The CSIPM said that the guidelines do not guide the transformation and redirection of current dominant food systems. They do not embrace a holistic food systems lens, do not recognize the public interest of food systems and fail to take a holistic view of human rights as universal, interdependent and indivisible. They do not promote a sustainable healthy diet, nor do they recognize harms caused by current agriculture and trade policies or the damage caused by ultra-processed food and beverages and anti-microbial use for growth promotion of livestock. And finally, they fail to prioritize local, resilient and agroecological food systems (CSIPM 2021c). In short, the VGFSyN were designed to shore up the current neoliberal industrialized food system, with minor tweaks, while CSIPM wanted a transformation of that system. There were some positive aspects of the VGFSyN (SIANI 2021), but they did not point toward a real transformation of food systems. By adopting the VGFSyN in plenary, CFS Member States demonstrated that they are satisfied that this narrative is sufficient to address food system deficiencies, making clear that most Member States are ambivalent at best about transformation.

More narrative clashes came out in discussions of agroecology, which the CSIPM and many Member States support. Getting approval from CFS to commission a report on agroecology took years of work, and it was only approved if it also included "other innovations," at the insistence of a few large agro-exporting countries. The HLPE recruited internationally recognized experts who developed an excellent report describing agroecology and comparing it with other approaches to food systems such as sustainable intensification. Colin Anderson and Chris Maughan (2021) analyzed comments submitted as part of the online consultation on the HLPE report, in addition to participant observation and related UN literature, to discern the competing narratives at play. They distinguished an innovation frame and an agroecological narrative:

> Innovation is used to reinforce dominant conceptions of agency—overwhelmingly those exercised by individuals through markets—in ways

> that maintain the political status quo... [P]roponents of agroecology put forward a counter-discourse for the collective rights and agency of the "most affected"... [which] challenges the centrality of agribusiness, the hegemony of abstract indicators, the notion that technology is the most important form of innovation and the casting of food producers as end-users or consumers ... Centering the collective protagonism, voice, agency and autonomy of food producers and their communities in decision-making on the governance of food systems is a radical shift that is ... side-lined by the innovation imperative.
>
> *(2021, 12)*

As is customary, the HLPE report on agroecology and other innovations concluded with recommendations. The CSIPM thought that the recommendations were quite weak and did not go far enough to encourage agroecology, which the report had demonstrated to have superior outcomes on food security and nutrition in many dimensions. Then the policy negotiation weakened some of these already-weak recommendations significantly. For example, the HLPE report (2019, 22) recommended that regulations on the use of chemical harmful for human health and the environment in agriculture and food systems be strengthened, alternatives to their use promoted, and practices that produce without them be rewarded. However, the way this showed up in the negotiated text (CFS 2021b, 8–9) was:

> Recognizing the importance of the optimization, proper management and the reduction, as appropriate, of the risk of and the reliance on chemical pesticides and other agrochemicals for the protection and improvement of human, animal, plant health and the environment:
>
> h Raise policymakers' and public awareness, using a science and evidence-based approach, about the risks of pesticides and other agrochemicals, to human, animal and plant health and the environment;
>
> i Promote, based on agroecological and other innovative approaches, alternatives to chemical pesticides and the greater integration of biodiversity for food and agriculture. Promote the removal of highly hazardous pesticides, in line with recommendation 7.5 of the WHO/FAO International Code of Conduct on Pesticide Management and depending on specific context and national capacities;
>
> j Promote the human rights of all and recognize the importance of the values and interests of peasants, Indigenous peoples, local communities, family farmers, and other people working in rural areas, and the importance of strengthening

their ability to avoid exposure and poisoning from hazardous agrochemicals;

k Drawing on the International Code of Conduct for the Sustainable Use and Management of Fertilizers, the Voluntary Guidelines for Sustainable Soil Management, and consistent with national strategies and contexts, recognize the value of, and strengthen support for, agroecological and other innovative approaches that promote recycling, optimizing, or reducing, as appropriate, the reliance on external inputs, and facilitate the regeneration of soil health

Language from the HLPE recommendations that recommended bolstering regulation and finding alternatives was weakened in earlier drafts of the policy recommendations with phrases such as "as appropriate," "responsible use," "optimize the use of pesticides … and phase them out to the extent possible" and "optimize the use of synthetic fertilizers." CSIPM delegates were successful to some extent at damage control, but the final draft still included "promote the removal of highly hazardous pesticides" rather than simply removing them, and "optimizing, or reducing, as appropriate, the reliance on external inputs."

CSIPM members stated that the policy recommendations on agroecology and other innovations fell short of providing a normative framework that could effectively guide the urgently needed overhaul of industrial food systems. Furthermore, they normalized status quo arrangements of power held by agribusiness corporations and dominant agricultural exporting countries, at the expense of protecting vulnerable people by prioritizing human rights such as by referencing UNDROP, UNDRIP and CEDAW. The recommendations put agroecology on an equal level with so-called "innovative approaches" that are at best unproven and at worst unsustainable, and which either preserve or deepen the inequality, exploitation and power imbalances behind the current food system. They failed to recognize the social, economic and environmental impacts of the extractive industrial food system. And they did not recognize Indigenous and ancestral knowledge that contributes to agroecology (CSIPM 2021a). The negotiations of this set of policy recommendations was rushed to fit the timeline of the approached UN Food Systems Summit, and CSIPM members did not believe that they had equal opportunities to participate because of connectivity issues, timing of meetings, and lack of translation.

Policy recommendations drafted for negotiation are not required to strictly follow their corresponding HLPE reports, although by refusing to follow the report, Member States are explicitly rejecting the available evidence, which the HLPE compiles. The purpose of negotiation is to find language to which all parties can agree. The negotiations on agroecological and other innovative approaches and food systems and nutrition failed in this respect: CSIPM did not approve the final drafts, although they were accepted in plenary. CSIPM had presented coherent alternatives to the policy recommendations, which were not given full consideration; but they were blamed by some senior officials for being obstinate and unwilling to compromise. Another interpretation might be that CFS Member States had been obstinate and unwilling to compromise. However, given CSIPM's commitment to working within the constraints of the CFS, these criticisms led to soul-searching about the best way forward during subsequent policy negotiations.

Negotiations over policy recommendations regarding youth's role in food systems were contentious, as expected given the very different views held by CSIPM members and neoliberal governments. One of the big issues in the youth negotiations was whether youth should have agency to choose production systems that are not in the food-as-commodity narrative. The "modernist" trope of industrialized farming assumes that youth don't want to work on farms unless they can be "agripreneurs" and most see their future in moving to cities. While urbanization and migration to cities have been major demographic shifts in most countries, assuming that young people do not want to farm is a big leap from that. I explained in Chapter 2 that less than half of the 89 percent of smaller US farms where farming is still the principal occupation have positive incomes. US agricultural and food system policies favor large-scale farmers in many ways, and farmers do not receive prices above operating costs for most of their products. If it were possible to make a decent living from small- and mid-scale farming, I believe that we would see a reverse of the urbanization trend. In my home state of Vermont, the director of Vermont Land Trust said that he has a list of 250–300 young people at any given time who want to farm, if they can acquire land. These are people who have worked on farms, not starry-eyed romantics. But land concentration, aggravated by financializaton and farmland purchases by wealthy individuals such as Bill Gates and Ted Turner and asset management firms such as TIAA have driven up the cost of farmland exorbitantly. The cost of US farmland rose 14.3 percent between 2021 and 2022, then another 8.1 percent in 2023, pricing it out of reach of most young people (NASS 2023). Peter Rosset observed:

> …if we look at the last 50 years of human history, we've seen a massive migration from rural areas to cities. and where have those people gone? They've gone to urban slums, which has been the largest growing demographic segment of the world: urban and peri-urban slums. And those people who are now the majority of almost any Third World city—who are they? From my peasant-centric point of view, they are peasants—either peasants who are displaced, sons and daughters of peasants who are displaced, or grandkids of peasants who are displaced… [T]he MST [Landless Workers Movement in Brazil] is proof that many people in urban

> slums would love to be able to go back to the countryside if they could get a piece of land. And what holds them back usually is the fact that they can't get a piece of land.
>
> *(Rosset 2022)*

What has happened with land access in the US has been mirrored in other countries, with corporations and powerful governments buying up land in the Majority World to produce food or biofuels for the Minority World, as explained in Chapter 2.

The negotiations on Policy Recommendations for Promoting Youth Engagement and Employment in Agriculture laid bare the fundamental narrative clash between the status quo of neoliberal extractive economic structures and post-capitalist world-views. This clash emerges in other statements from the CSIPM but was especially well articulated by the youth. Their stated priorities included the need for land and power redistribution; creating enabling environments for agroecology and diversified food production; shortening supply chains and supporting local and territorial markets; climate justice; restitution and reparations to historically marginalized peoples, including Indigenous Peoples; confronting narratives of digitalization and entrepreneurship; ensuring dignified livelihoods for all youth and realizing the human rights of youth, in all their diversities. Each of these priorities was opposed by CFS Member States, especially the major agro-exporting countries, either explicitly or by weakening language in the policy recommendations. Supporting these priorities would require a genuine transformation of food systems, which is precisely what youth want and need (CSIPM 2020a) but which would turn current power relations upside-down. The CFS is not yet willing to accept such a transformation, even though existing neoliberal power relations are resulting in the polycrisis documented in Chapter 2: increasing hunger, loss of biodiversity, environmental disasters, pandemics and the destruction of rural communities worldwide.

Negotiations on Youth Policy Recommendations coincided with the COVID outbreak, and the youth explained steps that they were already taking in their respective regions to create a better food system:

> We, as a diverse community of Youth from around the globe, are active in developing solutions to the challenges facing our communities: we are organizing ourselves to continue providing food for our communities and caring for the elderly as well as our children; we are shortening the distance from producer to consumer; we are defending school feeding programs and local markets; we are rebuilding rural economies and territories, ensuring youth can stay and return in the countryside; we are caring for and healing the earth by growing nourishing food through agroecology; we are standing up to domestic violence against women and girls as

> well as racism, homophobia, xenophobia and the patriarchy; and, we are defending workers' and migrants' rights as well as the rights of rural people. We are also imagining new ways to organize the world: envisioning healthy, sustainable and dignified food systems, and taking steps towards achieving them. In our own constituencies and territories, and now here at the CFS, we are elaborating public policy demands to ensure that radical transformations occur NOW, before it is too late.
>
> *(CSIPM 2020a, 1)*

While the CSIPM supported the approval of the Policy Recommendations on youth, in a concession to criticisms that they had not been sufficiently willing to compromise on earlier negotiations, it had several critical reservations. The recommendations did not recognize the diversity of youth, particularly with respect to multiple, intersecting identities and the identities of persons historically subjected to discrimination based on their sexual orientation and gender identity. They did not explicitly recognize women's rights, and Youth dissociated themselves from the many caveats referring to internationally recognized human rights instruments. Since UNDROP and UNDRIP specify access to productive resources as human rights, the Youth objected to the term "equitable access." The agency of youth and the importance of food sovereignty had been discounted and replaced by references to "youth entrepreneurship." Youth ownership of digital tools and data was included only in a weak form, and the recommendations did not formulate a conception of innovation that acknowledges diverse forms of social, technical and cultural innovations that support transitions toward economies of well-being (which the Youth Declaration called for). And finally, the recommendations strayed far from the original HLPE report, which the Youth Working Group supported (CSIPM 2022b).

Negotiation of data recommendations was similarly contentious. CSIPM created a Vision Statement on Data for Food Security and Nutrition (CSIPM 2023), noting that the type of data collection that the CFS and governments are pursuing is led by powerful actors who own the technology and are expanding data collection and analysis as a new commodity. Through its discussions, the Data Working Group of CSIPM grew into a key space for global civil society to discuss the evolving effects of digital technologies on food and agriculture. They sought transparent and inclusive decision-making processes around the increasing role of data. Patti Naylor, the coordinator for the CSIPM Working Group on Data, commented:

> a lot of Member States didn't even understand what we were talking about. They didn't see it as anything that was concerning to them. They didn't realize the impact that it's going to have.
>
> *(2023)*

Ownership and control of data are rapidly consolidating, with harmful consequences for producers, food purchasers, communities and small businesses (e.g., African Centre for Biodiversity 2023; Montenegro de Wit and Canfield 2023; Seufert 2023). A narrative clash occurred in discussion of the data policy recommendations over whether governance should be included:

> [T]here were some member states that really did not want anything like that at all in there. And … right now, due to unfettered capitalism, corporations are collecting data on food production and making profits from it, and it will continue to do that. And that's what was not really challenged. And if we don't have some form of governance, you know,… that won't be challenged, that won't be controlled.
>
> *(Naylor 2023)*

This relates to different Member States' views on the appropriate role of CFS, with some wanting data governance to be handled by other agencies.

Narrative clashes *per se* are expected and should be welcomed in the CFS; but in many negotiations, civil society does not believe that its voice is being heard and respected. This is extremely important, if indeed the CFS is attempting to improve food security and nutrition of those who are most affected. Indubitably, the CSIPM is demanding a radical shift in how power and resources are distributed; but the neoliberal model that wealthy countries are defending simply does not deliver global public goods such as food security. The alternative from below that CSIPM wants to see is spelled out clearly in its Vision on Food Systems and Nutrition, the Youth Declaration, and the reports on how communities have been affected by COVID (CSIPM 2020b, 2021d). It is unfortunate that Member States are not willing to open up to discussion of these alternatives.

The world is undergoing major shifts in geopolitical alignments, from a unipolar world after the fall of the Soviet Union and the end of the Cold War to a multi-polar world with countries in the Majority World demanding more independence and reparations for the extensive damage caused by Minority-World policies which have led to climate chaos, plundered Majority-World resources, and forced developing countries into deep debt, preventing them from attending to the social welfare of their own people. Under the "Washington Consensus," developing countries were forced to reduce the size of the public sector and open up their economies to global trade in order to receive much-needed financial assistance. The results have been devastating for many developing countries, which are now heavily indebted net food importers and increasingly vulnerable (Margulis 2017; Guillen and Cortés Torres 2023). These re-alignments are shaking the CFS. Furthermore, every country has been forced to confront vulnerabilities related to the COVID pandemic, climate change and disruptions to supplies of fuel and fertilizer due to Russia's invasion of Ukraine. But rather than exploring alternative ways to organize food systems for the public good, wealthy countries seem to be hunkering down to maintain their current grasp on power.

While the original intent of the CFS reform was to provide greater coherence to food system governance, stepping beyond national priorities in a time of re-alignments and threats seems to be almost impossible for some countries. CFS was supposed to be a space for learning, enabled by HLPE reports and listening to other participants. Learning from those who experience hunger and malnutrition is especially important, since they understand best the obstacles that must be overcome in their own countries. But asking country delegates to respectfully consider other ways to govern food systems beyond what their own governments support may be a step too far. CFS is after all a political forum and as such reflects the diversity of political arrangements of Member States. Olivier De Schutter (2014, 236) called for collective learning and monitoring as key components of the work of CFS:

> The various parties in the CFS each have their own views, shaped by diverse historical experiences and ideologies, about where hunger and malnutrition stem from, and what should be done about them. Only by agreeing to question the presuppositions, and by accepting that the framing by each of the questions to be addressed may not be the only framing possible, can true collective learning take place.

If Member States are not open at least to considering alternatives and learning from civil society, we have little prospect of food security and adequate nutrition for all people. This is the reason why countries purportedly invest time in the CFS, and no other UN body is able to develop these solutions.

How might narrative clashes in the CFS be handled such that opposing sides could work together toward shared policies? Narrative clashes should be openly recognized and examined for underlying evidence from many sources. In particular, CFS needs a resolution of how human rights will be included in its policy recommendations and guidelines, since this is a constant source of conflict. Closer interaction with the Human Rights Council might help with this, although many countries are moving away from human rights as an anchor for discussing how to address current crises, in favor of the Sustainable Development Goals (Duncan et al. 2021). This may be due mostly to some countries' wish to devalue human rights, but they remain as a strong guiding framework with legally binding agreements. Movement toward the SDGs instead of human rights may also be due to the opportunities that they provide to the private sector. As the Head of Corporate Sustainability and Public Affairs for a Danish corporation enthused:

> The SDGs are a gift to business because the economic rewards for delivering to the needs defined in the SDGs are very significant. According to the

> Business & Sustainable Development Commission, the potential economic reward from delivering solutions to the SDGs could be worth at least $12 trillion each year in market opportunities and generate up to 380 million new jobs by 2030.
>
> *(Pedersen 2018, 23)*

Rights-based approaches are not nearly as lucrative and often entail cutting corporate profits to allow adequate salaries for workers. As explained in Chapter 8, cutting profits is a red line for corporations (which have amassed spectacular profits during COVID and repeated food price crises).

The 2009 reform decision to include representatives from other agencies that deal with food systems in some way was intended to provide consistency across different forums, but some CFS Member States do not allow discussion of trade, which has obvious ramifications on food security, or other topics beyond a strict focus on food security and nutrition. This hobbles CFS's ability to create coherent policies. Olivier De Schutter's observation still rings true: "What we need is not more separation, but instead more consistency across policy areas that cannot be considered in isolation" (2014, 228). This might be facilitated if CFS had more leeway to consider *all* topics that have impacts on food security and nutrition and closer connections with other agencies such as the Human Rights Council and the UN Conference on Trade and Development (UNCTAD), so that policies are congruent.

Just as CFS needs wider scope, the HLPE needs to be able to identify emerging issues and develop reports on them as the experts see fit instead of waiting to be commissioned by CFS. The HLPE provides solid, evidence-based reports to inform CFS decisions, with ample and transparent opportunities for feedback from different constituencies of CFS; and it integrates different sources of knowledge. A wider scope for HLPE would require a larger budget. More discussion of HLPE and CSIPM reports through seminars and events might help Member States understand how these apply to their own countries (Guttal 2021).

Lack of transparency and conflict-of-interest policies is another major impediment for CFS, combined with private sector funding for some workstreams. The Bill & Melinda Gates Foundation (BMGF) pushed for and funded the data negotiations; selection of this topic was surely influenced by BMGF's generous funding of FAO with $11M in 2022 and $10M in 2023 (FAO 2022, 2023). Exactly how much FAO depends on the BMGF for funding is not clear, because FAO does not make contributions public. CFS and FAO could start with the World Health Organization's framework for conflict-of-interest policies (designed for companies that sell tobacco and breast-milk substitutes), although policies need to limit where companies with conflicts of interest can participate in CFS and not simply require that conflicts be declared. In addition, CFS and CSIPM would both benefit from larger and less precarious budgets, with a larger percentage coming from public rather than private or foundation sources to avoid the perception or reality that the private sector is dictating decisions.

CFS is still struggling to reconcile different perspectives on how civil society, as the rights-holders whose right to food is not being realized, should be incorporated. The 2009 reform laid out one pathway, which sufficed for nearly two decades. But the PSM has steadily pushed for more control of decision-making through its request to have an equal number of seats as CSIPM holds in the Advisory Group and by advancing various agreements between FAO and private sector coalitions including the World Economic Forum, CropLife and the International Fertilizer Association (Naik et al. 2022) and individual companies including Danone, Syngenta, Mars, Rabobank and Unilever (Liaison Group 2023). These moves have weakened the relative strength of CSIPM. FAO has opened the door and encourages more partnerships with the private sector in its Strategy for Private Sector Engagement 2021–2025 (FAO 2021). FAO's strategy has clear impacts on the CFS, but it is heading in a quite different direction from CFS products and commitments. For example, the private sector does not acknowledge food security as a public good and is committed to providing food through markets rather than federal or international social protection. It wants governance of food systems through multistakeholder coalitions, rather than through the multilateral one-country-one-vote of the CFS, despite the many weaknesses of multistakeholderism described in Chapter 6.

The multilateral system in the CFS is far from perfect: stronger Member States overpower weaker states and have funding to keep permanent staff in Rome, able to engage across many different policy areas. But multistakeholderism and strengthening corporate roles in governance are not the solution. To a large extent, corporations have been successful in wresting greater control, and the UN Food Systems Summit of 2021 and its sequelae demonstrated the consequences. As Jomo Sundaram warned before the Summit: "the UNFSS seems like a Trojan Horse to advance particular corporate interests, inadvertently undermining what UN-led multilateralism has come to mean" (Sundaram 2021, n.p.).

THE UN Food Systems Summit and its Aftermath

The Food Systems Summit (UNFSS) did not come from CFS, despite CFS's recognized role in addressing food security and nutrition. It bypassed Member States as well. Its organizing team did not even include representatives from CFS until their absence became an embarrassment. The CFS Chair initially was given a very minor role in the "Champions Network," but later elevated to be part of the Advisory Committee. The Scientific Group of the UNFSS invited the Chair of the HLPE in his personal capacity to join, but there was no recognition of the 15 reports by the HLPE nor of the CFS Voluntary Guidelines on Food Systems and Nutrition. These developments obviously baffled the CFS Secretariat and left many issues hanging, especially as the Deputy Secretary-General of the UN, Amina Mohammed, promised that no new structures would be established through the UNFSS. Would the CFS be expected to pick up the pieces after the Summit and coordinate Coalitions or review financial pledges? Given that the HLPE was the UN system's only formal science-policy interface on issues of food security and nutrition, how would the new Scientific Group build on its work and avoid undermining it? How would the products of CFS such as the VGGT and right to food guidelines be incorporated in national dialogs and transition pathways? (CFS 2021c). These questions were never really answered before the Summit, and it became increasingly clear that the Summit was designed to usurp the role of CFS.

The UNFSS was unusual in many respects, as compared with previous world food summits. First, it addressed food systems instead of just production and food security. Food systems are hardly a new idea; scholars had used the term for a couple of decades. But the Scientific Group of the UNFSS felt a need to define them and did so in a mechanistic way that did not take advantage of previous work (von Braun et al. 2021a). Second, the conference did not come out of the FAO (or CFS), the UN bodies with responsibility for food systems. Previous summits have been organized by the FAO with a political mandate conferred by Member States and negotiated outcomes. While the Secretary-General has the right to organize brief summits on issues which he feels to be important, these generally don't involve lengthy preparation or follow-up. Third, it involved national representatives only as members of multistakeholder partnerships; and MSIs were the basic structure of all of the groups formed through the Summit. This undermined the multilateral institutional structure of the UN. Fourth, human rights were invisible in early iterations of Summit documents, and only included at the insistence of civil society. This was especially peculiar since the UN Secretary-General had presented a "Call to Action for Human Rights" to the UN HRC in February, 2020, calling on countries to "put human rights principles and mechanisms front and centre in the implementation of the Sustainable Development Goals" (Fakhri 2021b). Fifth, corporations put their stamp on the Summit from the very beginning through the WEF/UN partnership agreement and the revolving door of corporate and WEF executives who played leadership roles in the Summit. The early appointment of Agnes Kalibata, President of the Alliance for a Green Revolution in Africa, as Special Envoy of the Summit was the most prominent of these alliances between corporate and UN interests. And sixth, it re-created existing structure in the UN System, most obviously by establishing a new "Scientific Group" whose Chair actively advocated for a permanent replacement of the HLPE (World Food Journal 2021; von

Braun et al. 2021b). Its efforts to build a platform for civil society replicated the CSIPM (poorly) and the Summit itself replicated many of the goals of the CFS (see Canfield et al. 2021; Canfield, Duncan et al. 2021; McMichael 2021; Fakhri 2022 for additional details).

I attended many of the Summit sessions virtually and participated in most of the meetings of an "Action Track" on "Nature Positive Production." I also participated in *ad hoc* groups on governance of food systems and governance of the Summit itself (whose coordinator resigned after several months of work due to lack of transparency by the Summit leadership). A dizzying array of Action Tracks, Action Areas, Levers of Change, networks, Working Groups, dialogues and coalitions held calls and produced reports which were overwhelming in sum. Since COVID was officially recognized as a pandemic in spring of 2020, most Summit activities were virtual, which limited participation of people who do not speak English, lack connectivity to the Internet or are outside European time-zones. The Summit consumed vast amounts of time and money, but the Special Rapporteur on the Right to Food, Michael Fakhri (2022, 35), wrote that it

> left the world with a jumble of ideas and no clear path forward for transforming the world's food systems. The Summit was touted as the ultimate place to provide the world with solutions—but it never clarified the problems with the dominant food systems leaving participants with no coherent or cohesive framework. Most distressingly, the Food Systems Summit did not put the COVID-19 pandemic and ensuing food crisis anywhere on its agenda.

Many competent people committed their time to the UNFSS, in hopes that something positive could come from it despite the chaotic organizing and lack of transparency (Anderson et al. 2022). It was an extraordinary production mounted with ambition and USD $24 million (Fakhri 2022). So how did it achieve so little? In this section, I give a short overview of the Summit and its aftermath, followed by description of narrative clashes that emerged. Many of these, not surprisingly, mirror CFS clashes. I suggest that failing to recognize and respect these clashes was a big contributor to the underwhelming results of the Summit.

UN Secretary-General António Guterres announced the Summit in October 2019, acknowledging that food insecurity and malnutrition were increasing and the world was not on track to end hunger by 2030, the goal of SDG2. This announcement was preceded by a Memorandum of Understanding between the World Economic Forum, whose members are the world's largest multinational corporations, and the Deputy Director-General. The Summit in September of 2021 was preceded by a Pre-Summit in late July of the same year and "Science Days," a two-day event in early July. One of the commitments made by the Secretary-General during the Summit was to hold "stocktaking" events every two years until 2030 to show progress made. The first one took place in 2023.

The first clash to consider is what is meant by "inclusivity," something that conference organizers believed that they were achieving. The FSS was billed as a "People's Summit" and adhered to a principle of inclusion known as "all affected," whereby anyone was able to participate in one way or another (Lagerspetz 2015). This principle actually excludes some voices because it does not recognize existing power asymmetries and how some participants can dominate others. Matt Canfield, Jessica Duncan and Priscilla Claeys (2021) contrasted this approach with participation of the "most-affected," which underlies the choice of constituencies in the CSIPM. At a press conference, Jennifer Peltz of the Associated Press asked Deputy Secretary-General Amina Mohammed about the concern that the summit was "too topdown, too tech-focused, and too corporate" and got a defensive response:

> In terms of inclusiveness, I actually don't know of a more inclusive process than the one that has been had on the food systems process. I've heard that this is "elite capture". I'm not sure which part of it is elite, and it would be good to hear about that.
>
> *(Moran 2021, n.p.)*

Although the organizers may have believed that they were being "inclusive," they controlled the agenda of both the Pre-Summit and Summit, giving the floor early on to corporate spokespeople from Nestlé, Unilever, PepsiCo, Syngenta, Yara and Bayer and only inviting civil society representatives at later points. They maintained "strategic silence" on corporate power and its domination of food systems and promoted "solutions" based on technology and innovation coming from corporations. The Scientific Group glued science to technology and innovation, as if that is the main purpose of science, even though the words "technology" and "innovation" did not appear in their terms of reference (Clapp et al. 2021).

The biggest omission, in terms of inclusivity, was the CFS and especially the CSIPM, as the largest formally recognized organization of civil society working on food security and nutrition in the UN system. In letters to the CFS Chair and the Secretary-General in September 2019, March 2020 and February 2021, CSIPM laid out its concerns regarding the Summit and the partnership with WEF. It said that it "could not jump on a train that is heading in the wrong direction," and as a condition for its involvement, asked for an additional Action Track on the transformation of corporate food systems to be organized by CSIPM (CSIPM 2021e, n.p.). When Ms. Mohammed finally met with members of the CSIPM more than a year after the March 2020 letter, which had been signed by nearly 550 international, regional and domestic organizations, she made clear that this Action Track would not be established and disagreed with many concerns that the CSIPM had raised (CSIPM 2021f). However, UNFSS organizers had understood the message that they had to include civil society more prominently. Cherry-picked representatives from civil society who would not be critical of the UNFSS were invited, after conference organizers saw that their failure to work with CSIPM was undercutting the potential success of the Summit.

Many civil society organizations did choose to participate in the FSS, and some of the largest international NGOs co-led Action Tracks. Civil society is quite diverse, and participation advanced the agendas of some organizations. For many small, local organizations in the Majority World suffering from governmental oppression, the UNFSS was seen as an opportunity to gain voice in a global forum; and they did not have the information and analysis to consider the down-sides. Other organizations sincerely believed that they could play roles both from within and from without. Given the lack of clarity on how input would be used, it was tempting to think that participation might influence the outcomes. But by and large, civil society other than organizations that support market-oriented policies was completely drowned out by corporate voices and the FSS further entrenched problematic power dynamics.

In addition to ignoring CSIPM and its supporters, Summit organizers did not understand the need for self-organization of civil society. They repeatedly suggested to Michael Fakhri that civil society should voice their concerns through Food System Summit Dialogues, even though civil society "has always had an autonomous space in international food institutions and processes" since the World Food Summit of 1996. He had spoken with several civil society organizations, who told him that "Food Systems Summit Dialogues as currently structured do not provide an enabling environment and autonomous space for full and meaningful participation" (Fakhri 2021b, n.p.).

The second major clash regarded the role of the private sector and in particular large multinational corporations that have been responsible for much of the environmental, health and social degradation of industrialized, extractive agriculture. The fundamental clash between extractive and regenerative systems was apparent in many ways: for instance, agroecology did not even appear in the program for a full year and was only added at the insistence of civil society, the Special Rapporteur on the Right to Food and several scholars. When asked about agroecology in an interview, the Chair of the Scientific Group responded:

> [T]he Summit must not get bogged down in ideological battles, but must focus on the challenges, especially with regard to smallholder farmers in developing countries and the question of how they can move from a low level of productivity in arable and livestock farming to more income with productivity and sustainability.
>
> *(World Food Journal 2021, n.p.)*

Agroecology was only mentioned as one of multiple innovations at landscape level in the introductory chapter that the Scientific Group prepared for the Action Track on nature positive solutions, but two chapters on agroecology were added to the reader of papers by the Scientific Group published online in 2023 (well after the Summit had taken place). Agroecology was never elevated during the Summit as a priority, despite its strong international support and solid evidence base for providing better nutrition, resilience, environmental protection and livelihoods (see Chapter 7 for more on agroecology).

Summit leadership did not allow a critique of the overweening power that agri-food corporations hold over the food system, as CSIPM had demanded. But that power was evident throughout the preparatory stage, Science Days, the Pre-Summit and the Summit. MSIs were the only mode of participation in Action Tracks, working groups, coalitions, national dialogues to develop national pathways and other spaces set up for participation. By bypassing multilateral decision-making, the Summit bypassed the foremost avenues of accountability by which people hold their own governments responsible for their actions. Accountability and whether it is essential was another significant narrative clash. As explained in civil society and scholarly critiques before and during the Summit (e.g., Gleckman 2013; McKeon 2017; ETC Group 2021; La Via Campesina 2021; Liaison Group 2021), MSIs privilege corporate-friendly perspectives, ignore asymmetries of power, subsume human rights to private profits and lack any systems of accountability. Just as the structure of the corporation is designed to allow individuals as shareholders to evade any personal liability for human rights abuses or financial malfeasance of the corporation, the structure of MSIs evades accountability. It also contributes to fragmentation of global food governance (Fakhri 2021a).

Blurring the roles of the private and public sectors obscured who should be at the UNFSS. As mentioned above, the choice of Agnes Kalibata as Special Envoy signaled that market-friendly "solutions" such as those promoted by AGRA would dominate the outcomes and proceedings. In an early meeting with the CSIPM at CFS, she referred disparagingly to "peasants" and clearly believed that they were inferior to farmers using "advanced" technology. In November 2020, the World Economic Forum organized a virtual pre-event that mirrored the themes that became apparent in the Summit. It included as speakers and participants "all members of Summit leadership, heads of State, government ministers, the World Farmers Organization, national and international civil servants, leaders from major agri-food corporations, representatives from philanthropic organizations and academics" (Fakhri 2021a, 12/24). If it wasn't already obvious, this event clarified who was in the Summit driver's seat and "inside circle."

Just as in the CFS, how and even whether human rights would be considered in the UNFSS became a point of contention. Michael Fakhri, the UN Special Rapporteur on the Right to Food, advocated tirelessly for greater attention to human rights for more than a year before he gained a role in the leadership team. He pointed out that human rights were lacking in nearly all of the Action Tracks and generously offered his assistance to the Summit. His post-Summit assessment was:

> When it came to human rights, the Summit leadership oscillated between hostility and ambivalence. This contradicted the sixty-year history of UN food summits, a period during which the right to food gained prominence on the agenda and civil society organizations gained clout within the process.
>
> *(Fakhri 2022, 16)*

The next major narrative clash, closely related to how the private sector's views were elevated in the Summit, was over the kinds of knowledge that are needed. Indigenous and traditional knowledge was consistently ignored or demoted, and science leading to new technology and innovations was advanced. The Chair of the Scientific Group, Joachim von Braun, is an agricultural economist "deeply embedded in the corporate-philanthropic network that has promoted market-based and technology-driven approaches to food systems" (Canfield et al. 2021, 184). The group that he recruited comprised 20 natural scientists and nine economists, with no representation from other social sciences, no Indigenous scholars and no scholars with expertise in food system transition. High-tech "solutions" that were promoted included genetic engineering, genome editing, digital farming and the use of blockchain technologies, sometimes with the goal of making these technologies more accessible to women, Indigenous people and other marginalized groups so that they are not "left behind." The Scientific Group ignored controversies over these technologies and the fact that they are products of an increasingly privatized agricultural innovation system (Clapp et al. 2021). At best, the Scientific Group that was established for the Summit was reformist, advising on ways to advance market-friendly approaches to food systems without addressing the need to transform power relations. But its insidious efforts to replace the HLPE with a new Scientific Group established for the Coordination Hub meant that it refused to be silenced or to share the "expert" role (see IPES-Food 2021).

What narrative did civil society critics of the UNFSS advance, to counter this elitist agenda? Civil society organized a massive counter-mobilization in July during the Pre-Summit to lay out its own agenda (CSIPM 2021g). The counter-mobilization was attended by around 9000 people who saw and heard from African seed sovereignty networks; eco-feminist collectives; Native land and water protectors; and peasant organizations from Africa, Europe, Asia, Latin America and the Caribbean. They made their demands clear: recognition of the urgent need for real transformation of power relations in the food system; public policies and support for food sovereignty; agroecology; human rights as indivisible and universal; youth agency; social, gender and economic justice; regulation of corporate control and the financialization of food systems; preservation of biodiversity; and full, effective participation in policymaking processes (FoodSystems4People 2023).

Taking these steps would return FAO and the CFS to the conception of food as a public good and human right. Initially, FAO's mandate was to stabilize and manage food security on a world scale, with food to be treated as an essential of life rather than primarily as merchandise. This vision of food as a public good was weakened by the World Bank redefining food security as "the ability to purchase food" (Canfield et al 2021, 4), then further weakened as the corporate food regime deepened its reach, with the complicity of powerful governments.

Food Systems Summit leadership back-tracked on its commitment not to establish any new institutions by setting up a Coordination Hub to be hosted by FAO and jointly led by the UN Deputy Secretary-General and the heads of the FAO, WFP, IFAD, WHO and UNEP. The new structure has a biennial budget of USD $14 million, more than double the budget of the CFS. The Coordination Hub does not include national governments in its governance structure, but it does have a new Scientific Policy Interface (led by von Braun), as well as a new hand-picked Stakeholder Engagement and Networking Advisory Group, duplicating the functions of the CFS and HLPE. However, as in the 2021 Summit, the Coordination Hub fails to respect the right of civil society to autonomous self-organization and reinforces the corporate-friendly approaches of the Food Systems Summit, where discussions on regulation or limitations on corporate expansion and concentration were conspicuously absent (FoodSystems4People 2023).

The first Summit "stock-taking" event in July of 2023 reiterated the themes of the 2021 Summit: more technology, more innovation and "investment" are needed, but there will be no criticism of existing power relations. Another counter-mobilization was organized, but the Coordination Hub leadership was impervious to criticism. Perhaps the biggest danger of this non-event is that it may segue into the Summit of the Future, based on the Secretary-General's report *Our Common Future* and the High Level Advisory Board's elaboration of how this will play out through MSIs, renamed "networked multilateralism" (UN Secretary-General 2021; HLAB 2023).

Given this increasingly bleak portrait of international food forums, what is happening at the local and sub-national scales to promote regenerative food systems? After being thwarted or simply overwhelmed by happenings at the international level, many people have turned to cultivating their own gardens, as "the Turk" advised Candide in Voltaire's famous satire (Voltaire 2002). The next chapter addresses various fledgling and well-established grassroots initiatives to transform food systems.

References

African Centre for Biodiversity. 2023. The rise of digital agriculture and dispossession in Africa: implications for smallholder farmers. *Fact Sheet*. Johannesburg, South Africa. https://acbio.org.za/wp-content/uploads/2023/08/Rise-of-digital-agriculture_dispossession_Africa_and_smallholder-farmers_factsheet.pdf

Anderson, CR and C Maughan. 2021. "The Innovation Imperative": the struggle over agroecology in the international food policy arena. *Front Sustain Food Syst* 5(18 February 2021). https://doi.org/10.3389/fsufs.2021.619185

Anderson, M, L Hoey, P Hurst, M Miller and M Montenegro de Wit. 2022. Debrief on the United Nations Food Systems Summit (UNFSS). *J Agric Food Systems Comm Dev* 11(2). https://doi.org/10.5304/jafscd.2022.112.008

Bread for the World. 2023. What are the challenges of smallholder farmers around the world? https://www.bread.org/article/challenges-of-smallholder-farmers/

Canfield, M, M Anderson and P McMichael. 2021. UN Food Systems Summit 2021: dismantling democracy and resetting corporate control of food systems. *Front Sust Food Syst* 5(April 2021). https://doi.org/10.3389/fsufs.2021.661552

Canfield, M, J Duncan and P Claeys. 2021. Reconfiguring food systems governance: the UNFSS and the battle over authority and legitimacy. *Development* 64:181–191. https://doi.org/10.1057/s41301-021-00312-1

Civil Society and Indigenous Peoples Mechanism (CSIPM). 2020a. Youth policy demands for a radical transformation of our food system. Youth Working Group. https://www.csm4cfs.org/csm-youth-policy-declaration-covid-19/

Civil Society and Indigenous Peoples Mechanism (CSIPM). 2020b. *Voices from the ground: from COVID-19 to Radical Transformation of our food systems*. https://www.csm4cfs.org/wp-content/uploads/2020/12/EN-COVID_FULL_REPORT-2020.pdf

Civil Society and Indigenous Peoples Mechanism (CSIPM). 2021a. CSM Positioning on the CFS Policy Recommendations on agroecological and other innovative approaches https://www.csm4cfs.org/csm-positioning-on-the-cfs-policy-recommendations-on-agroecological-and-other-innovative-approaches/

Civil Society and Indigenous Peoples Mechanism (CSIPM). 2021b. CSM vision on food systems and nutrition. An alternative to the CFS Voluntary Guidelines on Food Systems and Nutrition (VGFSYN). https://www.csm4cfs.org/wp-content/uploads/2021/04/EN-vision-VGFSyN.pdf

Civil Society and Indigenous Peoples Mechanism (CSIPM). 2021c. Public briefing on final CSIPM assessment of the Voluntary Guidelines on Food Systems and Nutrition. https://www.csm4cfs.org/csm-public-briefing-transcript/

Civil Society and Indigenous Peoples Mechanism (CSIPM). 2021d. *Voices from the ground 2: Transformative solutions to the Global Systemic food crisis*. https://www.csm4cfs.org/wp-content/uploads/2022/09/layout-CSIPM-report-EN.pdf

Civil Society and Indigenous Peoples Mechanism (CSIPM). 2021e. CSM Letter to the CFS Chair on the UN Food Systems Summit. https://www.csm4cfs.org/letter-csm-coordination-committee-cfs-chair/

Civil Society and Indigenous Peoples Mechanism (CSIPM). 2021f. Multilateralism and transformation of corporate food systems: different visions, different pathways. https://www.csm4cfs.org/multilateralism-transformation-corporate-food-systems-different-visions-different-pathways/

Civil Society and Indigenous Peoples Mechanism (CSIPM). 2021g. Thousands mobilize to call for food systems that empower people, not companies. https://www.csm4cfs.org/thousands-mobilize-to-call-for-food-systems-that-empower-people-not-companies/

Civil Society and Indigenous Peoples Mechanism (CSIPM). 2022a. A CSIPM update on the reconvened CFS 50th plenary session. https://www.csm4cfs.org/a-csipm-update-on-the-reconvened-cfs-50th-session/

Civil Society and Indigenous Peoples Mechanism (CSIPM). 2022b. Youth reservations on the CFS policy recommendations. https://www.csm4cfs.org/youth-reservations-on-the-cfs-policy-recommendations/

Civil Society and Indigenous Peoples Mechanism (CSIPM). 2023. Vision Statement on Data for Food Security and Nutrition. https://www.csm4cfs.org/csipm-vision-statement-on-data-for-food-security-and-nutrition/

Clapp, J, I Noyes and Z Grant. 2021. The Food Systems Summit's failure to address corporate power. *Development* 64:192–198. https://doi.org/10.1057/s41301-021-00303-2

Collins, AM. 2022. Empowerment, rights, and global food governance: gender in the UN Committee for World Food Security. *Globalizations* 19(2):220–237. https://doi.org/10.1080/14747731.2021.1877006

Committee on World Food Security (CFS). 2009. Reform of the Committee on World Food Security. Final Version. CFS:2009/2 Rev. 2. https://www.fao.org/3/k7197e/k7197e.pdf

Committee on World Food Security (CFS). 2021a. Voluntary Guidelines on Food Security and Nutrition. CFS 2021/49/Inf.14 https://www.fao.org/3/ng550en/ng550en.pdf

Committee on World Food Security (CFS). 2021b. CFS Policy Recommendations on Agroecological and Other Innovative Approaches for Sustainable Agriculture and Food Systems that Enhance Food Security and Nutrition. CFS 2021/48/2. https://www.fao.org/3/nf777en/nf777en.pdf

Committee on World Food Security (CFS). 2021c. The UN Food Systems Summit and its implications for CFS. CFS 2021/49/Inf.15.

De Schutter, O. 2014. The reform of the Committee on World Food Security: the quest for coherence in global governance. Pp. 219–238. In: NCS Lambek, P Claeys, A Wong and L Brilmeyer (Eds.) *Rethinking Food Systems. Structural Challenges, New Strategies and the Law*. Dordrecht: Springer.

Duncan, J and D Barling. 2012. Renewal through participation in global food security governance: implementing the International Food Security and Nutrition Civil Society Mechanism to the Committee on World Food Security. *Int J Soc Agric Food* 19(2):143–161. https://doi.org/10.48416/ijsaf.v19i2.221

Duncan, J, N Lambek and P Claeys. 2021. The Committee on World Food Security: advances and challenges 10 years after the reform. https://edepot.wur.nl/554200

ETC Group. 2021. *Hijacking Food Systems: Technofix takeover at the FSS*. Communiqué #118.

ETC Group. 2022. *Backgrounder: Small Scale Farmers and Peasants Still Feed the World*. https://www.etcgroup.org/content/backgrounder-small-scale-farmers-and-peasants-still-feed-world

Fakhri, M. 2021a. Interim report of the Special Rapporteur on the right to food, Michael Fakhri. UN General Assembly, 76th Session. A/76/237.

Fakhri, M. 2021b. Open letter by the UN Food Rapporteur to Agnes Kalibata, Special Envoy of the UN Secretary-General. https://quota.media/open-letter-by-the-un-food-rapporteur-to-agnes-kalibata-special-envoy-of-the-un-secretary-general/

Fakhri, M. 2022. The Food System Summit's disconnection from people's real needs. *J Agric Env Ethics* 35(3):16. 10.1007/s10806-022-09882-7

Food and Agriculture Organization (FAO). 2021. FAO Strategy for Private Sector Engagement, 2021–2025. Rome. https://doi.org/10.4060/cb3352en

Food and Agriculture Organization (FAO). 2022. FAO launches new phase of agriculture policy initiative with $11 million grant from Bill and Melinda Gates Foundation. https://www.fao.org/newsroom/detail/fao-launches-new-phase-of-MAFAP-initiative-with-11-million-from-gates-foundation/en

Food and Agriculture Organization (FAO). 2023. FAO welcomes $10 million donation from Bill & Melinda Gates Foundation to fight Desert Locust upsurge in East Africa. https://www.fao.org/news/story/en/item/1263404/icode/

FAO, IFAD, UNICEF, WFP and WHO. 2023. The State of Food Security and Nutrition in the World 2023. Urbanization, agrifood systems transformation and healthy diets across the rural–urban continuum. Rome, FAO. https://doi.org/10.4060/cc3017en

FoodSystems4People. 2023. To overcome the global food crisis, we need real food systems change for people and the planet. https://foodsystems4people.org/to-overcome-the-global-food-crisis-we-need-real-food-systems-change-for-people-and-the-planet/

Gleckman, H. 2012. Reader's Guide: Global Redesign Initiative. https://staging.umb.edu/gri

Gleckman, H. 2013. Multi-stakeholder governance seeks to dislodge multilateralism. *Civicus* http://www.civicus.org/images/A%20critical%20assessment%20of%20the%20World%20Economic%20Forums.pdf

Guillen, A and I Cortés Torres. 2023. The decline of American hegemony: Biden's foreign policy toward China. *Agrarian South: J Polit Econ* 12(3): 247–272. https://doi.org/10.1177/22779760231185860

Guttal, S. 2021. Re-imagining the UN Committee on World Food Security. *Development* 64:227–235. https://doi.org/10.1057/s41301-021-00322-z

High Level Advisory Board (HLAB). 2023. A Breakthrough for People and Planet: Effective and Inclusive Global Governance for Today and the Future. https://highleveladvisoryboard.org/new-blueprint-calls-for-reinvigorated-global-governance/

International Agri-Food Network (IAFN). 2011. CFS Private Sector modalities. https://www.fao.org/fileadmin/templates/cfs/Docs1112/WGs/PWB/PriorityInfoSession21March/Private_Sector_Modalities_Approved_FINAL.pdf

International Panel of Experts for Sustainable Food Systems (IPES-Food). 2021. An 'IPCC for Food'? *How the UN Food Systems Summit is being used to advance a problematic new science-policy agenda.* https://www.ipes-food.org/_img/upload/files/GovBrief.pdf

Klein, N. 2008. *The Shock Doctrine: The Rise of Disaster Capitalism.* London: Picador.

Lagerspetz, E. 2015. Democracy and the all-affected principle. *Res Cogitans* 10(1):6–23.

Lambek, N. 2014. The UN Committee on World Food Security's break from the agricultural productivity trap. *Transnat Legal Theory* 9(3/4):415–429. https://doi.org/10.1080/20414005.2018.1573406

La Via Campesina. 2021. A Summit under siege: La Via Campesina position paper on the UN Food Systems Summit 2021. https://viacampesina.org/en/position-paper-a-summit-under-siege-corporate-control-of-2021-un-food-summit-endangers-food-sovereignty/

Liaison Group, CSIPM. 2021. Risks of the increased systemic corporate capture fueled by the UN Food Systems Summit (UNFSS) and its follow up process. https://www.foodsystems4people.org/wp-content/uploads/2022/05/UNFSSAnalysisReportMay2022_FS4P.pdf

Liaison Group, CSIPM. 2023. Multistakeholderism and the corporate capture of global food governance. What is at risk in 2023? https://reliefweb.int/report/world/multistakeholderism-and-corporate-capture-global-food-governance-what-risk-2023

MacInnis, J, N Wiebe, AA Desmarais and M Montenegro de Wit. 2022. "This feminism is transformative, rebellious and autonomous": inside struggles to shape the CFS Voluntary Guidelines on Gender Equality and Women's Empowerment. *Agroecol Sust Food Syst* 46(7):955–968. https://doi.org/10.1080/21683565.2022.2091717

Margulis, ME. 2017. The forgotten history of food security in multilateral trade negotiations. *World Trade Rev* 16(1):25–57. https://doi.org/10.1017/S1474745616000410

McKeon, N. 2009. *The United Nations and Civil Society: Legitimating Global Governance—Whose Voice?* London: Zed Books.

McKeon, N. 2015a. *Food Security Governance: Empowering Communities, Regulating Corporations*. London: Routledge.

McKeon, N. 2015b. Global food governance in an era of crisis: lessons from the United Nations Committee on World Food Security. *Canadian Food Stud/RCEA* 2(2): 328–334. https://doi.org/10.15353/cfs-rcea.v2i2.134

McKeon, N. 2017. Are equity and sustainability a likely outcome when foxes and chickens share the same coop? Critiquing the concept of multistakeholder governance of food security. *Globalizations* 14(3):379–398. https://doi.org/10.1080/14747731.2017.1286168

McMichael, P. 2021. Shock and awe in the UNFSS. *Development* 64:162–171. https://doi.org/10.1057/s41301-021-00304-1

Montenegro de Wit, M and M Canfield. 2023. 'Feeding the world, byte by byte': emergent imaginaries of data productivism. *J Peasant Stud* 51(2):381–420. https://doi.org/10.1080/03066150.2023.2232997

Moran, G. 2021. Did the first UN Food Systems Summit give corporations too much of a voice? *Civil Eats*. https://civileats.com/2021/09/29/did-the-first-un-food-systems-summit-give-corporations-too-much-of-a-voice/

Naik, A, TJ Faircloth, C Dreger and S Adler. 2022. Corporate capture of FAO: industry's deepening influence on global food governance. Corporate Accountability, FIAN International and Pesticide Action Network International. https://corporateaccountability.org/resources/corporate-capture-of-fao/

National Agricultural Statistics Service (2023). Land values. US Department of Agriculture. https://www.nass.usda.gov/Charts_and_Maps/graphics/crop_value_hist_chart_lv.pdf

Naylor, P. 2023. Coordinator of CSIPM-North America. Personal communication. Used by permission.

Office of the High Commissioner on Human Rights. N.d. Human Rights Dashboard. https://indicators.ohchr.org/

Patel, R and P McMichael. 2009. A political economy of the food riot. *Review (Fernand Braudel Center)* 32:9–35. http://www.jstor.org/stable/40647787

Pedersen, CS. 2018. The UN Sustainable Development Goals (SDGs) are a great gift to business! *Procedia CIRP* 69:21–24. https://doi.org/10.1016/j.procir.2018.01.003

Rosset, P. 2022. Personal communication. Used by permission.

Schuftan, C. 2022. Commentary on CFS50, FAO Committee on Food Security. *World Nutrition* 13(4):90–91.

Seufert, P. 2023. How digital technologies affect the human rights of peasants and small-scale food producers. FIAN International. https://www.fian.org/files/is/htdocs/wp11102127_GNIAANVR7U/www/files/policy%20paper%20digitalization_rev.pdf

Sundaram, JK. 2021. Beware UN Food Systems Summit Trojan horse. *IPS News*. http://www.ipsnews.net/2021/07/beware-un-food-systems-summit-trojan-horse/

Swedish International Agricultural Network Initiative (SIANI). 2021. Five take-aways from the CFS Voluntary Guidelines on Food Systems and Nutrition. https://www.siani.se/news-story/five-takeaways-from-the-cfs-voluntary-guidelines-on-food-systems-and-nutrition/

UN Secretary-General. 2021. Our Common Agenda. https://www.un.org/en/common-agenda

Voltaire. 2002 [1759]. *Candide*. New York: Modern Library.

Von Braun, J, K Afsana, L Fresco, M Hassan and M Torero. 2021a. Food systems—definition, concept and application for the UN Food Systems Summit. A paper from the Scientific Group of the UNFSS. https://www.un.org/sites/un2.un.org/files/2020/12/food_systems_paper-draft_oct-25.pdf

Von Braun, J, K Afsana, LO Fresco and M Hassan. 2021b. Food systems: seven priorities to end hunger and protect the planet. *Nature* 597:28–30. https://doi.org/10.1038/d41586-021-02331-x

World Economic Forum. 2010. Everybody's Business: Strengthening International Cooperation in a More Interdependent World. Report of the Global Redesign Initiative. https://www3.weforum.org/docs/WEF_GRI_EverybodysBusiness_Report_2010.pdf

World Food Journal. 2021. "This summit must not become bogged down in ideological battles" *Welt Hunger Hilfe* (27 April). https://www.welthungerhilfe.org/news/latest-articles/2021/un-food-summit-whats-at-stake/

10

GRASSROOTS INITIATIVES TO DE-COMMODIFY FOOD SYSTEMS

Most people's reality is shaped by local circumstances, which seem far removed from global forums such as the CFS and the UN Food Systems Summit. For many, that reality is one of suffering and exploitation. There are clear commonalities across local struggles from Mali to Mississippi: people trying to hold onto their land, resources and way of life are pitted against policymakers aligned with business interests eager to eke out as much profit as possible from land, water, biodiversity and minerals as long as they last and not hesitating to displace the original inhabitants. The degree of suffering is very unequal however, with the heavy hand of colonialism and debt still holding many people in the Majority World under.

While resistance is essential and indeed unavoidable for many threatened communities, it is important to acknowledge the rise of alternative ways of meeting people's needs and desires that disrupt the dominant power relations in neoliberal food systems. These are being initiated and implemented by civil society to defend people from extractive food system actors. The initiatives are manifestations of the diverse economy that Gibson-Graham described (2006). There are many terms in the literature to describe "alternatives" to capitalist food systems: alternative food networks, local food systems, short food-supply chains, etc. Marit Rosol (2020) distinguished between alternative food (e.g., organic) and alternative food economies (e.g., social enterprises, cooperatives, food sharing). Gusztáv Nemes and his co-authors introduced the term "values-based territorial food networks" (Nemes et al. 2022) to emphasize both the place-based nature of these alternatives and ways that they incorporate values beyond profit. Amanda DiVito Wilson used the term "autonomous" to convey the values of self-governing and self-sufficiency, and noted that "the lens of autonomy looks for the potential to forge new

DOI: 10.4324/9781003260264-14

relationships and collective identities beyond the typical categories under capitalism of worker, producer, consumer and owner" (DiVito Wilson 2012, 729). The term "prosumption" is being used to describe ways that people can co-create the value of production, even when they are not the primary producers (Toffler 1980; Xie et al. 2008).

Alternative food systems encompass new business arrangements and markets, commoning needed resources, public education/training and projects rooted in social/solidarity economy principles. Often initiatives work in multiple areas; for example, commoning projects may work on policy and public education that will make starting commons more feasible. These initiatives have a shared challenge: how to maintain provision of public goods (food security, a healthy environment, biodiversity, etc.) in a society where privatization is condoned and promoted. The theme that binds these initiatives is de-commodifying the food system. Commodifying entails stripping away the multiple values of food and food systems to reduce them to goods that are sold for profit, privatizing property and services, relying on markets rather than public policy to determine exchanges, emphasizing individualism rather than collective action and exploiting nature. De-commodification is enacted through common practices across the food system:

a reinforcing additional values of food and the food system (food quality, connections between producers and their customers, conviviality, preservation of agrobiodiversity, decent working conditions, etc.);
b removing resources needed for food production and access from impersonal global or domestic markets to enable wider access by people whom these markets marginalize;
c collective action;
d strengthening the role of public policy (e.g., to realize the right to food, restrict corporate dominance of the food system and conserve agrobiodiversity) and
e protecting natural systems from degradation.

Part of the significance of place, and a primary reason why local food systems attract growing attention, is that local food systems allow relationships among producers, citizens and other food system actors to deepen and sometimes blur the distinctions between roles, as when citizens work for their share in a community-supported agriculture enterprise, get food in return for work at a food cooperative or engage with city government in a local food policy council.

The literature on "alternative food networks" emphasizes strengthening producer-consumer relations, but it is more important to find out what can undermine neoliberalism's commodification of life and health. Local food systems allow benefits of food exchanges to circulate within a community (the multiplier effect): local farmers purchase seeds, supplies and equipment from local dealers, helping to keep them afloat and hiring workers, and participate in the local school system and local politics. However, in many communities now, the only seed and equipment suppliers are outlets of national or international corporations due to rapid consolidation and concentration in the seed and equipment industries. Policy reform has the potential to reverse this consolidation, in addition to reviving the importance of place as a means of adding values beyond profits to interactions among food system actors. Giuseppe Feola et al. (2021, 2) stressed the need to both unmake and make, in transitions to sustainability:

> [S]ustainability transformation might not come about through the mere *addition* of supposed solutions, values or social imperative, but rather by *subtracting* problematic existing institutions, forms of knowledge, practices, imaginaries, power structure, and human-non-human relations in the first place.
>
> *(emphases in original)*

As we look for initiatives that have the potential to undermine neoliberal extractive food systems by de-commodifying, it is especially important to focus on those that serve everyone without any discrimination or that serve marginalized people who have not benefited as much from the current food system as wealthy white people in the Minority World. In the US, this marginalized group is quite large and made up of people of color, Indigenous, workers (especially farmworkers and workers in processing plants and other food businesses), women (especially single mothers), youth, small-scale food producers and people who have been formerly incarcerated, and those who are disabled or non-cisgender (i.e., those whose identity does not correspond to their reported sex at birth). In Majority World countries, marginalized populations may consist of small-scale farmers and fishers, women and people from ethnic minorities. Rapidly increasing inequality in wealth and income has resulted in only a small group of people being on the inside of global policymaking and privilege. As Marjorie Kelly explained in her book Wealth Supremacy: How the Extractive Economy and the Biased Rules of Capitalism Drive Today's Crises (2023, 13):

> It's about status, in a culture where the wealthy are revered as the possessors of godlike powers. It's about influence, including the power to control philanthropy. It's about political and legal power—including the power to finance candidates, to influence lawmaking through lobbying, and to escape the justice system that ensnares those without wealth.

It is also important to focus on initiatives that are run by and for disadvantaged populations, rather than those run by well-meaning citizens who are trying to "bring good food to others" (Guthman 2008). These projects reinforce the agency of people who are struggling to nourish themselves and their families and apply the unique knowledge that they have about the barriers they encounter. There is a tendency in the US for alternative food initiatives to be enclaves of whiteness, initiated and managed by white people, where people of color do not feel that they belong. Similarly, foreign aid programs may hire "experts" from the Minority World to develop projects and policies for impoverished people in the Majority World, rather than hiring locals or providing funds directly to organizations initiated in the Majority World. Although these projects may help the movement toward environmentally regenerative food, they do little for social justice. However, more and more food system organizations are tackling this problem in the US wake of growing awareness of police brutality and continuing discrimination against people of color and Indigenous.

This chapter examines projects that have the potential to de-commodify land, knowledge and other resources needed for food production and access to food. It ends with policy work that seeks to institutionalize the transformations that these projects are making in how people interact with each other and with nature and an explanation of how agroecology, food sovereignty and civil society enable these forms of de-commodification. The chapter emphasizes initiatives in the US and those about which I have direct knowledge. This is not meant to imply that US projects are better or more numerous than those in other countries; in fact, some kinds of initiatives are flourishing much better in other countries. For example, agroecological farming projects and organizations abound in Mexico, Central America and South America; and land commons are more prevalent in some European countries than in the US. My aim here is not to make comparisons between projects or countries, but to demonstrate that alternatives to the extractive food system with its food-as-commodity narrative are alive and well.

De-commodifying Land

Land can be de-commodified by taking it out of markets that are financialized by banks, asset management companies and other investors, thus susceptible to speculation and concentration. It can also be de-commodified by making access to it easier for youth and new farmers, small-holders and marginalized people. Due to the history of slavery and colonization in the US and continuing severe discrimination, Black and Indigenous people have less access than white people to healthy food, land and other resources needed for food production, and a higher prevalence of diet-related disease. As we think about healing the injustices and inequities in the US food system, they are among the groups that most deserve assistance. However, finding ways to liberate ourselves from the strictures of neoliberalism is important for the planet and for *everyone* who is not benefiting from its extractive practices and exploitation, i.e., every person outside the class of the wealthy elite. Inspirational and courageous leaders are taking on this task around the world.

Half a century ago, the Black nationalist Malcolm X told his audience, "land is the basis of all independence. Land is the basis of freedom, justice, and equality" (Malcolm X 1963, n.p.). Land ownership and access are bedrocks of freedom for people who have been oppressed, as is food sovereignty. As Leah Penniman, one of the founders of Soul Fire Farm in New York, said:

> If you can feed yourself, you can quite literally free yourself. We have always seen, and continue to see, food sovereignty as linked to freedom for people. If you don't have any control over your food system, it essentially puts you at the whim of a racist, capitalist food system in terms of your basic survival needs.
>
> *(Penniman in Frisch 2019, n.p.)*

This section begins with three ways that marginalized people living under conditions of gross inequity in land distribution have claimed or reclaimed land: occupations by landless people, land-back to Indigenous people, and the establishment of autonomous territories. The Movimento dos Trabalhadores Rurais Sem Terra (MST) in Brazil consists of landless workers who organize to claim arable land from concentrated land-holdings, then grow food and establish settlements on the claimed land. Brazil is an extreme case of land concentration in the hands of a few landowners. According to the most recent census in Brazil (2017), roughly one percent of landowners control almost 50 percent of the rural land (Tricontinental 2020). Brazilian law recognizes that rural properties should have a social function, and the federal government has granted landless workers the right to use and live on land that they had occupied. Families who settle on claimed land use diversified production and regenerative practices. In addition to providing for their own food security, they sell produce in nearby cities. According to the Ministry of Agriculture, Livestock and Supply, there are 959,186 families living in 9444 settlements focused on agrarian reform. MST's website states that 370,000 of these are MST families who currently own the land they work, and 150,000 more are living in 900 active encampments waiting for the government to process their paperwork to make the settlements official (Froio 2023).

Other inspiring examples of land justice come from North America, where tribal nations have won back some of the land and waters that were stolen from them during the European invasion. Successes include purchase by Mi'kmaq tribes of Clearwater Seafoods, which gives them ownership of Clearwater's offshore fishing licenses and freedom to harvest lobster, scallop, crab and clams in a large area extending from Georges Bank to the Laurentian Channel off Cape Breton. Other major victories have been won by the Wiyok, Quapaw, Yurok, Gila and Tohono O'odham peoples (Montalvo 2021; Poole 2021).

Autonomous communities have been established by peasants in Mexico and Columbia to transform society beyond capitalism at a territorial level. The Zapatista Army of National Liberation (EZLN) took over seven municipalities in Chiapas, Mexico, in 1994 in a challenge to representative democracy and neoliberal governance exercised by the federal government. They have created systems for bottom-up decision-making, autonomous justice, education, healthcare and a cooperative economy. In 2019, the EZLN announced the creation of the Caracoles and the Good Government Councils, replacing the Zapatista Autonomous Rebel Municipalities as a way to separate the army from civilian functions and provide better mediation and conflict resolutions (Reyes and Kaufman 2011; Rebrii 2020; Gómez 2022). The Zapatista municipalities have faced many internal challenges and aggression from outside, yet they maintain their autonomy. In Colombia, *territorios campesinos agroalimentarios* (agro-food farming territories) are emerging as transformations beyond capitalism that preserve peasants' cultural identity. The territories are based on principles of campesino autonomy, coexistence, participation and profound respect for life and nature. They have created an *economia propia* (appropriate economy) with principles of sufficiency, just production and exchange, food sovereignty and the protection of the environment and human relations (Feola et al. 2021). Creating these new territories has necessitated unmaking existing institutions of governance, defense and development and creating new institutions that replace socially and ecologically destructive industries and agribusiness. The territories practice agroecology and farmers share knowledge through the *campesino-a-campesino* (peasant to peasant) model, a distributed network of municipal agrarian committees (Feola et al. 2021).

At a larger scale, Rojava (Autonomous Administration of North and East Syria) is an experiment in radical democracy, feminism and anti-capitalism, surrounded by reactionary forces of the Islamic State. Decades of colonialism, capitalism and war resulted in serious environmental degradation; efforts are underway to plant trees and restore ecological integrity (Make Rojava Green Again 2019). Abdullah Öcalan is a thought-leader of Rojava, and called for a "renewed, conscious and enlightened unification towards a natural, organic society" (Make Rojava Green Again 2019, n.p.). He was influenced by and further developed the work on "social ecology" of the US social theorist Murray Bookchin. The core argument of social ecology is that capitalist modernity causes environmental destruction and ecological crises and that it goes hand in hand with oppression and exploitation of people. The Mesopotamian Ecology movement has an informal presence in Rojava, seeking to rebuild ecological resilience by decreasing the Kurdish region's dependence on imports, returning to traditional water-conserving cultivation techniques, advocating for ecological policymaking at the municipal level, promoting local crops and livestock and traditional construction methods, organizing educational activities and working against destructive and exploitative "investment" and infrastructure projects such as dams and mines (Keller 2018). The agricultural policy of the autonomous administration has been to create short supply chains to link productive resources to consumption needs in the region and suppress speculation on scarce but crucial items, including food and fuel as well as land. The aim is to secure the local provisioning of food at fair prices for both producers and customers. Food provisioning for regional markets has been a key feature in the economy, along with the stimulation of family farms and cooperatives and the development of processing and manufacturing capacities (Jongerden 2022).

Land commoning is a very old practice that has been revived periodically in resistance to waves of enclosure and exploitation to allow people to access land communally that has been privatized. Elinor Ostrom's research showed that land commons can be sustained for long periods of time; they are not inherently prone to collapse. But they do require effort on the part of commoners, to resist encroachment from beyond their boundaries. Trauger and Passidomo (2012, 297) commented that, "[t]he generation of the commons requires food-citizen engagement in a particular place through the creation of a mutually dependent stake in the outcomes of agriculture." But beyond this, the ancient practice of "beating the bounds" in necessary, or active resistance to the forces that try to usurp commons property, by regularly re-establishing commons boundaries (Bollier 2014). Policy reforms may be the most effective way to beat the bounds of contemporary commons.

Several examples of land commoning exist near where I live in the rural state of Vermont. A non-profit organization called Intervale Center, situated on 360 acres of rich bottomland on the bank of the Winooski River, rents land to different enterprises that are growing food. They are creating a community food system through farming with sustainable practices, stewarding the natural environment and advancing a community food movement. Intervale has a fascinating mix of farming business models: a community-supported agriculture farm (CSA), community gardens, and Diggers' Mirth in which five people co-manage and farm a plot together. It also hosts a food hub, amalgamating produce from smaller farms so that it can be sold to larger markets, an Abenaki Garden where Indigenous people are growing traditional plants, and a farm where refugees from many different African and Asian countries can grow their preferred crops (New Farms for New Americans). Growers at Intervale share large farm equipment and a food processing shed. Volunteers glean extra produce from farms in the surrounding county and provide it for free through a Fair Share Market. Visitors to Intervale also can get free produce at a pick-your-own garden. A winter market allows customers who are on federal food assistance to get food at a 50 percent discount. Intervale has provided incubation space for beginning farmers in the past, but graduates have had trouble finding farmland of their own. Celebrations through the year bring hundreds of people to Intervale to hear music, dance and eat. It is a beautiful and beloved center for the Burlington, Vermont, food community that has benefited from decades of work by talented planners, farmers and policymakers.

People struggle more to create land commons in less urban areas where volunteers are a bit more sparse but assistance with land access is still greatly needed. Land trusts in the US have provided an essential service by buying up arable land and selling it at affordable prices to people who want to farm. In central Vermont, the White River Land Collaborative is a farmer-led, community-driven project that aims to provide young farmers affordable land and housing on an old dairy farm, offer other support to the region's farmers and economy, generate green power and provide community space. The Collaborative entered into a partnership to buy the farm with Vermont Land Trust because the asking price of $700,000 was too high for an individual farmer to cover on farm proceeds and they wanted to create a shared space. An "anchor farmer," Shona Sanford-Long, grew up in Tunbridge next door to the farm and brought her livestock to the Collaborative. The group has been renovating a farm store, working to deepen connections with the Abenaki community, planting native species in the forest, and planning farm and forest projects.

Other examples of providing land access to aspiring farmers in the US are farms for immigrants and refugees from Africa, the Mideast, Latin America and Asia, sometimes established with support from state governments but generally initiated and run by civil society. Many immigrants are skilled producers from agrarian backgrounds, seeking to make a new life for themselves while preserving their cultural identity. These farms are places where immigrants can learn about growing food in a new climate and share experiences with others. Some examples include the Maya Regeneration Project in Omaha, Nebraska; Plant It Forward in Houston, Texas; Flats Mentor Farm in Lancaster, Massachusetts and Cultivating Community in Maine. The best of these projects involve immigrants as managers and decision-makers, and have stable access to the resources that the farmers need.

Community gardens, urban farms and urban food forests are other examples of land commoning to enable access for people who would not otherwise be able to grow food. The Detroit Black Community Food Security Network created D-Town Farm in 2008 after Detroit went into a steep recession. Automobile factories, the main employer, had closed down and many people had fled the downtown areas. African Americans are the vast majority of Detroit residents now, and they are leading the food movement. D-Town Farm is the largest of Detroit's many gardens and farms, situated on a little over seven acres in the City of Detroit's Rouge Park. It is maintained by a small staff and volunteers who grow over 30 different fruits, vegetables and herbs every year using regenerative methods. In addition to running D-Town farm, the Black Community Food Security Network holds trainings on Black Food Sovereignty, sustainable production and land stewardship methods, and local policies affecting environmental justice. Executive Director Malik Yakini summarized the mission of the Network:

> Justice requires a conscious, vigilant and active populace. Building towards food justice requires that we conduct public education campaigns to make communities aware of the impact of the current food system on our planet, our health and the economies of our communities. It requires that we provide local food–related models of what sustainability and justice might look like. These models must provide real ways that people can participate in growing, processing, distributing and selling healthy foods and realizing economic benefit from their efforts.
>
> *(Yakini 2023, n.p.)*

D-Town Farm has been a model for other farms and projects that help create food justice for Black people. Soul Fire Farm in the Hudson Valley of New York is another well-known model of training for Black liberation. It is an Afro-Indigenous-centered community farm committed to uprooting racism and seeding sovereignty in the food system, raising food and distributing it in Albany and New York City. It brings diverse communities together to share skills on sustainable agriculture, natural building, spiritual activism, health, and environmental justice; to train the next generation of activist-farmers; and to strengthen the movements for food sovereignty and community self-determination. It holds farmer trainings for Black and Brown growers and food justice workshops for urban youth, fights for reparations and land return initiatives for Northeast farmers, builds home gardens for city-dwellers living under food apartheid, makes food deliveries to food-insecure households and teaches public decision-makers about systems and policy for food sovereignty (Soul Fire Farm 2023).

Like D-Town Farm and Soul Fire Farm, community gardens often provide education as well as shared space to grow food. The Food Project in Boston was an early example, founded in 1991 to educate youth in community, anti-racism and food production. It employs 120 teenagers on 70 acres of urban and suburban farmland each year, selling the produce in farmers' markets and businesses in low-income neighborhoods at affordable prices (The Food Project 2023). The Food Project hires teenagers from inner-city Boston communities and wealthy suburbs, who work side-by-side through the growing season. The Food Project's focus on youth employment and anti-racism makes it stand out, but nearly every city in the US has at least one community garden or farm now.

Urban food forests also are starting to pop up in the US, where residents can graze on fruit grown on public lands. A food forest is an agricultural system that mimics a woodland ecosystem by substituting edible trees, shrubs, perennials and annuals for non-edible forest plants. Fruit and nut trees make up the canopy; and berry shrubs, edible perennials and annuals make up the understory. Food forests are relatively low maintenance, resilient, productive agricultural systems, capable of meeting significant portions of the caloric and nutrient needs of large numbers of people on relatively small amounts of space. City agencies, the State University of New York and civil society created an urban food forest in Syracuse in 2019 and received a federal grant under the Great Lakes Restoration Initiative to expand in 2022 to plant and promote wild foraging of nutritious species along a 7-mile corridor through a poor part of town (Syracuse Urban Food Forest Project n.d.). Syracuse is the 14th-worst city in the US in terms of overall poverty and also has very high prevalence of child poverty (Tampone 2022). Free access to fresh food can make a real difference under these circumstances.

In Boston, the Food Forest Coalition acquires city-owned parcels of land which they place into community control to remain protected in perpetuity. They prioritize neighborhoods with less equitable access to open space and green space, and have nine different food forests across the city. A network of local educators offers regenerative permaculture and environmental workshops for the stewards who caretake food forests and for the general public (BFFC 2023). In England "Incredible Edible" based in Todmorden in Yorkshire has also converted public areas into food-producing spaces. They have expanded to 100 sites in the UK and more than 700 worldwide. They are explicit in their desire to repurpose public land for food production for the public and for agricultural biodiversity (Maughan and Ferrando 2018).

Land commons are prevalent in Europe and the UK, where they date back to medieval times. They sometimes join together in networks that help create commons-friendly local policies such as the Common Lands Network, which maintains a map and website to support commons and Territories of Life in Europe, the Middle East and North Africa. In Italy, about 10 percent of land is held in common for "civic uses" including grazing, hunting, felling timber, gathering firewood and sowing crops. Italian commons were medieval land management institutions carried forward to the present day. However, recent legislation and governments have tried to sell common land and impose regulations without considering collective management (Battisti and Pisano 2022; Maughan and Ferrando 2018). Mondeggi Bene Comune in Italy is part of a new group of more radical efforts to create a just, democratic and ecological food system on common property. Residents occupied a historic farm near Florence with a villa and farm buildings to resist its privatization, hoping to establish a local food system centered on Mondeggi. Local residents were invited to help care for olive trees on the property and share the harvest. Since its inception in 2013, Mondeggi has created ties with surrounding communities and become a venue for arts performances, a laboratory to preserve agricultural traditions and a place where adults and children can reconnect with nature (Maughan and Ferrando 2018). Mondeggi is part of an Italian network called Genuine Clandestine that seeks to support and spread territorial communities and commons, promote peasant agriculture and foods, promote self-determination, safeguard cultural food diversity and support city-countryside collaboration (Mondeggi Bene Comune n.d.; Genuine Clandestine n.d.).

De-commodifying Resources Needed for Production: Water, Knowledge, Seeds, Equipment

Other resources needed for food production include water, knowledge, seeds and equipment. Enabling public access to water entails many of the same struggles as access to land and privatization of public water systems has been rampant under neoliberalism (Jaffee 2020). Large corporations such as Coca-Cola are privatizing water sources for private profit in a new round of enclosure of the commons. Much has been written about water privatization and resistance to it; my intention here is simply to note that water is a human right and essential for food production, processing and meal preparation in addition to being essential for survival. Particularly with increasing drought under climate change, growing numbers of people are unable to realize their right to drinking water (UN News 2022).

Knowledge is a second essential resource. The previous section on de-commodifying land described several community projects that are providing trainings for producers or the wider public, including how to grow one's own food in addition to how to produce food to sell or barter. Farmer organizations are helping to common knowledge about agroecological practices that will create more regenerative food systems. For example, the Alliance for Food Sovereignty in Africa and the Seed Knowledge Initiative train farmers on practices to avoid soil degradation through the Healthy Soil Healthy Food Initiative (AFSA 2023a). This project combines training and extension, a community of practice across 10 countries, research, advocacy to publicize agroecology and entrepreneurship to assist local enterprises/businesses supplying high-quality organic fertilizers and products. Other examples include the farmer-led *campesino-a-campesino* movement which has spread through Mexico and Central America (Holt-Giménez 2006) and Sustainable Harvest International, a nonprofit started by Florence Reed after a stint in the Peace Corps, that partners with smallholder farmers in Central America to adopt regenerative practices. Program graduates make a commitment to teach additional farmers about the practices that they learn (Sustainable Harvest International 2023).

In the US, Black Dirt Farm Collective in Maryland was created by Black farmers, builders, educators, scientists, agrarians, seed keepers, organizers, and political educators. They share a vision of Black liberation based on "Afroecology," which they define as:

> a form of art, movement, practice and process of social and ecological transformation that involves the re-evaluation of our sacred relationships with land, water, air, seeds and food; (re)recognizes humans as co-creators that are an aspect of the planet's life support systems; values the Afro-Indigenous experience of reality and ways of knowing; cherishes ancestral and communal forms of knowledge, experience and lifeways that began in Africa and continue throughout the Diaspora; and is rooted in the agrarian traditions, legacies and struggles of the Black experience in the Americas.
>
> *(de Wolfe 2023 n.p.)*

The group purchased 24 acres in Marlboro, Maryland, where they are creating a safe haven that will also function as a residential farm, a small business incubator, and a home for the agroecology movement. Sharing leadership and knowledge about agroecology and healing are important principles of the group. Other Black agroecological training/learning centers include the Lola Hampton-Frank Pinder Center for Agroecology at Florida A&M University (a historically Black university) and Soul Fire Farm, described above.

Enabling access to seeds has become extremely important in many countries in the Majority World, particularly in Africa, where corporations in partnership with governments have re-written seed laws to make seed-saving and planting of "non-registered" seed varieties illegal (Wise 2019). Saving seeds has therefore become a criminal activity, yet essential for farmers without the income to purchase seed every year. Several African organizations including the Alliance for Food Sovereignty in Africa are fighting for seed sovereignty; AFSA has proposed a legal framework for the recognition and promotion of farmer managed seed systems and the protection of biodiversity. In the US, Maywa Montenegro de Wit (2019) described how the Open Source Seed Initiative resists the enclosure of seed commons via patents on seeds or plant traits. The OSSI was started in 2012 by US-based social scientists, plant breeders, organic farmers and small seed companies to sidestep traditional intellectual property rights with a "protected common," in which plant genetic material can be shared with access rights guaranteed by a simple pledge:

> You have the freedom to use these OSSI seeds in any way you choose. In return, you pledge not to restrict others' use of these seeds or their

derivatives by patents or other means, and to include this Pledge with any transfer of these seeds or their derivatives.

(OSSI 2023)

This pledge is similar to "copy-left" patents for software, by which users are free to use and alter code but not patent what they have done to restrict use by others.

Sharing equipment also can help small-scale farmers, given that most farming equipment is extremely expensive. For example, John Deere (the top-ranked tractor company in the US) sells "compact" tractors for around $20,000 and larger, more powerful tractors sell for over $200,000. Sharing equipment is not always practical, however, since many farms may be doing the same tasks at the same time. Sometimes the right kind of equipment is not available in the US. A small-scale Vermont rice farmer, Erik Andrus, who grows rice in fields that are prone to flooding, has started advising farmers in New York state who are trying to diversify production. He imported a small-scale rice planter and harvester from Japan, ideal for the small farms that are prevalent in both Japan and Vermont, because the only equipment available in the US is designed for much larger fields. He hopes to start an equipment common for the beginning rice farmers in New York.

Another way to resist neoliberalism as it plays out in the world of farm equipment is to share knowledge instead of the equipment itself. Farm-hacking brings together technologists and agrarians. Farmers have been accustomed to making and repairing their own equipment since farming began, but recent laws have criminalized repair by a non-authorized service provider. The ostensible reason is that self-repair will result in safety flaws, but the laws are flagrant attempts to control what farmers do. Farm Hack is an all-volunteer organization established in 2011 that partners with open source and maker communities in the US and EU. Through its website and training events, Farm Hack is providing a template for autonomous local manufacturing and control. It recognizes that innovation is happening on farms all the time, not only in universities and labs, and promotes a culture of trust and sharing (Cox 2015).

De-commodifying Access to Food

Food access can be de-commodified by acknowledging the values of food beyond profits in markets, creating mechanisms by which people who have been excluded can access food, democratizing decision-making about markets and access, aiming for a greater share of the value going to producers rather than corporate owners, lessening the distance between producers and their customers and imposing social and environmental standards on markets and transactions. While civil society is often seen as the "third force" in society, balancing the public sector and business, there are numerous hybrid arrangements by which businesses involved in food access are taking on functions usually managed by civil society, such as public education. Claire Lamine and her co-authors noted (2012, 250),

> [i]n response to multi-dimensional food-related health and sustainability concerns in recent years, a range of initiatives from civil society organizations, (local and regional) governments and sometimes also market partners has emerged. Together these new food practices compose a new alternative and local food geography which is grounded in a different logic and incorporates different values.

These authors examined solidarity-based purchase groups in Italy and two regions of France in which producers were experimenting with different kinds of market outlets, such as collective shops run by producers and a local fruit cooperative.

Jan van der Ploeg et al. (2022, 19) dug into exactly what is different about the logic and values of nested "peasant markets" in Brazil, China and the Netherlands compared with "general markets" (run on capitalist principles):

> First, general markets operate through profit-oriented activities that enlarge the *return on capital*, while the nested markets discussed here are oriented at defending and improving labor incomes. Second, general markets are governed by capital, whereas peasant markets are governed by labor (in the form of peasant producers and food consumers). Third, the capital-controlled markets are constructed as webs of dependencies, whereas peasant markets are structured as patterns of complementarities.
> *(italics in original)*

These authors saw peasant markets having potential to contribute to wider transformations in society; indeed, the Brazilian peasant market that they examined helps producers to sell agroecological food at better prices for the grower but cheaper prices for customers than they would pay in "general markets." They argued against the premise that peasant markets will be taken over eventually by capital, subordinated and neutralized, as has happened to parts of the organic market. There is no *a priori* reason to assume that peasant markets cannot persist.

Examples of markets that operate beyond neoliberal tenets (yet are still solidly embedded in capitalist economies) are direct marketing strategies including farmstands, farmers' markets, territorial markets and community-supported agriculture. In all of these the middleman is eliminated, so producers receive all of the cost of the product, and supply chains are shorter. Territorial markets were the main ways that food was exchanged before the advent of supermarkets and supercenters. They are sub-national (and sub-global), use short supply chains and often enable a more direct connection between producers and their customers. The idea of territorial markets is related to foodsheds, city-region food systems, organic districts and rural-urban linkages: in all cases, a population center draws its food from the surrounding area instead of through global or national supply chains. This helps to strengthen the regional economy. Territoriality also can help to overcome the alienation of producers from their customers, encourage cultural embeddedness, and promote decentralized governance of market spaces. When supply chains broke down during the COVID pandemic, territorial markets proved to be very resilient (Urgenci 2021).

In San Cristóbal de las Casas, Chiapas, Mexico, students from El Colegio de Frontera Sur (ECOSUR) helped to set up an agroecological territorial market in which producers sell a wide range of products including honey, meat, coffee, produce, cheese and prepared foods. They use a participatory guarantee system to decide which people can sell in the market. An assurance of agroecological, safe production practices is especially important in this area because there is no public sanitation system and some commercial producers use untreated water containing sewage to irrigate their crops. The market convenes twice a week in an old warehouse near the city center and it is always crowded with customers. It is one of a network of Tianguis Indígena which aim to increase the income of small-holders through market exchange, provide equal participation for women, preserve traditional agriculture and increase resilience to climate change (Carranza López 2012).

Solidarity purchasing groups (mainly in Italy) and community-supported agriculture (CSA) are distinctive marketing arrangements in which customers buy products from one or more selected farmers. In solidarity purchasing groups, the customers coordinate to buy food and other products (shoes, clothes, detergents, etc.) directly from producers, who are selected in accordance with ethical and solidarity principles, the most important of which are respect for the environment and for people (Fonte 2013). They do not have a contract with the producers, however. In CSAs, customers share the risks of farming by paying for a "share" before the growing season begins and then receiving whatever the farm is able to produce. This provides both income for the producers when it is most needed, as the growing season begins, and also a form of insurance in case bad weather wipes out a significant portion of some crops. CSAs also build stronger personal connections between growers and customers: the grower learns what customers want, and the customers learn about the inherent risks and constraints of diversified crop production. Many CSAs intentionally build community through shared dinners, meetings and other events. "Community-building" aspects of CSAs might be overblown, however; some customers participate simply to have access to fresh, local, in-season produce (Pole and Gray 2013). Several CSAs increase access to shares through donations or by asking people who can afford to pay more to subsidize shares for people who have tighter income constraints.

Another scheme to improve grower livelihoods has emerged through international fair trade, in which growers adhere to rigorous standards for regenerative production and receive a price which is set as the average in that region for such practices. They sell products at a premium, and the fair trade company distributes the products and solicits customers who are willing to pay extra when they know that growers are getting a fair price. In a survey by Fairtrade America, despite increases in the cost of living in the US, the percentage of customers who recognized the Fair Trade label had increased 118 percent since 2019, and nearly 80 percent of customers who knew Fairtrade were willing to pay more (Fairtrade America 2023). Fair trade started with international imports of bananas and coffee; but a wide range of crops, flowers, fruits, vegetables and spices are now available. A domestic version of fair trade in the US, the Agricultural Justice Project, uses a participatory guarantee certification in which both farmers and farmworkers agree whether inspected farms are following production and labor practices. This is still a relatively small program, compared to organic certification; but the inclusion of fair labor standards makes it stand out.

Other programs work on a business-to-business basis instead of selling directly to customers. One example is the Equitable Food Initiative (EFI) in the US, which certifies products as responsibly grown and "farmworker assured." Their certification standards were created through collaboration with farmer, farmworker, customer and retailer organizations. Standards address working conditions, pest management and food safety. They are able to meet multiple retail standards dealing with social responsibility, pest management and pollinator impacts and food safety through a single audit (Equitable Food Initiative 2023). Although fair trade and the work of EFI sound great in principle, they have come under fire from the organization Corporate Accountability for failing to protect farmworkers in the Mexican produce industry (Daria and Canning 2023). Their critique of EFI echoes the familiar weaknesses of MSI standards described in Chapter 6.

Food cooperatives deserve mention as another marketing system that can promote regenerative food systems. They share organizational values of self-help, self-responsibility, democracy, equality, equity, and solidarity and believe in ethical principles of honesty, openness, social responsibility and caring for others. They operate according to seven principles set by the International Cooperative Alliance (2023):

- voluntary and open membership;
- democratic member control;
- member economic participation;
- autonomy and independence;

- education, training, and information;
- cooperation among cooperatives and
- concern for community.

Most food coops have a large quantity of organic products and seek out local suppliers; some also try to purchase from businesses operated by women, people of color and Indigenous people. Some food coops allow members to work in the store to receive a discount, although this has become somewhat more difficult to manage with food safety laws. Members invest in the coop when they join, then receive a dividend at the end of each year based on the coop's profits. They are also able to vote on major coop policies. While coops don't always provide the cheapest prices possible, they try to set fair prices that balance the needs of suppliers, customers and workers.

Grower cooperatives have assisted many small-scale and marginalized producers to amass enough product to sell to retailers. Amy Trauger and Catarina Passidomo (2012) investigated Tuscarora Organic Growers in Southeastern Pennsylvania, which is helping to make organic produce affordable for low-income customers through transportation and marketing efficiencies and shared access to skills, capital and resources. The Federation of Southern Cooperatives is one of the oldest Black cooperatives in the US, coming out of the 1960s Civil Rights Movement. It reverses Black land loss through education, outreach and technical assistance. It also helps to establish new cooperative business enterprises and advocates for policy that will benefit its members. It has fought against continuing discrimination aimed at Black farmers in the South for over half a century (Federation of Southern Cooperatives 2023).

A unique marketing system was set up by the nonprofit organization Red Tomato to link small and mid-sized farms in nine Northeastern US states with markets. In this region, four percent of farmers are classified as "mid-sized," yet they farm 20 percent of all farmland and are responsible for 28 percent of the agricultural markets. Red Tomato was started in 1997 by Michael Rozyne, a co-founder of Equal Exchange fair trade company. He wanted to apply the principles of fairness, transparency, and sustainability to produce sales from farms in the Northeastern US. Red Tomato started out trucking apples and peaches and owning a warehouse, but in 2003 changed to a logistics and marketing operation in which it doesn't own trucks or hire drivers but arranges for marketing fruit and vegetables to several supermarkets and food coops. It delivers whole truckloads of product to distribution centers, which then send fruit and vegetables on to retailers. In 2014, Red Tomato initiated a direct store delivery model relying on aggregation and distribution partnerships with growers and other companies so that they can interact more directly with store purchasing teams and final customers. Fruit growers who work with Red Tomato are "eco-certified" to follow Integrated Pest

Management protocols; organic production of high-quality fruit is extremely difficult in the Northeast because of pest pressure and moisture (Red Tomato 2023). Red Tomato exemplifies how an innovative marketing organization has to continually re-invent itself in response to changing market conditions and competition that keeps driving down prices.

Although civil society has responded to customer interest in a range of values associated with food systems by providing ways that people can purchase food guaranteed to be more regenerative, business entrepreneurs have also recognized that they can capitalize on changing customer values. Thus, most organic food in the US is now purchased through supermarkets or supercenters, not directly from producers. Whether initiated by civil society or by business, most of the initiatives in this chapter have an educational as well as a sales angle, to help inform customers about the benefits of what they are buying. They have helped to familiarize the public with the problems of industrialized food systems and the alternatives available to spend dollars in values-based purchasing. And by making demand for regenerative products apparent to producers and large-scale businesses, they are helping to grow the market and increase supply. However, as Chapter 8 argued, the capacity to create a more regenerative food system through purchasing alone is limited; preferential purchasing needs to be combined with other strategies.

Food consumption as well as marketing is being de-commodified by sharing food preparation and building convivial relationships in which people eat together. Community kitchens are sites where people can come together to prepare food products for sale. They allow small-scale manufacturers to have access to equipment for cooking, packing and labelling that they could not otherwise afford and to work in a site that meets local food safety standards.

Slow Food International is a global, grassroots organization, founded in 1989 by Carlo Petrini and a group of activists to prevent the disappearance of local food cultures and traditions, counteract the rise of "fast" life and combat people's dwindling interest in the food they eat, where it comes from and how our food choices affect the world around us. Slow Food communities at the local level are made up of at least 10 people who share and promote the values of the international Slow Food movement. The community is based first and foremost on the assumption that everyone has the right to good, clean and fair food. Since its beginnings, Slow Food has grown into a global movement involving millions of people in over 160 countries (Slow Food International n.d.).

Coming out of the right to food movement in Brazil, the city of Belo Horizonte in Brazil created very popular *Restaurantes Populares* (People's Cafeterias) that serve 12,000 people every day from all walks of life. The food is mostly locally grown and costs the equivalent of less than 50 cents a meal. According to Frances Moore Lappé, "no one has to prove they're poor to eat in a People's Restaurant, although about 85 percent of the diners are. The mixed clientele erases stigma and allows 'food with dignity'" (Lappé 2019, n.p.). And in Rio de Janeiro, Refettorio Gastromotiva is a unique restaurant serving homeless people for free. The food is donated by companies that would otherwise throw it away, and prepared by a team of trainees led by professional chefs. Most of the cooks are from favelas and low-income communities and all were selected through tough competition to participate in a three-month training course leading to a diploma. The restaurant is part of a new movement for "social gastronomy," which trains chefs from disadvantaged backgrounds and serves low-income clients (Phillips 2018).

Many projects that provide free food rely on donations or food that would otherwise be sent to a landfill or allowed to rot. When people understand that the amount of food produced in the world is sufficient to feed everyone, they sometimes jump to the narrative that hunger is simply a problem of poor distribution of available food. While re-purposing food that is still edible is worthwhile, the idea that this will eliminate hunger is deeply flawed. At worst, it is an elitist "let them eat waste" attitude; free food initiatives must maintain dignity and choice for clients. Gleaning projects allow volunteers to harvest any food left over in fields after the producer has harvested what she can; these projects often donate the produce to a local pantry serving low-income people. In Bar Harbor, Maine, I volunteered at a community kitchen, using a church basement, that made soup every week for any community members who arrived. The chef raised pigs which ended up sometimes in the soup, and collected donated food from local supermarkets. Another Maine project on the other side of Mt. Desert Island was a restaurant that charged full prices during the tourist season, but remained open on a "pay-as-you-are-led" basis during the winter when unemployment was high.

De-commodification through the Solidarity Economy

According to the UN Inter-agency Task Force on Social and Solidarity Economy, the SSE includes organizations that:

1 have explicit economic and social (and often environmental) objectives;
2 involve varying degrees and forms of cooperative, associative and solidarity relations between workers, producers and consumers and
3 practice workplace democracy and self-management.

It includes traditional forms of cooperatives and mutual associations, as well as women's self-help groups, community forestry groups, social provisioning organizations or "proximity services," fair trade organizations, associations of informal sector workers, social enterprises, and community currency and alternative finance schemes (UNTFSSE 2023). The UN, recognizing the value of social innovation, has become a supporter of the social/solidarity economy as an alternative approach to sustainable development and meeting the SDGs.

The UN definition above includes most of the initiatives described in this chapter, but for some people the social/solidarity economy goes farther into post-capitalism. Its initiatives involve more radical, autonomous forms of governance and greater economic localization and self-reliance. In these projects, there is a resurgence of ways of life that center respect of nature, co-existence, and justice. Bringing these groups together is the purpose of the Global Tapestry of Alternatives (Kothari and Bajpai 2023). A more ambitious definition of the SSE (Kawano and Matthaei 2020, n.p.) described it as:

1. a global movement;
2. a broad set of practices that align with its values:
   - solidarity
   - participatory democracy
   - equity in all dimensions
   - sustainability
   - pluralism (not a one-size-fits-all approach) and
3. framework that connects SE practices to articulate a post-capitalist system and world.

Some people distinguish the "social economy" from the "solidarity economy." The social economy seeks to achieve "limited, progressive change within the confines of the current social order by ameliorating the effects of market failure, unemployment and poverty" while the solidarity economy is a "transformative vision of society based on democratic self-management, redistribution, solidarity and reciprocity" (Solidarity Economy Principles 2023).

Social and solidarity economies deal with much more than food, of course: labor, money, housing, energy, etc. But in this section, I am most interested in exploring how people are creating a "pluriverse" of economic alternatives for growing and obtaining food. The pluriverse is another name for the transformative initiatives and alternatives to the currently dominant processes of globalized development, and a critique of its structural roots in modernity, capitalism, state domination, and patriarchal values. Ashish Kothari and a group of co-editors working in this domain compiled a "dictionary" of these approaches and critiques, with authors from many different countries (Kothari et al. 2019). The pluriverse entries draw heavily from Indigenous world-views that link the human, natural and spiritual worlds.

Food sharing is a prominent way to express solidarity economy principles in the food system. The organization Food Not Bombs in the US, with chapters in many cities, provides vegetarian food for free to anyone who shows up at their distribution sites. It provides food for demonstrations and public events and contests unequal power relations in the food system. Food is provided not as charity but as a right, to build community and forge new identities. Free food provision has been criminalized in many US cities, and Food Not Bombs members have been arrested for violating city bylaws that prohibit giving food to unhoused people (DiVito Wilson 2012). Food Not Bombs has been criticized because the cooks and food distributors often are able to take the time to engage only because of their social status. "Economic constraints, care obligations and oppressive systems within capitalism can all work to limit the ability to experiment and curtail an imagination for possibilities other than the current reality" (DiVito Wilson 2012, 734). One of the most common recommendations for moving toward degrowth is to reduce the work week, which would allow more time for volunteer work.

The organization SHARECITY started in Dublin in 2016 with EU funding to analyze the potential of urban food sharing to reduce consumption; conserve resources, prevent waste and provide new forms of socio-economic relations. They used mapping, ethnographies, comparative governance analysis, sustainability impact assessment and a futures-oriented analysis. They studied food-sharing in Dublin, Melbourne, Berlin, Singapore, Barcelona, San Francisco, New York, Athens and London, creating city profiles and a "Manifesto for Food Sharing" (SHARECITY 2021) to help guide new initiatives.

Sharing is not antithetical to gaining a livelihood and often expresses deeply held values of care. In Vermont, the Executive Director of ACORN, Lindsey Berk, noted:

> I see [farmers] giving away food (to community members directly and to food shelves) that could be sold through other market channels, but their ethics lean more towards giving the food away than finding the highest market price. I can think of a few (organic, vegetable) farmers who are not farming for the money, but because of a moral pursuit. We'd also heard from farmers during our 2020 focus groups that they would prioritize feeding their immediate community over sending food to an urban market (where the price might be higher).
>
> *(Berk 2023)*

ACORN is an organization that works to relocalize the food system through creating better and more stable markets for local producers and hosting numerous events each year that raise public interest in and funds for the local food system.

Attention to caretakers and an "ethic of care," understood as "a consideration of, and preparedness to take action about the needs of others (not only human) is central to the identities, motives and practices" (Kneafsey et al. 2008, 49) of many grassroots initiatives. Care is a way to overcome disconnects between producers and their market, customers with products and where/how they were produced, and people with nature. The desire to re-connect drives many efforts to de-commodify the food system.

Some people are creating solidarity economy projects to transform their entire community, not just the ways that people access food. Transition Towns are:

> working for a low-carbon, socially just future with resilient communities, more active participation in society, and caring culture focused on supporting each other ... In practice, they are using participatory methods to imagine the changes we need, setting up renewable energy projects, re-localising food systems, and creating community and green spaces. They are nurturing the Inner Transition of the cultural and mindset changes that support social and environmental change. They are sparking entrepreneurship, working with municipalities, building community connection and care, repairing and re-skilling.
>
> *(Transition Network 2021, n.p.)*

The movement started in England and has since spread to 48 countries and thousands of groups in towns, villages, cities, universities and schools. Local Transition Town initiatives are linked into a global "learning network" which has facilitated its rapid spread (Haxeltine et al. 2017; Transition Network 2021).

At the local level, communities have defined the solidarity economy in ways that meet their own needs. For example, in the Friuli Venezia Giulia (FVG) region of Northern Italy, the Regional Council passed a law that citizens had brought forward to promote self-sufficiency and resilience. It defines solidarity economy supply chains as:

> integrated systems whose satisfaction of basic needs shall primarily be based on: local resources, raw materials and energy saving; respect for the environment and the local landscape; protection of the rights of workers and consumers; health; and active participation of citizens.
>
> *(Piani et al. 2021, 2)*

In the FVG, local communities are identified as the protagonists for moving toward a different socioeconomic model. In Ecuador, the solidarity economy is formally recognized at the constitutional level, and Brazil and Colombia have specific framework laws. France and Greece both passed national laws recognizing the social solidarity economy. The EU model of solidarity economies is based on traditions of cooperativism such as proximity services in France and social cooperatives in Italy (Piani et al. 2021). In the US,

Transition Towns are being built from scratch, grounded in citizens' concerns about the polycrisis of climate change, financial volatility, environmental degradation and food access during social breakdowns.

That said, there is a strong tradition in the US and other countries of mutual aid which re-emerged during the COVID pandemic. Mutual aid is neighbors helping each other instead of waiting for governmental assistance, and it played a vital role in the first defense of communities assaulted by COVID (Carstensen et al. 2021). Oli Mould et al. (2022) warned against governments neglecting their responsibilities for social welfare when mutual aid is picking up the slack. Mutual aid can be strengthened by governmental recognition of its role and funds directed to community organizations that understand the specific needs of their areas better than state or national agencies do.

A final example of grassroots rejection of the neoliberal economy is ecovillages, which are intentional communities that work to consciously pursue economic, social and ecological sustainability. Every ecovillage is different, because they build from the values and aspirations of the residents. However, they share concepts and principles from commoning, degrowth and co-housing. Olea Morris (2022) analyzed how Mexican ecovillagers think about "profitability" and claimed that they consider ecological and social as well as economic abundance. The Global Ecovillage Network catalogs over 10,000 ecovillages around the world that are rooted in local participatory processes, use a whole systems approach to sustainability and actively restore and regenerate their social and natural environments (GEN n.d).

Working through Policy

Civil society has long recognized that changing policy will help to create more favorable environments for regenerative food systems. Many of these organizations only work on a part of regenerative food systems, but in concert their work is helping to pull public policy in a favorable direction. Work on policy reform is necessary to support the grassroots initiatives above and to weaken the neoliberal food system. Chapter 5 introduced several policy reforms that could slow down or reverse the concentration and dominance of food system corporations. For a transition toward regenerative food systems, it is not enough to create and obtain food through alternatives such as the ones highlighted in this chapter: it is also necessary to de-construct neoliberalism through policy.

A good place to begin is with realizing the right to food. Even though the US as a nation does not recognize the right to food, many people in the country do. The alternative, that people should only have access to healthy food if they can afford to pay for it, is deeply offensive. There is a growing movement to implement right-to-food legislation at the state level, with the hope that eventually this will rise to the national level.

The state of Maine has been a leader in this movement, building on decades of implementing food sovereignty statutes at the municipal level. The Town of Sedgwick, Maine, passed an ordinance in 2011 that granted residents the "right to produce, process, sell, purchase, and consume local foods of their choosing" (Trauger 2014). The action was provoked by passage of the US Food Safety and Modernization Act, which created new constraints on production and distribution of food that were especially onerous for small-scale producers. It was also inspired by the international movement for food sovereignty, although there are notable differences between La Via Campesina's food sovereignty and the version that Mainers achieved (Alkon and Mares 2012; Kurtz 2015). The food sovereignty ordinances enacted in Maine encountered pushback from the state and some producers who were fearful that a food safety scare might damage Maine's reputation. But in 2017, the Maine legislature passed a state-wide Act to Recognize Local Control Regarding Food Systems, LD725, which applies to sales conducted at farms and homes where the food was produced in towns that have formally declared food sovereignty. The law was amended in October to exclude meat and poultry processing, and to exclude sales at farmers' markets or other public venues. Then in 2021, voters approved a constitutional amendment saying that "all individuals have a natural, inherent and unalienable right to grow, raise, harvest, produce and consume the food of their own choosing for their nourishment, sustenance, bodily health and well-being." As of 2023, at least 97 towns in Maine have food sovereignty ordinances (Local Food Rules 2023), which means that LD725 applies in these towns. Similar "food freedom" laws were passed in 2021 in Wyoming, Montana and Colorado. These laws focus on deregulating food, rather than on food access as a social right (Larsen 2023).

In Maine, activists originally proposed the following language for the Constitutional amendment:

> **Right to food, food sovereignty and freedom from hunger.** All people have a natural, inherent and unalienable right to food, including the right to acquire, produce, process, prepare, preserve and consume the food of their own choosing by hunting, gathering, foraging, farming, fishing, gardening and saving and exchanging seeds or by barter, trade or purchase from sources of their own choosing, for their nourishment, sustenance, bodily health and well-being, as long as an individual does not commit trespassing, theft, poaching or other abuses of private property rights, public lands or natural resources in the acquisition of food; furthermore, all people have a fundamental right to be free from hunger, malnutrition, starvation and the endangerment of life from the scarcity of or lack of access to nourishing food.
>
> *(as reported by Cohen 2023)*

The Maine legislature pared this down and eliminated the final statement about the right to be free from hunger, malnutrition, starvation and the endangerment of life. However, activists in West Virginia working with West Virginia University are using this original language in their efforts to secure a constitutional amendment. The growing Right-to-Food community of practice, coordinated by Alison Cohen (formerly with WhyHunger) is aligned with the international conceptualization of the right to food, which the original language from Maine reflects. Whether sufficient public pressure can be mobilized to get this into state constitutions is still a question; but guaranteeing food and nutrition as a human right is increasingly important given unusually high food price inflation since 2020 (US Inflation Calculator 2023), the overtaxed charitable food assistance network that runs pantries and food banks, the roll-back of programs that helped food-insecure families to access food during COVID-19 and relentless Republican efforts to reduce federal food assistance. States that accept food and nutrition as a human right would be obligated to maintain existing food assistance, in addition to addressing the root causes of food insecurity and undertaking efforts to identify and remove barriers to food security.

Other organizations working on policy to implement access to regenerative food systems' products for everyone focus on institutional procurement. As stated in a previous chapter, three of these organizations have come together recently to create the Anchors in Action standards framework. Procurement standards that push institutions to purchase regenerative food benefit poor children most, since school meals may be the only nutritionally balanced meal of the day for them and make up a substantial proportion of the food they consume. But they also benefit the environment, producers and food businesses selling foods produced regeneratively, because they can lead to long-term contracts for high-quality products. In a similar vein, Farm to Institution New England (FINE) helps producers to secure direct contracts with different kinds of institutions so that they can get a higher percentage of the price. In Canada, Local Food Plus got started in 2005 by establishing standards for University of Toronto food purchasing. The standards were eventually adopted in many Canadian provinces to help local food suppliers scale up to sell in larger markets (Friedmann 2007). This was the earliest certification scheme in Canada to include labor standards (Stahlbrand 2023).

HEAL Food Alliance, based in Oakland California, was started by the Food Chain Workers Alliance, the National Black Food & Justice Alliance, Real Food Generation and the Union of Concerned Scientists. It is a multi-sector, multi-racial coalition building collective power to transform food and farm systems. Its member organizations represent over two million rural and urban farmers, fishers, farm and food chain workers, Indigenous groups, scientists, public health advocates, policy experts, community organizers and activists. Its food policy platform consists of dignity for food workers; opportunity for all producers; fair and competitive markets; resilient regional economies; getting rid of junk food and its marketing; increasing food literacy and transparency; phasing out factory farming; sustainable food production; and closing the loop on waste, runoff and energy. HEAL Food Alliance also supports worker ownership and control, improved land access, self-determination in food production, more food entrepreneurship and increased federal food assistance (HEAL Food Alliance 2022). It is an ambitious platform that encompasses workers' rights, better opportunities for low-income communities and ecological integrity. HEAL Food Alliance has been successful in its advocacy for environmental justice and racial justice.

Migrant farm workers have organized independently in several states to protect their rights. The Coalition of Immokalee Workers (CIW) in Florida was one of the first and was able to win seven cases against labor contractors who were guilty of slavery (CIW 2023). The group has won compliance by fourteen multi-billion dollar food retailers (supermarkets and fast-food companies) with a Fair Food Agreement that ensures humane working conditions including higher wages, decent living conditions and recourse for complaints. The stores and companies that have signed on include Walmart, Ahold USA, McDonald's, Subway, and Compass Group. The Fair Food Program's success has inspired similar programs across the US, in South Africa, Mexico, Chile and the UK (Fair Food Program 2023). In Vermont, the migrant-led Migrant Justice organization modelled its Milk with Dignity campaign after the Fair Food Program and has signed on Ben & Jerry's ice cream company to its code of conduct that provides humane conditions for dairy farmworkers. They have also called attention to racial profiling by police in many communities and secured the right for undocumented migrants to obtain driver's licenses. Migrant Justice and CIW were two of the founding members of the Worker-Driven Social Responsibility Network, which advocates for fair labor standards in industries across the globe. They have had victories in Lesotho and Bangladesh, in addition to those secured by CIW and Migrant Justice (Worker-Driven Social Responsibility Network 2023).

Local food policy councils (FPCs) are other places in the US where people are addressing food system policy. FPCs generally work within or in partnership with existing governmental institutions. They are organized groups of stakeholders, sanctioned by a government body or existing independently, which address food system issues and needs at the local, state, regional or tribal nation levels. They get laws and ordinances passed, secure funding and implementation for policies and programs and work with public and private institutions. They address a wide range of issues, including healthy food financing, food and nutrition incentives at farmers' markets, and school wellness policies and economic recovery from COVID. Given the converging crises of 2020 that affected food access, FPCs often were "first responders" in coordinating action across government agencies and civil society organizations. Although FPCs are not "radical" or anti-capitalist spaces by any means, they are improving well-being for many people.

As of November 2020, 288 US FPCs were active, in development or in transition in the US and tribal nations. In a 2020 survey, 68 percent of the reported FPCs operated at the local level (e.g., county, city/municipality, or both city/municipality and county); 19 percent focused on multi-county or multi-state regions; 11 percent worked at the state level, and two percent worked within tribal nations. Most were housed in non-profit organizations, although one-quarter were embedded in government and the overwhelming majority had some kind of relationship with government (Santo et al. 2022). Brazil has a much more extensive network of nested food policy councils, ranging from the local to the federal level, called CONSEAs, which engage civil society extensively to address food security and nutrition (Duarte de Moraes et al. 2021). The US does not have any similar organized policy network at the national level that brings together civil society and government stakeholders; although there are posted opportunities to comment individually on proposed policies through the Federal Register, people do not come together to deliberate on their merits and problems. Spaces to deliberate together are among the essential features of food democracy (Anderson 2023). Without such shared spaces, the "demos" or common people are stripped from food democracy. Websites for providing individual comments are likely to be used only by those with time, strong interest and access to the Internet.

Many other countries and regions have grassroots organizations that work on food system policy. Just a few examples: the African Centre for Biodiversity seeks to resist seed policies that prohibit small-holder farmers from adapting and reproducing agricultural biodiversity. The Alliance for Food Sovereignty in Africa (AFSA) has been developing a common food policy for Africa since 2019. They note that African countries do not have a food policy, but a variety of frameworks for agriculture, food safety and public health, trade, environmental protection, climate and energy, economic and social cohesion, rural development and international development, employment and education (AFSA 2023b). A few African countries developed food policies between the UN Food Systems Summit and the two-year "stocktaking," but these are not coordinated across the region. As noted above, several organizations are working to reverse seed privatization in Africa and other regions.

In the EU, the Agricultural and Rural Convention (ARC2020) has created a Sustainable Food Systems Law (ARC2020 2023) and is calling on countries to develop National Sustainable Food Plans that will revise national dietary guidelines, set minimum requirements for the food environment, and support the accessibility and affordability of food. They share stories about initiatives happening around the region in a regular newsletter, highlighting local efforts to build resilience. They belong to the EU Food Policy Coalition along with about 60 other civil society organizations, the European Environmental Bureau, and a few institutes and think-tanks. Food First Information and Action Network Europe (FIAN), based in Heidelberg, advocates for right to food policies and works through chapters in Africa, the Americas, Asia and Europe. Pesticide Action Network Europe works on policy to reduce or eliminate the use of pesticides, and has chapters in Asia, North America and South America.

In summarizing, what can we make of the rich array of alternatives in this chapter? Do they actually have potential to create an emancipatory regenerative de-commodified food system in which all people can be nourished, grow food or work in food businesses without oppression, and support ecological integrity? Although some are small and incipient, the simple fact that communities keep creating and re-creating such food system alternatives that go beyond capitalism is telling. It is obvious that people are hungry for a better food future than the extractive industrialized food system is offering us.

Olivier De Schutter (2017) described three possibilities for grassroots initiatives: (1) co-optation by the mainstream system, (2) providing inspiration to mainstream actors if exogenous shocks to the food system require it to change or (3) replacing the mainstream if a crisis leads to breakdown of the mainstream regime or the grassroots innovation exerts pressure that cannot be co-opted without a fundamental re-alignment of the regime. The initiatives described in this chapter may have different fates, but some may ultimately "win out" over the practices of the extractive industrialized food system.

Regardless of whether the grassroots initiatives are strong enough to overcome pressures of neoliberalism, participation by citizens has multiple benefits. It reinforces the belief that people can accomplish worthwhile goals through collective action, thus undermining neoliberalism's emphasis on individualism. It causes people to question whether food should be commodified, and how it can be de-commodified. It cracks apart the neoliberal narrative that industrialized exploitative food systems are essential to "feed the world." It allows people to care for their neighbors who are not benefiting from the current food system, overcoming distance and helplessness. And it nourishes participants with healthy food.

References

Alkon, A and T Mares. 2012. Food sovereignty in US food movements: radical visions and neoliberal constraints. *Agric Human Values* 39:347–359.

Alliance for Food Sovereignty in Africa (AFSA). 2023a. Healthy soil healthy food. https://afsafrica.org/healthy-soil-healthy-food/

Alliance for Food Sovereignty in Africa (AFSA). 2023b. Toward a food policy for Africa. A 3-year process of research, reflection and citizen engagement. https://afsafrica.org/towards-a-common-food-policy-for-africa/

Anderson, MD. 2023. Expanding food democracy: a perspective from the United States. *Front Sustain Food Syst* 7. https://doi.org/10.3389/fsufs.2023.1144090

ARC2020. 2023. Sustainable food systems law: policy recommendations for a meaningful transition. https://www.arc2020.eu/wp-content/uploads/2023/04/SUSTAINABLE-FOOD-SYSTEMS-LAW-POLICY-RECOMMENDATIONS-FOR-A-MEANINGFUL-TRANSITION_A.pdf

Battisti, F and C Pisano. 2022. Common property in Italy. Unresolved issues and an appraisal approach: towards a definition of environmental-economic civic value. *Land* 11:1927. https://doi.org/10.3390/land11111927

Berk, L. 2023. Executive Director, ACORN Vermont. Personal communication. Used by permission.

Bollier, D. 2014. *Think Like a Commoner. A Short Introduction to the Life of the Commons*. Gabriola Island: New Society Press.

Boston Food Forest Coalition (BFFC). 2023. About Us. https://www.bostonfoodforest.org/ourwork

Carranza López, T. 2012. Tianguis Indígena: the solidarity economy and indigenous women in Mexico. *Development* 55(3):393–396.

Carstensen, N, M Mudhar and F Schurmann Munksgaard. 2021. 'Let communities do their work': the role of mutual aid and self-help groups in the Covid-19 pandemic response. *Disasters* 45(S1):S146–S173. https://doi.org/10.1111/disa.12515

Coalition of Immokalee Workers (CIW). 2023. Anti-slavery program and Campaign for Fair Food. https://ciw-online.org/

Cohen, A. 2023. General Coordinator, Right to Food Community of Practice. Personal communication. Used by permission.

Cox, D. 2015. Farm Hack: a commons for agricultural innovation. Pp. 145–150 In: D Bollier and S Helfrich (Eds.). *Patterns of Commoning*. Amherst, MA: Commons Strategies Group and Off the Common Books.

Daria, J and A Canning. 2023. *Certified Exploitation: How Equitable Food Initiative and Fair Trade USA Fail to Protect Farmworkers in the Mexican Produce Industry. Corporate Accountability Lab*. https://corpaccountabilitylab.org/certified-exploitation

De Schutter, O. 2017. The political economy of food system reform. *Eur Rev Agric Econ* 44(4): 705–731. https://doi.org/10.1093/erae/jbx009

De Wolfe, SY. 2023. The Black Dirt Farm Collective. https://farmersfootprint.us/the-black-dirt-farm-collective/

DiVito Wilson, A. 2012. Beyond alternative: exploring the potential for autonomous food spaces. *Antipode* 45(3):719–737. https://doi.org/10.1111/j.1467-8330.2012.01020.x

Duarte de Moraes, V, CV Machado and Magalhães. 2021. The National Council for Food and Nutrition Security: dynamics and agenda (2006–2016). *Ciência & Saúde Coletiva* 26(12):6175–6187.

Equitable Food Initiative. 2023. About us. https://equitablefood.org/

Fair Food Program. 2023. Partners. https://fairfoodprogram.org/partners/

Fairtrade America. 2023. Recognition of Fairtrade more than doubles in four years, per 2023 consumer market research. https://www.fairtradeamerica.org/news-insights/recognition-of-fairtrade-more-than-doubles-in-four-years-per-2023-consumer-market-research/

Federation of Southern Cooperatives. 2023. History. https://www.federation.coop/history-archives

Feola, G, O Koretskaya and D Moore. 2021. (Un)making in sustainability transformation beyond capitalism. *Global Env Change* 69:102290. https://doi.org/10.1016/j.gloenvcha.2021.102290

Fonte, M. 2013. Food consumption as social practice: Solidarity Purchasing Groups in Rome, Italy. *J Rural Stud* 32:230–239. https://doi.org/10.1016/j.jrurstud.2013.07.003

Friedmann, H. 2007. Scaling up: bringing public institutions and food service corporations into the project for a local, sustainable food system in Ontario. *Agric Human Values* 24(3):389–398.

Frisch, T. 2019. To free ourselves, we must feed ourselves. Leah Penniman on bringing people of color back to the land. *The Sun Magazine*. https://www.thesunmagazine.org/issues/523/to-free-ourselves-we-must-feed-ourselves

Froio, N. 2023. Landless workers fight for fair food. *Yes! Magazine* 107:34–39. https://www.yesmagazine.org/issue/growth/2023/08/31/brazil-mst-landless-workers-fair-food

Genuine Clandestine. N.d. Comunitàin lotta per l'autodeterminazione alimentare. https://genuinoclandestino.it/il-manifesto/

Gibson-Graham, JK. 2006. *A Post Capitalist Politics*. Minneapolis, MN: Minnesota University Press.

Global Ecovillage Network (GEN). n.d. What is an ecovillage? https://ecovillage.org/ecovillages/what-is-an-ecovillage/

Gómez, M. 2022. Autonomía contra viento y marea: 19 aniversario de los *caracoles* zapatistas *La Jornada* (2 August). https://www.jornada.com.mx/2022/08/02/opinion/015a1pol

Guthman, J. 2008. Bringing good food to others: investigating the subjects of alternative food practice. *Cultural Geogr* 15:431–447.

Haxeltine, A, F Avelino, JM Wittmayer, I Kunze, N Longhurst, A Dumitru and T O'Riordan. 2017. Conceptualizing the role of social innovation in sustainability transformations. Pp. 12–25 In: J Bakhaus, A Genus, S Lorek, E Vadovics and JM Wittmayer (Eds.) *Sustainable Innovation and Sustainable Consumption: Research and Action for Societal Transformation*. London: Routledge.

HEAL Food Alliance. 2022. Who we are. https://healfoodalliance.org/who-is-heal/

Holt-Giménez, E. 2006. *Campesino A Campesino: Voices from Latin America's Farmer to Farmer Movement for Sustainable Agriculture*. Oakland, CA: Food First Books.

International Cooperative Alliance. 2023. Cooperative identity, values & principles. https://www.ica.coop/en/cooperatives/cooperative-identity

Jaffee, D. 2020. Enclosing water: privatization, commodification, and access. Pp. 303–323 In: K Legun, J Keller, M Bell and M Carolan (Eds.) *The Cambridge Handbook of Environmental Sociology* (Vol. 2). Cambridge: Cambridge University Press.

Jongerden, J. 2022. Autonomy as a third mode of ordering: agriculture and the Kurdish movement in Rojava and North and East Syria. *J Agrarian Change* 22(3):592–607. https://doi.org/10.1111/joac.12449

Kawano, E and J Matthaei. 2020. System change: a basic primer to the solidarity economy. *Nonprofit Quarterly*. https://nonprofitquarterly.org/system-change-a-basic-primer-to-the-solidarity-economy/

Keller, S. 2018. Agriculture and autonomy in the Middle East. *Local Futures*. https://localfutures.medium.com/agriculture-autonomy-in-the-middle-east-bf9f0fa23a7d

Kelly, M. 2023. *Wealth Supremacy: How the Extractive Economy and the Biased Rules of Capitalism Drive Today's Crises*. Oakland, CA: Berrett-Koehler Publishers.

Kneafsey, M, R Cox, L Holloway, E Dowler, L Venn and H Tuomainen. 2008. *Reconnecting Consumers, Producers and Food: Exploring Alternatives*. Oxford, UK: Berg.

Kothari, A and S Bajpai. 2023. Global Tapestry of Alternatives: weaving transformative connections. Opening essay for a Global Transitions Forum. https://greattransition.org/gti-forum/global-tapestry-kothari-bajpai

Kothari, A, A Salleh, A Escobar, F Demaria and A Acosta (Eds.). 2019. *Pluriverse: A Post-Development Dictionary*. New Delhi: Tulika Books.

Kurtz, HE. 2015. Framing multiple food sovereignties. Comparing the Nyéléni declaration and the local food and selfgovernance ordinance in Maine. Pp. 163–176 In: A Trauger (Ed.). *Food Sovereignty in International Context: Discourse, Politics and Practice*. London: Routledge.

Lamine, C, H Renting, A Rossi, JSC Wiskerke and G Brunori. 2012. Agri-food systems and territorial development: innovations, new dynamics and changing governance mechanisms. Pp. 229–256 In: I Darnhofer, D Gibbon and B Dedieu (Eds.) *Farming Systems Research into the 21st Ccntury: The New Dynamic*. Dordrecht: Springer.

Lappé, FM. 2019. This city made access to food a right of citizenship. *Yes! Magazine*. https://www.yesmagazine.org/issue/food-everyone/2019/01/29/this-city-made-access-to-food-a-right-of-citizenship

Larsen, R. 2023. Food for thought: the emergence of right-to-food legislation in the United States. *Minnesota Law Review* (February 13). https://minnesotalawreview.org/2023/02/13/food-for-thought-the-emergence-of-right-to-food-legislation-in-the-united-states/

Local Food Rules. 2023. List of municipalities with a LFCSGO. https://www.localfoodrules.org/wp-content/uploads/2020/04/LFCSGOsList-Adopted.pdf

Make Rojava Green Again. 2019. *Rojava: building an ecological society*. https://degrowth.info/en/blog/rojava-building-an-ecological-society

Malcolm X. 1963. Message to the grassroots. https://www.blackpast.org/african-american-history/speeches-african-american-history/1963-malcolm-x-message-grassroots/

Maughan, C and T Ferrando. 2018. Land as a commons: examples from the UK and Italy. Pp. 329–341 In: JL Vivero, T Ferrando, O De Schutter & U Mattei (Eds.) *Routledge Handbook of Food as a Commons*. London: Routledge.

Mondeggi Bene Comune. N.d. Chi siamo. https://mondeggibenecomune.noblogs.org/chi-siamo/

Montalvo, M. 2021. Indigenous food sovereignty movements are taking back ancestral land. *Civil Eats* (March 31). https://civileats.com/2021/03/31/indigenous-food-sovereignty-movements-are-taking-back-ancestral-land/

Montenegro de Wit, M. 2019. Beating the bounds: how does 'open source' become a seed commons? *J Peasant Studies* 46:44–79. https://doi.org/10.1080/03066150.2017.1383395

Morris, O. 2022. How ecovillages work: more-than-human understandings of *rentabilidad* in Mexican ecovillages. *Sust Sci* 17:1235–1246. https://doi.org/10.1007/s11625-022-01162-7

Mould, O, J Cole, A Badger and P Brown. 2022. Solidarity, not charity: Learning the lessons of the COVID-19 pandemic to reconceptualise the radicality of mutual aid. *Trans Inst Brit Geographers* 47(4): 866–879 https://doi.org/10.1111/tran.12553

Nemes, G, R Reckinger, V Lajos and S Zollet. 2022. 'Values-based territorial food networks'—benefits, challenges and controversies. *Sociologia Ruralis* 63:3–19.

Open Source Seed Initiative (OSSI). 2023. The Open Source Seed Initiative. https://osseeds.org/

Phillips, D. 2018. More than a meal: the swanky Rio restaurant for homeless people. *The Guardian* (5 November). https://www.theguardian.com/global-development/2018/nov/05/more-than-a-meal-swanky-rio-de-janeiro-restaurant-for-homeless-people-refettorio-gastromotiva

Piani, L, M Carzedda and N Cerestiato. 2021. Food solidarity economy: evaluating transition community initiatives in Friulia Venezia Giulia region. *Agric Econ* 9:32. https://doi.org/10.1186/s40100-021-00203-6

Pole, A and M Gray. 2013. Farming alone? What's up with the "C" in community supported agriculture. *Agric Human Values* 30:85–100. https://doi.org/10.1007/s10460-012-9391-9

Poole, B. 2021. Tribal influence over Arizona water growing. *Courthouse News* https://www.courthousenews.com/tribal-influence-over-arizona-water-growing/

Red Tomato. 2023. Who we are. https://redtomato.org/who-we-are/

Reyes, A and M Kaufman. 2011. Sovereignty, indigeneity, territory: Zapatista autonomy and the new practices of decolonization. *South Atlantic Quart* 110(2):505–525.

Rebrii, A. 2020. Zapatistas: Lessons in community self-organisation in Mexico. *Open Democracy*. https://www.opendemocracy.net/en/democraciaabierta/zapatistas-lecciones-de-auto-organizaci%C3%B3n-comunitaria-en/

Rosol, M. 2020. On the significance of alternative economic practices: reconceptualizing alterity in alternative food networks. *Econ Geog* 96(1):52–76. https://doi.org/10.1080/00130095.2019.1701430

Santo, R, C Misiaszek, K Bassarab, D Harris and A Palmer. 2022. *Pivoting policy, Programs and Partnerships: Food Policy Councils' Responses to the Crises of 2020.* Center for a Livable Future, Johns Hopkins University, Baltimore, Maryland.

SHARECITY. 2021. SHARECITY Manifesto. https://sharecity.ie/wp-content/uploads/2021/08/SHARECITY-Manifesto_h.png

Slow Food International. N.d. About us. https://www.slowfood.com/about-us/

Solidarity Economy Principles. 2023. What do we mean by solidarity economy? https://solidarityeconomyprinciples.org/what-do-we-mean-by-solidarity-economy-3/

Soul Fire Farm. 2023. Mission. https://www.soulfirefarm.org/

Stahlbrand, L. 2023. Co-founder of Local Food Plus. Personal communication. Used by permission.

Sustainable Harvest International. Our work. https://www.sustainableharvest.org/

Syracuse Urban Food Policy Project. N.d. https://falk.syr.edu/faculty-research/syracuse-urban-food-forest-project-suffp/

The Food Project. 2023. What we do. https://thefoodproject.org/what-we-do/

Tampone, K. 2022. Child poverty improves in Syracuse; it's still among highest in US, Census says. https://www.syracuse.com/data/2022/09/child-poverty-improves-in-syracuse-its-still-among-highest-in-us-census-says.html

Toffler, A. 1980. *The Third Wave*. New York: William Collins Sons & Co. Ltd.

Transition Network. 2021. What is transition? https://transitionnetwork.org/about-the-movement/what-is-transition/

Trauger, A. 2014. Toward a political geography of food sovereignty: transforming territory, exchange and power in the liberal sovereign state. *J Peasant Studies* 41(6):1131–1152. https://doi.org/10.1080/03066150.2014.937339

Trauger, A and C Passidomo. 2012. Towards a post-capitalist-politics of food: cultivating subjects of community economies. *ACME* 11(2):282–303. https://acme-journal.org/index.php/acme/article/view/934

Tricontinental: Institute for Social Research. 2020. *Popular Agrarian reform and the struggle for land in Brazil*. Dossier No. 27. https://www.mstbrazil.org/sites/default/files/Popular percent20Agrarian percent20Reform percent20and percent 20the percent20Struggle percent20for percent20Land percent20in percent20 Brazil.pdf

United Nations Inter-Agency Task Force on Social and Solidarity Economy (UN-TFSS). 2023. What is the social and solidarity economy? https://unsse.org/sse-and-the-sdgs/https://unsse.org/sse-and-the-sdgs/

UN News. 2022. Climate change threatening access to water and sanitation. https://news.un.org/en/story/2022/05/1118722

US Inflation Calculator. 2023. Food inflation in the United States, 1968-2023. https://www.usinflationcalculator.com/inflation/food-inflation-in-the-united-states/

Urgenci. 2021. Enacting resilience: the response of local solidarity-based partnerships for agroecology to the COVID-19 crisis. *International Network of Local Solidarity-based Partnerships for Agroecology*. https://urgenci.net/wp-content/uploads/2021/01/Urgenci-rapport-Enacting-ResilienceFINAL-FINAL.pdf

Van der Ploeg, JD, J Ye and S Schneider. 2022. Reading markets politically: on the transformativity and relevance of peasant markets. *J Peasant Studies* 50(5):1–26. https://doi.org/10.1080/03066150.2021.2020258

Wise, TA. 2019. *Eating Tomorrow: Agribusiness, Family Farmers and the Battle for the Future of Food*. New York: New Press.

Worker-Driven Social Responsibility Network. 2023. About the WSR. https://wsr-network.org/about-us/

Xie, C, RP Bagozzi and SC Troye. 2008. Trying to prosume: toward a theory of consumers as co-creators of value. *J Acad Market Sci* 36(1):109–122. https://doi.org/10.1007/s11747-007-0060-2

Yakini, M. 2023. *Environmental Justice. Detroit Black Community Food Security Network*. https://www.dbcfsn.org/environment

SECTION 5
Can Food System Narratives Be Melded Together?

11 FUTURE FOOD SYSTEM NARRATIVES

The number of papers and reports with recommendations for how to transform the food system, globally or within a single country, has grown exponentially over the last decade. A database search on "food system" and "transformation" delivers thousands of articles, and that does not include papers using "transition," "agrifood" or specific desired outcomes such as resilience or freedom from hunger. If only we could review all of these recommendations, compare the pathways that they suggest, and be confident that we know the best option based on the number of people promoting it or the number of times it appears in the literature! But cataloging and comparing recommendations is quite difficult.

Even when we examine only global recommendations, versus those discussing the EU or single countries, there are difficulties in making comparisons. Many times the recommendations use vague wording or terms without a clear definition. For example, what exactly do authors mean by "put people first" (De Cleene and Strauss 2021, n.p.) or "[increase] capabilities for data-driven agrifood systems" (FAO 2022, 396)? Is the latter the same as investing in the "ecosystem for a digital enabling environment" (Barrett et al. 2020)? Recalling Chapter 2 in which there is considerable agreement on problems with current food systems, the fact that these recommendations appear might simply mean that authors recognize that some people have been left out of food system solutions, and digital systems are taking over much more rapidly than the ability to use them well and equitably. But little will be accomplished by recommendations that are ambiguous and open to interpretation.

The second big problem in comparing recommendations is the lack of criteria by which options are selected. The Intergovernmental Panel on Climate

DOI: 10.4324/9781003260264-16

Change is a notable exception, in its charts of options for adaptation and mitigation (IPCC 2022, SPM7). It ranks options by how much GHG emissions are reduced, the relative cost of implementing the practice and the confidence that authors place on estimates. No comparable ranking by costs and confidence exists for food system recommendations.

A third barrier to comparing recommendations is lack of clear targets. Some articles on transformation are focused on one outcome, such as greenhouse gas emissions (as the IPCC report is), hunger or malnutrition; others include a diversity of outcomes. Is "resilience" or "sustainability" the same as regeneration of communities, institutions and ecosystems, for authors writing these reports? It is not possible to talk meaningfully about transformation without specifying its aims and what problems it is trying to overcome. What will improve? What will disappear? Who will benefit?

A fourth barrier is the lack of attention to trade-offs. Occasionally, recommendations from a single source are mutually incompatible, or result in very different outcomes. For example, FAO (2022) recommended both "market access for smallholders" and "competitiveness of international and national markets"; the latter probably will not be increased by providing more market access to smallholders. In other papers, trade-offs are simply ignored. Shenggen Fan and his co-authors (2021) recommended both "scale up productive and regenerative agriculture" and "promote sustainable intensification of agriculture"; but surely they are aware of the debates over "sustainable intensification." In an exception to this tendency, Christophe Béné and his co-authors (2019) raised the problem of meeting recommendations to reduce loss and waste by providing more cold-storage facilities in rural areas of poor countries to prevent post-harvest losses. They noted that there would be clear energy costs of this intervention with a probable increase in use of fossil fuels and greenhouse gas emissions.

A fifth barrier is lack of attention to feed-backs and the dynamic nature of interventions. If a recommendation is taken up, what will be the results and to whom? Is it likely to catalyze further positive changes in the system? In Chapter 5 of this book, feedback loops are highlighted as the way that a system learns and changes. Resilience theory also indicates that appropriate responses to feedback and "system learning" are essential for resilience (Walker and Salt 2006). They are equally important for regeneration; actors in the food system need to learn constantly from what works and what doesn't.

Finally, looking for universally applicable recommendations is futile because transformation is complex and highly context-dependent (Candel and Pereira 2017; Babu 2019; Lamine et al. 2019; HLPE 2020; Stefanovic et al. 2020; Dengerink et al. 2021; Leeuwis et al. 2021). Policy and practice changes needed in a highly industrialized country like the US are different than policies and practices needed in Nigeria or Mongolia.

Given these problems in reviewing recommendations, I limited my literature review for the purposes of this chapter to papers and reports that addressed the global food system and multiple outcomes (i.e., not just reducing greenhouse gas emissions or hunger); used the term "transformation" rather than "transition" or "change" in the title, abstract or text; and took a normative approach of making specific recommendations for action, rather than simply writing about recommendations or making recommendations for research. I am sure that these constraints led to my missing important papers and reports, but the sheer number of publications required setting some limits. I used different criteria in reviewing the literature on specific options described in Chapters 6 and 7, which were not necessarily global. In those chapters, the criteria I used were potential to result in regenerative food systems with diverse outcomes, inclusion of more food system actors and where the option fit in Donella Meadows's scheme of leverage points. That is, I am most interested in transformation options that have the greatest potential to spread through the system and catalyze self-organizing changes in different parts of the system. I also emphasized recommendations from grassroots organizations that serve marginalized people because they have closer connections with the people who are not being served by the current food system and better understand the barriers these people face in realizing their rights to food, decent work, a healthy environment and other human rights spelled out in UNDROP and UNDRIP.

A reader might argue that there are obvious "no-regrets" practices and policies for food system transformation. The recommendations raised most frequently in the literature I reviewed were:

- shifting to regenerative, nature-based or agroecological practices (e.g., Foley et al. 2011; Schipanski et al. 2016; Campbell et al. 2018; Caron et al. 2018; CSIPM 2020; Rockström et al 2020; Stefanovic et al. 2020; Dinesh et al. 2021; Fan et al. 2021; GAFF 2021; HLPE 2020; CSIPM 2022; Dornelles et al. 2022; Elechi et al 2022; McGreevy et al. 2022; Pimbert 2022; Ewert et al. 2023; Fakhri 2023; Food Systems Partnership 2023; Jones et al. 2023; Wolpold-Bosien 2023; Woodhill 2023);
- shifting to plant-based, diverse and more sustainable diets for all people to reduce GHG emissions from livestock and allow human food production on land currently used for growing animal feed (e.g., Foley et al. 2011; Caron et al. 2018; Dinesh et al. 2018; Béné et al. 2019; Gerten et al. 2020; Kennedy et al. 2020; Rockström et al. 2020; Vermeulen et al. 2020; Webb et al. 2020; Weber et al. 2020; Fan et al. 2021; Gaupp et al. 2021; GAFF 2021; FAO 2022; Food Systems Partnership 2023; Stefanovic et al. 2020; Dornelles et al. 2022; Elechi et al. 2022; Jones et al. 2023; Woodhill 2023);
- reducing food loss and waste (e.g., Schipanski et al. 2016; Béné et al. 2019; Gerten et al. 2020; Rockström et al. 2020; Stefanovic et al. 2020;

Webb et al. 2020; Ellen MacArthur Foundation 2021; Gaupp et al. 2021; Elechi et al. 2022; FAO 2022; McGreevy et al. 2022; Food Systems Partnership 2023; Jones et al. 2023; Nierenberg 2023);
- being open to pluralist knowledge sources (e.g., Dahlberg 2001; Abson et al. 2017; Arora et al. 2020; Scoones et al. 2020; Sonnino and Milbourne 2022; GAFF 2021; den Boer et al. 2021b; Leeuwis et al. 2021; Béné 2022; Elechi et al. 2022; Pimbert 2022; Tschersich and Kok 2022; Vijayan et al. 2022);
- deepening democratic governance (e.g., Dahlberg 2001; Candel and Pereira 2017; Arora et al. 2020; CSIPM 2020; Stefanovic et al. 2020; Ruben et al. 2021; Arthur et al. 2022; CSIPM 2022; Pimbert 2022; Bezner Kerr 2023; Food Systems Partnership 2023; Woodhill 2023) and
- creating new streams of stable finance or redirecting existing funding (e.g., Campbell et al. 2018; Dinesh et al. 2018; Barrett et al. 2020; Herrero et al. 2020; Kennedy et al. 2020; Swinnen et al. 2021; Dinesh et al. 2021; Fan et al. 2021; GAFF 2021; Elechi et al. 2022; Food Systems Partnership 2023; Woodhill 2023).

As mentioned above, it is often not possible to know exactly what authors mean by a recommendation; so some of the examples above might not be equivalent. Implicit in many recommendations but seldom stated explicitly, except in the context of reducing red meat intake, is the goal of reducing greenhouse gas emissions from food systems. And there are disputes even over "no-regrets" options, with the advocates and lobbyists who don't want to see reductions in red meat consumption the most vehement (Neslen 2023).

The next tier of recommendations includes those made somewhat less frequently, but still often:

- achieving greater policy coherence across the value chain (e.g., Candel and Pereira 2017; Caron et al. 2018; Vermeulen et al. 2020; Webb et al. 2020; Gaupp et al. 2021; One Planet Network 2020; Elechi et al. 2022; Sonnino and Milbourne 2022; Ewert et al. 2023) and
- innovation (e.g., Campbell et al. 2018; Béné et al. 2019; Barrett et al. 2020; Herrero et al. 2020; Fan et al. 2021; den Boer et al. 2021a; Elechi et al. 2022; FAO 2022; Tschersich and Kok 2022).

Recommendation areas that appear even less frequently include changing wealth distribution, supporting more diverse markets, power changes, better planning for transitions, social protection and transforming vision and values. Yet each of these areas of intervention has strong advocates.

My arguments for changing the cultural narrative require a new vision and values. In their analysis of major food system reports, Scott Slater and his co-authors (2022) found that "recommendations tended to ignore political economy factors, including power asymmetries between actors" (1), and were limited to adjusting or reforming rather than transforming food systems despite the rhetoric supporting transformation. This suggested to them "a dominant paradigm of 'improving' the current system by applying adjustments to broken system components, rather than a paradigm shifting and truly transformative food systems change" (2022, 15). They also found a low acknowledgment of feedback loops in policy, which means that authors were not applying a systemic approach to change. Hamid El Bilali and his co-authors (2021) found a need to address social issues, economics, politics, governance and trade-offs in the 1289 papers that they reviewed in 2020 (but a significant increase in publications has occurred since that date, many of which deal with these issues). They also found biases in publication, with most of them dominated by researchers and organizations from developed countries. This still seems to be true.

We can draw a few lessons from successful efforts to move toward more regenerative and sustainable food systems. While no authors have reviewed the full slate of recommendations, some provide advice about the kinds of recommendations and their development that are most effective. Solid recommendations draw strength from broad coalitions across interest groups and audiences (reviewed in Rutting et al. 2023), common goals, shared discourse and joint strategy (Leeuwis et al. 2021). Grounded in MLP thinking, Cees Leeuwis and his co-authors stressed the importance of supporting varied interventions and capturing existing diversity, protecting niche-level initiatives temporarily and selectively, with an eye on landscape trends, fostering active destabilization of undesirable elements of the regime (industrialized exploitative agrifood systems) and fostering pressures at the landscape level (factors exogenous to the food system that are influencing openness to changes, such as awareness of sea level rise). Dentoni et al. (2017) drew on large systems change theory to argue that supporting, doing and forcing change are all ways to push a niche up to disrupt the regime level. Forcing change can have undesirable blowbacks, however.

In their review of over 200 papers on food system transformations toward sustainability, Hanna Weber and her co-authors (2020) suggested the following key components that emerged across studies:

- political action to support inclusive and participatory governance structures;
- close collaboration of stakeholders in new networks and platforms;
- education to support consumers, farmers and policymakers and
- a deep value shift.

They identified five clusters of transformation research with different recommendations in each for practical programs, personal values, political power shifts and interactions. Other authors, such as Benjamin Davis and his co-authors, cautioned against forgetting certain essential components of food system transformation. They were concerned that influential intergovernmental reports left out the livelihoods of poor rural people, and thus were likely to result in transforming food systems to reach environmental and nutritional objectives on the backs of the rural poor (Davis et al. 2022). This warning resonates with arguments that a "Green New Deal" in the Minority World is likely to exploit people in the Majority World who live in countries that have rare minerals needed for renewable energy and cheap labor (Kolinjivadi and Kothari 2020).

While some of the narratives described in Chapters 6–8 are harmonious and will augment each other, the two meta-narratives identified in Chapter 2 are deeply incompatible. There cannot be a reconciliation between exploiting people and nature solely for private profit and creating systems with multiple values, rooted in care and the public good. One meta-narrative expands death and destruction and the other seeks to enhance life and well-being. To reach the latter goal, the exploitative and extractive system must be weakened. Paula Juárez and her co-authors remarked (2018, 320) that:

> transformation is highly related to confrontation (e.g., the act of challenging, altering and /or replacing established institutions). This relationship entails a deep, persistent, and irreversible change in the social values, perspective, and behaviors of actors and social groups.

Neoliberalism is not going to go away without sustained confrontation. However, the food system that it has created is so deeply embedded in society that imagining the route from here to there can be difficult.

Food systems in industrialized capitalist countries have passed through the stage of growth and exploitation that resilience theorists proposed in their adaptive cycle (Holling and Gunderson 2002), and often seem to be heading straight into the collapse stage without passing through a conservation stage in which energy and materials are slowly accumulating. Accumulation in food systems has accelerated with concentration of industries in every sector and the relentless push for acquiring more land, water and fossil fuels. This is driving collapse of food systems, ecosystems and entire societies. Resilience theorists have another stage up their sleeves, however: after collapse comes re-organization of the elements of the system. This is what the grassroots initiatives described in Chapter 10 are doing, albeit in a fragmented way. No one would wish for general collapse of our current food system: where it is already happening due to climate change and conflicts, the suffering and displacement of people is horrendous. So our task is to find ways to strengthen these alternatives to the neoliberal food system so that more people can work within them and their capacity to fill gaps of food, knowledge and resources grows.

One of the clearest ways to strengthen the alternatives is to change the dominant cultural narrative because it has a catalyzing effect on many other food system components (Figure 7.1). The UN Human Development Report 2020 (UNDP 2020, 398) stated, "nothing short of a wholesale shift in mindsets, translated into reality by policy, is needed to navigate the brave new world of the Anthropocene, to ensure that all people flourish while easing planetary pressures." This is the significance of a changed dominant narrative. Cultural shifts and value shifts can drive a sustainability transition as more people become aware of food system problems and alternative ways to deal with them. The adoption of globalized, industrialized, extractive food systems in wealthy countries was due to a major cultural shift away from subsistence farming and simple market economies, pushed by industries manufacturing technological innovations; farmers enthusiastic about the labor-saving advantages of new technology; and policymakers who believed that increasing food production, productivity and trade would solve food insecurity and increase their own popularity. Labor-saving technology is wonderful, especially if it is designed for the use of women, farmworkers and others who are performing most of the work in the global food system and does not rely on fossil fuels. But technological innovation usually favors wealthy actors who can best afford its price and ignores significant environmental degradation that results from its use.

We will not be able to establish enduring alternatives to extractive food systems until we make another major cultural shift reflected in a new dominant narrative. While many people, such as animal welfare or local farming advocates, are working to change values in parts of the food system, the logic behind regenerative agriculture requires a completely different way of perceiving and interacting with the natural world than is customary in industrialized societies. This would lead to value shifts and cultural changes throughout the food system, not only in whether people eat meat or whether they shop at local markets.

The principles of the needed cultural shift are embedded in many traditional and Indigenous societies. Robin Wall Kimmerer, a member of the Potawatomi nation and botanist, outlined many of these principles in her book, Braiding Sweetgrass: Indigenous Wisdom, Scientific Knowledge and the Teachings of Plants (2020) through illustrative stories, a traditional method of teaching ethical behavior. The White/Wiphala Paper on Indigenous Food Systems (FAO 2021, xi–xii) began with an introduction to principles held by Indigenous Peoples:

- living in balance and harmony with nature and Mother Earth;
- food sovereignty as the right for Indigenous Peoples to choose, cultivate, and preserve their food practices and biocultural values;
- collective rights and communal or common resources;

- biocentrism (i.e., the belief that humans are simply one component of the ecosystem, deserving respect alongside other non-human living entities);
- food generation and production completed with respect for and understanding of ecosystems' carrying capacity to ensure the replenishment and protection of biodiversity;
- territorial management that maintains reciprocal relationships, storytelling, cosmogony and natural resources, generates food and preserves biodiversity;
- collective reciprocity and solidarity and
- non-market access to food (e.g., bartering) with a self-sufficiency and subsistence orientation and low levels of monetization.

The list included a few more general principles:

- Food is more than just eating. Food is an expression of the linkages between Indigenous Peoples, lands, waters, non-human relatives (species), and the spiritual world.
- Sustainability and resilience are inherent components of Indigenous Peoples' food systems, preceding the conceptualization of these terms in Western science.
- Many Indigenous Peoples' societies across the world are informed by principles of reciprocity and solidarity. Often food cannot be sold or stored and so is shared amongst and between communities.

These principles are reflected in the principles and values identified by Lyla June Johnston through her analysis of written materials by Indigenous authors, interviews with Indigenous land managers, and experiences growing up in an Indigenous culture in Turtle Island (as Indigenous people refer to North America). She found the following driving principles: non-humans are equal to or Elder to humans; non-human lifeforms are our relatives; all lifeforms have an ecological and spiritual role, including humans; humans have a sacred covenant to protect and care for their respective homelands; humans have a responsibility to create a home for future generations and creation is sacred. These principles are founded in values of relationality, reciprocity, respect, reverence, restraint, regenerative practice, responsibility to homeland, kinship with life, service to life, generosity, humility, efficiency and a notion that all life is equal (Johnston 2022). While community life based in these principles and values may seem impossibly utopian, the evidence is clear that Indigenous cultures fostered greater sustainability in interactions with the natural world and other people. They were able to survive in sometimes-hostile environments for millennia without degrading the places on which they depended, while contemporary industrialized cultures are rapidly destroying the ecosystems that are necessary to sustain human life. This is certainly not to say that Indigenous cultures were perfect or without conflict, but that most of them have been far more successful than settler societies at figuring out what attitudes must be cultivated to allow both humans and non-humans to thrive.

Settler peoples intentionally destroyed Indigenous food systems and are only beginning to see that they embody wisdom that is desperately needed in the world today about how to achieve widespread well-being. Many Indigenous people are willing to teach and share what they know, which is remarkable given how settler societies have tried to exterminate them. In The Nutmeg's Curse: Parables for a Planet in Crisis (2021, 174–175), Amitav Ghosh quoted a "leading advocate for the Americanization of Indians," who wrote in 1896 of:

> the absolute need of awakening in the savage Indian broader desires and ampler wants. To bring him out of savagery into citizenship we must make the Indian more intelligently selfish before we can make him unselfishly intelligent. We need to *awaken in him wants*. In his dull savagery he must be touched by the wings of the divine angel of discontent ... Discontent with the teepee and the starving rations of the Indian camp in winter is needed to get the Indian out of the blanket and into trousers,—and trousers with a pocket in them, and with a *pocket that aches to be filled with dollars*!

A blunter refutation of the wisdom of Indigenous ways of living is hard to imagine. The settler colonialists in North America were brutal in their efforts to exterminate Indigenous peoples and cultures through war, kidnapping their children and putting them in boarding schools, killing buffalo and destroying villages.

Although Indigenous wisdom is critically needed today, receptivity to and understanding of the principles above is low in capitalist societies that often instill their opposite in young people and set up institutions that undermine this way of being in the world. For example, individual ownership of property, Intellectual Property Rights and extraction of resources far beyond the ability of ecosystems to recover are diametrically opposed to Indigenous principles. Yet the more that non-Indigenous people respect Indigenous food systems and the wisdom that Indigenous people have accumulated through millennia of interaction with land and waters, the closer we will come to regenerative food systems.

A new cultural narrative that incorporates many aspects of Indigenous worldviews seems to be emerging, based on growing recognition of the destructive nature of the exploitative neoliberal food system:

> [I]f the practices of industrial agriculture are allowed to continue, they will eventually destroy the ecological foundations of any agriculture.

> [T]he only way to nourish all people adequately without undermining planetary support systems is to transform the food system into one where food is no longer a commodity that is captured and controlled to increase the profits of companies, shareholders, and investors.
>
> *(Gliessman 2022, 789–790)*

The emerging narrative has other key aspects: it "prioritizes living begins, their needs and rights and their balance with the environment ... according to principles/objectives of solidarity, environmental resilience and sustainability, fairness, inclusiveness and democracy" (Rossi et al. 2021, 548). Respect, protection and fulfillment of human rights—but also the rights of nature—are part of this new narrative, as are care and solidarity. This is the narrative promoted by many civil society organizations and scholars; and it offers solutions through agroecology and food sovereignty to climate, food and environmental crises facing the planet, while ensuring a life with dignity for peasants (Juárez et al. 2018).

Can a rights-based food system exist within a neoliberal society? Many of the grassroots initiatives introduced in the former chapter are trying to build this, but they are subject to harassment and attacks. For example, gifting food to strangers without shelter to realize their right to food has been criminalized in the US. In an earlier paper (Anderson 2008), I argued for a rights-based food system (RBFS) based on the following principles:

- absence of human exploitation;
- democratic decision-making on food system choices that have impacts on people in more than one sector of the system (e.g., consumers and producers, or distributors and producers);
- fair, transparent access by producers to all necessary resources for food production, including knowledge;
- multiple independent buyers;
- absence of resource exploitation and
- no impingement on the ability of people in other locales to meet these criteria (e.g., through trade relationships that undermine decent wages, fair prices, environmental quality, and transparency of access to information in other countries).

In those principles, I was trying to remedy some of the problems of globalized, concentrated food industries, such as few buyers for farm products and trade agreements that undermine human rights. It seemed to me that right-based food systems could exist in a market economy: "RBFS transcend market goals for food systems, but can work through markets and form a conceptual bridge between market goals and non-market goods and services that make life possible and worth living" (605). In hindsight, I think that there is no incompatibility with markets *per se*, but RBFS cannot coexist with neoliberalism. Human rights and neoliberalism operate with different logic, assumptions and principles.

How might the emerging narrative be impelled forward and strengthened? Jeroen J.L. Candera and Laura Pereira (2017) suggested that the first step toward an integrated food policy is constructing a resonating policy frame. This requires a shared understanding of the nature of the food system, its issues and the resulting need for a holistic policy framework. These authors noted that "changing existing ideas and preferences takes time and depends on broad and sustained public support" (90). In Chapter 9, one of the biggest shortcomings of the UN Food Systems Summit was its failure to identify what is badly malfunctioning in the current food system; thus, there was no agreement on which interventions out of a large bundle that were volunteered might be worthwhile.

Machteld Simoens and her co-authors posited three pathways of discursive change to overcome lock-ins in socio-technical systems, disruptive, dynamic and cross-sectoral; these are also applicable to food systems. The disruptive pathway occurs because of events exogenous to the food system, such as natural disasters, that alter values and assumptions. This is similar to the "collapse" stage of resilience theory but less complete. Unfortunately, the dominant cultural meta-narrative of the industrialized food system seems nearly impervious to natural disasters such as pandemics, crop failures and market failures. If anything, such disasters strengthen the hand of corporations that insist that their ability to move food around the world is essential to overcome the disaster. The dynamic pathway comes from within, challenging the values and assumptions of the meta-narrative and delegitimizing some of its elements. Without a strong and widely supported alternative to replace the meta-narrative, however, this pathway may not go far. The third pathway builds on deliberative learning across different discourses, such as energy and development, to create simultaneous structural changes (Simoen et al. 2022). This third option is the pathway that seems most promising to me.

Although he used different terminology than I have used in this book, Chris Reidy's ideas about "discursive entrepreneurship" are relevant to changing food system narratives (Reidy 2022). He started with the discursive landscape, or the "complex landscape of competing, cooperating and overlapping discourses at multiple scales" (545). For our purposes, discourses are roughly equivalent to narratives, although for Reidy they are more encompassing than the narrative. Discursive entrepreneurship is the practice of creating, performing and transforming memes, stories, narratives and discourses to promote a desired structure of the discursive landscape, i.e., intentionally changing a dominant narrative. Memes are the smallest elements of meaning in the discursive landscape. For food systems, they might include the Green Revolution or planetary boundaries.

Reidy included six key strategies for creating a desired narrative: *deconstruction* of the existing landscape, *framing* a planned communication by selecting memes, *construction* of a communication (such as a narrative) from those memes, *performance* of that communication and *connection* with audiences in the hope that memes will be transmitted and reproduced, and *collaboration* with audiences and other practitioners. The steps that he laid out are consistent with other sources on narrative change, but it is interesting that he included deconstruction as the first step. This echoes Julia Tschersich and Christian Kok's explanation of the importance of "unmaking" ideas about justice and democracy, in seeking just transitions in agri-food systems. Another place in which he went beyond other authors was in emphasizing the importance of interaction with the audience. Collaborating with audiences involves overcoming cognitive dissonance by shifting perspectives, and empowering people to do their own meaning-making rather than accepting pre-selected meanings. For food system narratives, telling stories about how agroecology and food sovereignty have enhanced personal, community and regional well-being can enable people to shift their perspective on the value of the industrialized food system.

In Chapter 4, I suggested that regeneration draws from movements for human rights, equity, degrowth and ecological integrity. The latter includes movements for climate justice, resisting fossil fuel extraction, protecting pollinators, restoring water quality of rivers and more. Figure 11.1 shows how

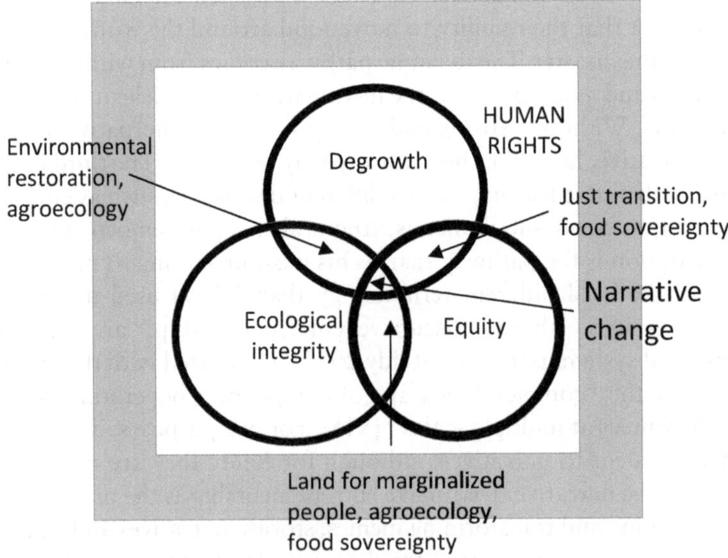

FIGURE 11.1 Contributions of agroecology and food sovereignty to regenerative food systems.

agroecology and food sovereignty support the interlocking goals of organizations that are trying to build regenerative food systems based in degrowth, equity and ecological integrity.

Agroecology fits in the intersection of ecological integrity and equity and serves both by facilitating food production with environmentally responsible practices by marginalized people. It is aligned with degrowth by eliminating inputs of fossil-fuel-intensive inputs, helping small-scale producers to make a living and resisting the mandate of capitalism for accumulation and exploitation. Degrowth has many intersections with equity, prominent in the call for a just transition to a more sustainable future and food sovereignty, to enable marginalized people to realize the right to food from healthy environments that are not polluted by extraction. Just transition should be inclusive of distributive, procedural, recognition and restorative justice principles and practice (Tschersich and Kok 2022) which lead to greater equity. A just transition will require that food system actors show greater care for humans and non-humans alike. In the center of these movements and driving them forward is a changed and life-affirming cultural narrative.

Regenerative food systems are embedded in a rights-based framework, but this brings accompanying responsibilities. Penobscot teacher Sherri Mitchell (2018, 91) reminded us,

> when we balance our demand for rights with an acceptance of our responsibility toward one another and all other living beings, we take back our power. When we do so, we build a foundation for a rights-based society that is balanced, just, and harmonious.

All of us have a responsibility to present and future generations, and non-human beings, to preserve ecological integrity. We also share the responsibility of stopping the juggernaut of fossil-fuel-enabled industrialization and excessive consumption. And we share the responsibility of creating an economy of care and solidarity, so that everyone enjoys the opportunity to realize their full potential. We know enough to act, and we have a responsibility to do so.

References

Abson, DJ, J Fischer, J Leventon, J Newig, T Schomerus, U Vilsmaier, H von Wehrden, P Abernethy, CD Ives, NW Jager and DJ Lang. 2017. Leverage points for sustainability transformation. *Ambio* 46:30–39. https://doi.org/10.1007/s13280-016-0800-y

Anderson, M. 2008. Rights-based food systems and the goals of food systems reform. *Agric Human Values* 25(4):593–608. https://doi.org/10.1007/s10460-008-9151-z

Arora, S, B Van Dyck, D Sharma and A Stirling. 2020. Control, care and conviviality in the politics of technology for sustainability. *Sustain: Sci, Practice Policy* 16(1):247–262. https://doi.org/10.1080/15487733.2020.1816687

Arthur, H, D Sanderson, P Tranter and A Thornton. 2022. A review of theoretical frameworks of food system governance, and the search for food system sustainability. *Agrocol Sust Food Syst* 46(8):1277–1300. https://doi.org/10.1080/21683565.2022.2104422

Babu, S. 2019. To transform the global food system and feed the world sustainably, start at the local level. International Food Policy Research Institute. https://www.ifpri.org/blog/transform-global-food-system-and-feed-world-sustainably-start-local-level

Barrett, CB, TG Benton, J Fanzo, M Herrero, RJ Nelson, E Bageant, E Buckler, K Cooper, I Culotta, S Fan, R Gandhi, S James, M Kahn, L Lawson-Lartego, J Liu, Q Marshall, D Mason-D'Croz, A Mathys, C Mathys, V Mazariegos-Anastassiou, A Miller, K Misra, AG Mude, J Shen, LM Sibande, C Song, R Steiner, P Thornton and S Wood. 2020. *Socio-technical innovation bundles for Agri-food systems transformation. Report of the International Expert Panel on Innovations to Build Sustainable, Equitable, Inclusive Food Value Chains.* Ithaca, NY and London: Cornell Atkinson Center for Sustainability and Springer Nature.

Béné, C. 2022. Why the great food transformation may not happen – a deep-dive into our food systems' political economy, controversies and politics of evidence. *World Dev* 154:105881. https://doi.org/10.1016/j.worlddev.2022.105881

Béné, C, P Oosterveer, L Lamotte, ID Brouwer, S de Haan, SD Proger, EF Talsma and CK Khoury. 2019. When food systems meet sustainability – current narratives and implications for action. *World Dev* 113:116–130. https://doi.org/10.1016/j.worlddev.2018.08.011

Bezner Kerr, R. 2023. Maladaptation in food systems and ways to avoid it. *Curr Opin Environ Sustain* 61:101269. https://doi.org/10.1016/j.cosust.2023.101269

Campbell, BM, J Hansen, J Rioux, CM Stirling, S Twomlow and E Wollenberg. 2018. Urgent action to combat climate change and its impacts (SDG 13): transforming agriculture and food systems. *Curr Opin Environ Sustain* 34-13-20. https://doi.org/10.1016/j.cosust.2018.06.005

Candel, JJL and L Pereira. 2017. Towards integrated food policy: main challenges and steps ahead. *Env Sci Policy* 73:89–92. https://doi.org/10.1016/j.envsci.2017.04.010

Caron, P, G Ferrero y de Loma-Osorio, D Nabarro, E Hainzelin, M Guillou, I Andersen, T Arnold, M Astralaga, M Beukeboom, S Bickersteth, M Bwalya, P Callero, BM Campbell, N Divine, S Fan, M Frick, A Friis, M Gallagher, J-P Halkin, C Hanson, F Lasbennes, T Ribera, J Rockström, M Schuepbach, A Steer, A Tutwiler and G Verburg. 2018. Food systems for sustainable development: proposals for a profound four-part transformation. *Agron Sust Dev* 38:41. https://doi.org/10.1007/s13593-018-0519-1

Civil Society and Indigenous Peoples Mechanism (CSIPM). 2020. *Youth Demands for a Radical Transformation of Our Food System.* https://www.csm4cfs.org/csm-youth-policy-declaration-covid-19/

Civil Society and Indigenous Peoples Mechanism (CSIPM). 2022. *Voices from the Ground 2: Transformative Solutions to the Global Systemic Food Crises.* https://www.csm4cfs.org/voices-from-the-ground-transformative-solutions-to-the-global-systemic-food-crises/

Dahlberg, KA. 2001. Democratizing society and food systems: or how do we transform modern structures of power? *Agric Human Values* 18:135–151. https://doi.org/10.1023/A:1011175626010

Davis, B, L Lipper and P Winters. 2022. Do not transform food systems on the backs of the rural poor. *Food Sec* 14:729–740. https://doi.org/10.1007/s12571-021-01214-3

De Cleene, S and T Strauss. 2021. 3 urgent actions to redesign the future of food in 2021. World Economic Forum. https://www.weforum.org/agenda/2021/01/how-to-redesign-food-systems-2021/

Den Boer, ACL, KPW Kok, M Gill, J Breda, J Cahill, C Callenius, P Caron, Z Damianova, M Gurinovic, L Lähteenmäki, T Lang, R Sonnino, G Verburg, H Westhoek, T Cesuroglu, BJ Regeer and JEW Broerse. 2021a. Research and innovation as a catalyst for food system transformation. *Trends Food Sci Tech* 107:150–156. https://doi.org/10.1016/j.tifs.2020.09.021

Den Boer, ACL, JEW Broerse and BJ Regeer. 2021b. The need for capacity building to accelerate food system transformation. *Curr Opinion Food Sci* 42:119–126. https://doi.org/10.1016/j.cofs.2021.05.009

Dengerink, J, F Dirks, E Likoko and J Guijt. 2021. One size doesn't fit all: regional differences in priorities for food system transformation. *Food Security* 31:1455–1466. https://doi.org/10.1007/s12571-021-01222-3

Dentoni, D, S Waddell and S Waddock. 2017. Pathways of transformation in global food and agricultural systems: implications from a large systems change theory perspective. *Curr Opinion Environ Sust* 29:8–13. https://doi.org/10.1016/j.cosust.2017.10.003

Dinesh, D, DLT Hegger, L Klerkx, J Vervoort, BM Campbell and PPJ Driessen. 2021. Enacting theories of change for food systems transformation under climate change. *Global Food Sec* 31:100583. https://doi.org/10.1016/j.gfs.2021.100583

Dinesh, D, AM Loboguerrero Rodríguez, A Millan, T Rawe, L Stringer, P Thornton, S Vermeulen and B Campbell. 2018. A 6-part action plan to transform food systems under climate change: creative actions to accelerate progress towards the SDGs. CCAFS Info Note. Wageningen, Netherlands: CGIAR Research Program on Climate Change, Agriculture and Food Security (CCAFS).

Dornelles, AZ, WJ Boonstra, I Delabre, JM Denney, RJ Nunes, A Jentsch, KA Nicholas, M Schroter, R Seppelt, J Settele, N Shackelford, RJ Standish and TH Oliver. 2022. Transformation archetypes in global food systems. *Sust Sci* 17:1827–1840. https://doi.org/10.1007/s11625-022-01102-5

El Bilali, H, C Strassner and T Ben Hassen. 2021. Sustainable agri-food systems: environment, economy, society, and policy. *Sustainability* 13:6260. https://doi.org/10.3390/su13116260

Elechi, JOG, IU Nwiyi and CS Adamu. 2022. Global food system transformation for resilience. Pp. 21–43 In: AI Ribeiro-Barros, DS Tevera, LF Goulao and LD Tivana. *Food Systems Resilience*. London: IntechOpen.

Ellen MacArthur Foundation. 2021. *Building a Healthy and Resilient Food System.* https://www.ellenmacarthurfoundation.org/articles/building-a-healthy-and-resilient-food-system

Ewert, F, R Baatz and R Finger. 2023. Agroecology for a sustainable agriculture and food system: from local solutions to large-scale adoption. *Annu Rev Resour Econ* 15:351–381. https://doi.org/10.1146/annurev-resource-102422-090105

Fakhri, M. 2023. Right to food for food system recovery and transformation. Interim report of the Special Rapporteur on the right to food A/78/202. UN General Assembly. https://daccess-ods.un.org/tmp/7819461.22646332.html

Fan, S, E EunYoung Cho, T Meng and C Rue. 2021. How to prevent and cope with coincidence of risks to the global food system. *Annu Rev Environ Resourc* 46:601–623. https://doi.org/10.1146/annurev-environ-012220-020844

Foley, JA, N Ramankutty, KA Brauman, ES Cassidy, JS Gerber, M Johnston, ND Mueller, C O'Connell, DK Ray, PC West, C Balzer, EM Bennett, SR Carpenter, J Hill, C Monfreda, S Polasky, J Röckstrom, J Sheehan, S Siebert, D Tilman and DPM Zaks. 2011. Solutions for a cultivated planet. *Nature* 278:337–342. https://doi.org/10.1038/nature10452

FAO. 2021. *The White/Wiphala Paper on Indigenous Peoples' Food Systems*. Rome. https://doi.org/10.4060/cb4932en

Food and Agriculture Organization (FAO). 2022. The Future of Food and Agriculture, No. 3. Drivers and Triggers for Transformation. Rome. https://doi.org/10.4060/cc0959en

Food Systems Partnership. 2023. Pathways for food systems transformation. Food Systems Pavilion, COP28. https://foodsystemspavilion.com/pathways-for-transforming-food-systems/.

Gaupp, F, CR Laderchi, H Lotze-Campen, F DeClerck, BL Bodirsky, S Lowder, A Popp, R Kanbur, O Edenhofer, R Nugent, J Fanzo, S Dietz, S Nordhagen and S Fan. 2021. Food system development pathways for healthy, nature-positive and inclusive food systems. *Nature Food* 21:928–934. https://doi.org/10.1038/s43016-021-00421-7

Gerten, D, V Heck, J Jägermeyr, BL Bodirsky, I Fetzer, M Jalava, M Kummu, W Lucht, J Rockström, S Schaphoff and HJ Schellnhuber. 2020. Feeding ten billion people is possible within four terrestrial planetary boundaries. *Nature Sustainability* 3:200–208. https://doi.org/ 10.1038/s41893-019-0465-1

Ghosh, A. 2021. *The Nutmeg's Curse: Parables for a Planet in Crisis*. Chicago: University of Chicago Press.

Gliessman, S. 2022. Changing the food system narrative. *Agroecol Sust Food Systems* 46(6):789–790. https://doi.org/10.1080/21683565.2022.2082569

Global Alliance for the Future of Food (GAFF) (2021). Principles for food system transformation: a framework for action. https://futureoffood.org/insights/principles-for-transformation/

Herrero, M, PK Thornton, D Mason-D'Croz, J Palmer, TG Benton, BL Bodirsky, JR Bogard, A Hall, B Lee, K Nyborg, P Pradhan, GD Bonnett, BA Bryan, BM Campbell, S Christensen, M Clark, MT Cook, IJM de Boer, C Downs, K Dizyee, C Folberth, CM Godde, JS Gerber, M Grundy, P Havlik, A Jarvis, R King, AM Logobuerrero, MA Lopes, CL McIntyre, R Naylor, J Navarro, m Obersteiner, A Parodi, MB Peoples, I Pikaar, A Popp, J Rockström, MJ Robertson, P Smith, E Stehfest, SM Swain, H Valin, M van Wijk, HHE van Zanten, S Vermeulen, J Vervoort and PC West. 2020. Innovation can accelerate the transition towards a sustainable food system. *Nature Food* 1:266–272. https://doi.org/10.1038/s43016-020-0074-1

High Level Panel of Experts of the Committee on World Food Security (HLPE). 2020. *Food Security and Nutrition: Building a Global Narrative Towards 2030*. Committee on World Food Security. Rome: FAO.

Intergovernmental Panel on Climate Change (IPCC). 2022. Summary for Policy-Makers of WGIII Report. Figure SPM7. https://www.ipcc.ch/report/ar6/wg3/figures/summary-for-policymakers

Holling, CS and LH Gunderson. 2002. Resilience and adaptive cycles. Pp. 25–62 In: LH Gunderson and CS Holling (Eds.) *Panarchy: Understanding Transformations in Human and Natural Systems*. Washington, DC: Island Press.

Johnston, LJ. 2022. *Architects of Abundance: Indigenous Regenerative Food and Land Management Systems and the Excavation of Hidden History*. PhD Dissertation, University of Alaska Fairbanks. https://scholarworks.alaska.edu/handle/11122/13122

Jones, SK, A Monjeau, K Perez-Guzman and PA Harrison. 2023. Integrated modeling to achieve global goals: lessons from the Food, Agriculture, Biodiversity, Land-use, and Energy (FABLE) Initiative. *Sust Sci* 18:323–333. https://doi.org/10.1007/s11625-023-01290-8

Juárez, P, F Trentini and L Becerra. 2018. Transformative social innovation for food sovereignty: the disruptive alternative. *Int J Soc Agri Food* 24(3):318–335. https://doi.org/10.48416/ijsaf.v24i3.3

Kennedy, E, P Webb, S Block, T Griffin, D Mozaffarian and R Kyte. 2020. Transforming food systems: the missing pieces needed to make them work. *Curr Dev Nutr* 5(1):nzaa177. https://doi.org/10.1093/cdn/nzaa177

Kimmerer, RW. 2020. *Braiding Sweetgrass: Indigenous Wisdom, Scientific Knowledge and the Teachings of Plants*. Minneapolis, MN: Milkweed Editions.

Kolinjivadi, V and A Kothari. 2020. No harm here is still harm there: the Green New Deal and the Global South. https://www.jamhoor.org/read/2020/5/20/no-harm-here-is-still-harm-there-looking-at-the-green-new-deal-from-the-global-south

Lamine, C, I Darnhofer and TK Marsden. 2019. What enables just sustainability transitions in agrifood systems? An exploration of conceptual approaches using international comparative case studies. *J Rur Stud* 68:144–146. https://doi.org/10.1016/j.jrurstud.2019.03.010

Leeuwis, C, BK Boogaard and K Atta-Krah. 2021. How food system change (or not): governance implications for food system transformation processes. *Food Sec* 13:761–780. https://doi.org/10.1007/s12571-021-01178-4

McGreevy, SR, CDD Rupprecht, D Niles, A Wiek, M Carolan, G Kallis, K Kantamaturapoj, A Mangnus, P Jehlicka, O Taherzadeh, M Sahakian, I Chabay, A Colby, J-L Vivero-Pol, R Chaudhuri, M Spiegelberg, M Kobayashi, B Balázs, K Tsuchiya, C Nicholls, K Tanaka, J Vervoort, M Akitsu, H Mallee, K ota, R Shinkai, A Khadse, N Tamura, K Abe, M Altieri, Y-I Sato and M Tachikawa. 2022. Sustainable agrifood systems for a post-growth world. *Nature Sust* 011–1017. https://doi.org/10.1038/s41893-022-00933-5

Mitchell, S. 2018. *Sacred Instructions: Indigenous Wisdom for Living Spirit-Based Change*. Berkeley, CA: North Atlantic Books.

Nierenberg, D. 2023. A manifesto for disrupting global food politics. *Forbes*. https://www.forbes.com/sites/daniellenierenberg/2023/01/06/a-manifesto-for-disrupting-global-food-politics/?sh=38a4c8dd3528

Neslen, A. 2023. "The anti-livestock people are a pest": how UN food body played down role of farming in climate change. *The Guardian* (20 October 2023). https://www.theguardian.com/environment/2023/oct/20/the-anti-livestock-people-are-a-pest-how-un-fao-played-down-role-of-farming-in-climate-change

One Planet Network. 2020. Achieving the SDGs through food systems transformation: On the road to the Food Systems Summit 2021. Outcome Document of the 3rd Global Conference of the One Planet network's (10YFP) Sustainable Food Systems (SFS) Programme. https://www.oneplanetnetwork.org/knowledge-centre/resources/outcome-document-3rd-global-conference-one-planet-networks-sustainable

Pimbert, M. 2022. Transforming food and agriculture: competing visions and major controversies. *Mondes en Développement* 3(199–200):361–384. https://doi.org/10.3917/med.199.0365

Riedy, C. 2022. Discursive entrepreneurship: ethical meaning making as a transformative practice for sustainable futures. *Sust Sci* 17:541–554.

Rockström, J, O Edenhofer, J Gaertner and F DeClerck. 2020. Planet-proofing the global food system. *Nature Food* 1:3–5. https://doi.org/10.1038/s43016-019-0010-4

Rossi, A, M Coscarello and D Biolghini. 2021. (Re)commoning food and food systems. The contribution of social innovation from solidarity economy. *Agriculture* 11:548. https://doi.org/10.3390/agriculture11060548

Ruben, R, R Cavatassi, L Lipper, E Smaling and Paul Winter. 2021. Towards food systems transformation—five paradigm shifts for healthy, inclusive and sustainable food systems. *Food Sec* 13:4423–1430. https://doi.org/10.1007/s12571-021-01221-4

Rutting, L, J Vervoort, H Mees, L Pereira, M Veeger, K Mulderman, A Mangnus, K Winkler, P Olsson, T Hichert, R Lane, B Bottega Pergher, L Christiaens, N Bansal, A Hendriks and P Driessen. 2023. Disruptive seeds: a scenario approach to explore power shifts in sustainability transformations. *Sust Sci* 18:1117–1133. https://doi.org/10.1007/s11625-022-01251-7

Schipanski, ME, GK MacDonald, S Rosenzweig, MJ Chappell, EM Bennett, R Bezner Kerr, J Blesh, T Crews, L Drinkwater, JG Lundgren and C Schnarr. 2016. Realizing resilient food systems. *BioScience* 66(7):600–610.

Scoones, I, A Stirling, D Abrol, J Atela, L Charli-Joseph, H Eakin, A Ely, P Olsson, L Pereira, R Priya, P van Zwanenberg and L Yang. 2020. Transformations to sustainability: combining structural, systemic and enabling approaches. *Curr Opinion Environ Sust* 41:65–75. https://doi.org/10.1016/j.cosust.2019.12.004

Simoen, MC, L Fuenfschilling and S Leipold. 2022. Discursive dynamics and lock-ins in socio-technical systems: an overview and a way forward. *Sust Sci* 17:1841–1853. https://doi.org/10.1007/s11625-022-01110-5

Slater, S, P Baker and M Lawrence. 2022. An analysis of the transformative potential of major food system report recommendations. *Glob Food Sec* 32:100610. https://doi.org/10.1016/j.gfs.2022.100610

Sonnino, R and P Milbourne. 2022. Food system transformation: a progressive place-based approach. *Local Env* 27(7):915–926. https://doi.org/10.1080/13549839.2022.2084723

Stefanovic, L, B Freytag-Leyer and J Kahl. 2020. Food system outcomes: an overview and the contribution to food systems transformation. *Front Sust Food Systems* 4:546167. https://doi.org/10.3389/fsufs.2020.546167

Swinnen, J, J McDermott, and S Josef. 2021. Beyond the pandemic: transforming food systems after COVID-19. Pp. 6–23 In: *Global Food Policy Report 2021: Transforming food systems after COVID-19*. Washington, DC: International Food Policy Research Institute. https://www.ifpri.org/publication/2021-global-food-policy-report-transforming-food-systems-after-covid-19

Tschersich, J and KPW Kok. 2022. Deepening democracy for the governance of just transitions in agri-food systems. *Environ Innov Soc Transitions* 43:358–374. https://doi.org/10.1016/j.eist.2022.04.012

United Nations Development Program (UNDP). 2020. *Human Development Report 2020. The Next Frontier: Human Development and the Anthropocene*. New York, NY. https://hdr.undp.org/system/files/documents/hdr2020pdf.pdf

Vermeulen, SJ, T Park, CK Khoury and C Bene. 2020. Changing diets and the transformation of the global food system. *Ann NY Acad Sci* 1478:3–17. https://doi.org/10.1111/nyas.14446

Vijayan, D, D Ludwig, C Rybak, H Kaechele, H Hoffmann, HC Schönfeldt, HA Mbwana, C Vacaflores Rivero and K Löhr. 2022. Indigenous knowledge in food system transformations. *Communications Earth & Environ* 3: 213. https://doi.org/10.1038/s43247-022-00543-1

Walker, B and D Salt. 2006. *Resilience Thinking: Sustaining Ecosystems and People in a Changing World*. Washington, DC: Island Press.

Webb, P, TG Benton, J Beddington, D Flynn, NM Kelly and SM Thomas. 2020. The urgency of food system transformation is now irrefutable. *Nature Food* 1:584–585. https://doi.org/10.1038/s43016-020-00161-0

Weber, H, K Poeggel, H Eakin, D Fischer, DJ Lang, H von Wehrden and A Wiek. 2020. What are the ingredients for food systems change towards sustainability?—insights from the literature. *Env Res Lett* 15:113001. https://doi.org/ 10.1088/1748–9326/ab99fd

Wolpold-Bosien, M. 2023. *Food Systems Transformation: In Which Direction?* FIAN International. https://www.fian.org/files/is/htdocs/wp11102127_GNIAANVR7U/www/files/FoodSystems_Directionality%20report_final.pdf

Woodhill, J. 2023. Why, what, and how: a framework for transforming food systems. Lead Foresight 4Food Initiative. https://foresight4food.net/why-what-and-how-a-framework-for-transforming-food-systems/

INDEX

Note: *Italic* page numbers refer to figures.